English Grammar in Context

Kitty Chen Dean

Nassau Community College

Allyn and Bacon
Boston • London • Toronto • Sydney • Tokyo • Singapore

Vice President, Humanities: Joseph Opiela
Editorial Assistant: Julie Hallett
Marketing Manager: Melanie Goulet
Editorial–Production Service: Matrix Productions Inc.
Composition and Prepress Buyer: Linda Cox
Manufacturing Buyer: Suzanne Lareau
Cover Administrator: Kristina Mose-Libon
Electronic Composition: Omegatype Typography, Inc.

Library of Congress Cataloging-in-Publication Data

Dean, Kitty Chen.
    English grammar in context / Kitty Chen Dean.
      p.   cm.
    Includes index.
    ISBN 0-205-30754-X
    1. English language—Grammar. I. Title.

PE1112 .D36 2000
428.2—dc21

                                   00-061104

Printed in the United States of America

10 9 8 7 6 5 4 3 2 1   05 04 03 02 01 00

Contents

PART III Clauses   145

11   *Independent Clauses: Simple and Compound Sentences*   *147*

12   *Dependent Clauses*   *160*

13   *Adjective Dependent Clauses*   *175*

Preface to the Instructor

English Grammar in Context hopes to serve college students who want or need to improve their command of grammar in order to write correctly and clearly. Grammar is a means to an end, not the end in itself. Thus, instruction in grammatical concepts and terminology is kept to a minimum, and terminology is limited to words already familiar to most students. Rather than simply introducing the grammatical concepts, the text emphasizes *using* the concepts in pieces of writing.

The thirty chapters are divided into six parts, each consisting of four to six chapters. They do not need to be taught in a particular order, although they do progress in a logical way.

Part I: Words discusses the parts of speech (nouns and pronouns; verbs; adjectives and adverbs; prepositions, conjunctions, and interjections), subjects and objects, and complements.

Part II: Phrases concentrates on the four types of phrase: prepositional phrases, adjective verbal phrases, infinitive verbal phrases, and noun verbal phrases (gerund phrases).

Part III: Clauses discusses simple and compound sentences, dependent clauses in general, adjective dependent clauses, noun dependent clauses, and adverb dependent clauses, as well as inverted sentences and passive voice.

Part IV: Sentence Structure deals with parallel construction, predication, subject-verb agreement, and pronoun-antecedent agreement.

Part V: Punctuation treats commas, semicolons and colons, quotation marks and italics, and apostrophes, as well as dashes, parentheses, brackets, slashes, hyphens, and a number of minor punctuation marks.

Part VI: Errors discusses fragments, run-together sentences, words often confused, dangling and misplaced modifiers, and pseudoerrors. The final chapter corrects some misconceptions about such "rules" as not starting a sentence with a conjunction or writing long sentences and calling them "run-ons."

These thirty chapters are independent of each other so that chapters may be omitted or may be taught in a different order depending on the needs of the class. For example, the chapter that discusses dependent clauses without differentiating the types may be adequate for the concept of dependent clauses, so the subsequent three chapters may be omitted. Or if students seem reasonably well versed in the parts of speech, the first four chapters may be skipped.

Each chapter begins with a pretest made up of paragraphs or a series of related sentences, from a professional source whenever possible. Before any instruction has occurred, students can test themselves on their knowledge of a particular concept and have a good idea of their understanding. Answers to the pretests, and only the pretests, are in the back of the book so that students can check their own answers without fear of exposing their inadequacies.

The instructional material in each chapter is kept to a minimum so that much of the learning will be through the exercises contained in each chapter. The exercises are graduated in difficulty and progress in the following manner:

1. *Recognition of the concept.* A piece of writing contains a number of examples of the particular grammatical point, which the student must underline or circle. Sometimes an additional exercise also calls for recognizing the grammatical concept but contains more difficult sentences that demand more precise understanding and discrimination.

2. *Controlled use of the concept.* A piece of writing asks for the insertion of words, phrases, or clauses that complete the sentences in order to form complete paragraphs or short essays. Thus students can demonstrate their understanding of the concept by inserting their own examples that are appropriate to the exercise.

3. *Correction of the concept.* A piece of writing contains elements that need changing so that students can practice their comprehension of the concept by making the necessary changes. For example, a series of simple sentences making up a complete paragraph has to be changed to contain compound and complex sentences through combining the simple sentences, or a short essay in the present tense has to be changed to another tense. Whenever possible, students do not just correct errors but change or improve a piece of writing, so they enhance their editing skills.

4. *Generation of the concept.* A series of related words, phrases, or clauses are presented for students to use in sentences or paragraphs. They then practice not only using the particular grammatical concept but also writing coherent paragraphs and short essays.

5. *Proofreading an essay.* A short essay contains some errors relating to a particular concept and asks for correction. Students are confronted with only one type of error that must be corrected. In order to do this final exercise, they must both understand the concept and know whether it is being used correctly or not.

All the exercises are contextual; that is, they form paragraphs, short essays, or, at the very least, related sentences on topics of interest to students. Some of them consist of personal narratives that should evoke similar stories from students. The emphasis, however, is not on personal narratives or literary endeavors but rather on subjects that occur in other classrooms, the business world, and the scientific realm. Since *English Grammar in Context* contains well over two hundred exercises on a variety of subjects, students should find much of interest to them.

Each chapter ends with a summary so that students can review what they have learned through seeing the individual topics in order, each with an example.

English Grammar in Context can be used alone in a class devoted to the study of grammar. The many topics of general interest, as well as a few personal narratives, can serve as springboards for discussion or as models for essays that further explore the topic. In a class that is not dedicated solely to the study of grammar, the textbook can be used along with a reader to further enforce the conjunction of reading and writing. Instructors should find that *English Grammar in Context* is easy to use, versatile, and interesting.

No text is completed without the help of many people. I want to thank my colleagues in the English Department of Nassau Community College; Joe Opiela at Allyn and Bacon; Merrill Peterson of Matrix Productions; the reviewers who added invaluable insight—James Vanden Bosch, Calvin College; Avon Crismore, Indiana University–Purdue University at Fort Wayne; Robert Funk, Eastern Illinois University; and Robert S. Sweazy, Vincennes University; my friends who appear in this book (they know who they are); and Richard and Cecilia, who help make all things possible.

Preface to the Student

Grammar is probably not your favorite subject, and it shouldn't be unless you want to become a grammarian, editor, linguist, or proofreader. A knowledge of grammar is a means to an end, not the end in itself. As you master concepts of grammar, you will improve your writing. Except in the unskilled, low-paying labor market, correct writing is essential in the working world.

Since you are studying grammar, use *English Grammar in Context* to its fullest to improve your skills and enhance your knowledge. Try following these directions to get the maximum benefit in the least amount of time and for the most enjoyment:

1. Do the pretest at the beginning of each chapter when it is assigned. Be honest in marking your answers and do not consult the answers at the end of the book until after you have finished. If you got all the answers right, you should feel confident that you know some basics of grammar. If you got most of the answers wrong, you have your work cut out for you. If you are a typical student, you will have a variety of scores. Concentrate, however, on learning new material that seems unclear to you.

2. Read the instructional pages of each chapter with close attention. Notice how the examples illustrate the grammatical point being made; don't concentrate on the subject matter of the examples (you may or may not like cats, but that fact is unimportant). Underline or highlight important definitions and points, not the examples.

3. Do the assigned exercises with care. The early ones in each chapter may seem tedious if you already understand the concept, but feel lucky about that. Don't be too lenient with yourself. You probably can get most of the answers right, but what about those you didn't? Ask yourself why you didn't get them, what you didn't understand about the concept. Don't let carelessness or haste be your response to incorrect answers.

4. Try to form coherent, well organized paragraphs, not just random sentences, when you have to write exercises that ask for several sentences using a particular grammatical construction. Use your imagination and be creative; use some humor if that is your style. You have the power to make grammar more interesting.

5. As you do your grammar exercises, try to develop an interest in the subject matter as well. The subjects won't all be fascinating to you, but if you find most of

the subjects boring or uninteresting, you might consider broadening your horizons by learning some new information.

6. Use the summary at the end of each chapter to review the concepts. Ask yourself if you really understand each point. Don't try to memorize the summary since it won't be of much help for tests or for comprehension.

To study for grammar tests, you will probably spend a lot of time memorizing grammatical terms and their definitions, as well as lists of uses for these grammatical functions. You will probably pass your tests with flying colors, but don't let yourself be satisfied. Make grammar part of your life. Look for examples of, say, prepositional phrases or, later on, of adverb dependent clauses in advertisements, your other textbooks, the newspapers, or any reading matter. See how these constructions work (or perhaps don't work). See if you can find any errors, such as dangling modifiers or fragments, in advertisements or the newspapers. If you do this occasionally, you will develop a growing awareness of how language works, and you will learn to appreciate good writing.

Conversely, when you do your own writing, whether for your personal use or for other classes, you should begin by writing down your thoughts clearly and coherently. When you have finished putting down all your thoughts on your subject, go back and look at the grammar. Notice, for example, what kinds of sentences you have written. If you have compound sentences, make sure they are punctuated correctly. Or you might combine some simple sentences into compound or complex sentences. You should check on words often confused by using a dictionary to make sure you have chosen the right ones. See if your verbs have the correct tense for your purposes and if you have changed tense for no reason. Also make sure that pronouns agree with their antecedents. Using the spell checker on the computer is simply not enough.

As you practice editing and correcting your own writing, you will find that some grammatical points become automatic. As in sports, with practice you will improve your skills so that you will wonder why you ever had trouble at all. Eventually you will just *know* when something is correct, even though you have forgotten the grammatical term for it. When you reach that level, you have used grammar as a means to an end. And that end is clear, effective writing.

Words

Chapter 1

Nouns and Pronouns

Read the following paragraph and underline the **nouns** and **pronouns.**

Edith Wharton was born Edith Jones on January 24, 1862, in New York, New York, and married Boston banker Edward Wharton in 1885. A member of upper-class society, she wrote about her world and criticized its rigid attitudes and customs. Her work has often been compared to that of another critic of social norms, Henry James, with whom she was acquainted. Wharton's first successful writing was a book entitled *The Decoration of Houses* (1897), an attack on upper-class interior decorating. Later she incorporated her interest in decorating and architecture in her fiction, using detailed settings and commenting on the order or disorder in her characters' homes and lives. (Patricia D. Netzley, *Encyclopedia of Social Protest Literature*)

Nouns

As you may already know, *nouns* name the things that are the topics of our sentences and paragraphs; that is, they tell us what we are reading or speaking about. Nouns are usually defined as persons, places, things, ideas, or concepts and are usually divided into these categories:

Proper Nouns and Common Nouns

Proper nouns are capitalized names of people and animals, places, titles, and brands (for example, Jane, Fido, London, Queen Elizabeth, Sony), and *common nouns* are all the others. Places and titles are capitalized when they refer to a particular person or place but not when they refer to people or places in general. Notice how *queen* and *palace* are used in this paragraph:

I just finished reading a biography about Queen Elizabeth II and her life in Buckingham Palace. Learning about the lives of kings and queens really fascinates me, but I would not want to be a queen or live in a palace.

In the same way, if you write about Hollywood High School, you capitalize *high* and *school.* But if you write about going to high school, you do not capitalize those words.

Concrete Nouns and Abstract Nouns

Concrete nouns refer to things that you can see, hear, taste, smell, or touch, while *abstract nouns* refer to things that the five senses do not perceive. Some nouns, such as *house, music, apple, odor,* or *tree,* are obviously concrete, but others, such as *air,* are less obvious. *Abstract nouns* deal mostly with ideas and concepts, such as *honesty, hate, democracy, frivolity.* Yet, as with concrete nouns, some nouns are difficult to categorize as abstract. For example, is *coalition* concrete (can you see a group of people?) or abstract (can you tell that they are united in a common cause?)? Use the noun's meaning in a sentence to decide whether, in that particular case, it is concrete or abstract.

Pronouns

Pronouns take the place of nouns and mean the same thing as the nouns they replace. You could just use nouns and eliminate pronouns, but pronouns help to keep sentences from being monotonous and repetitive. They also help give unity to a piece of writing. You will notice that you can name the noun that the pronoun replaces in the opening paragraph on Edith Wharton. For example, *she* and *her* refer to Wharton, while *its* refers to her world.

Like nouns, pronouns can be divided into categories. These categories are described in the sections that follow.

Subjective Case and Objective Case Pronouns

In grammar, *case* refers to the different forms taken by words depending on their grammatical use in sentences. Modern English has case forms only with subjective, objective, and possessive pronouns and no other part of speech.

Subjective pronouns (*I, you, he, she, it, we, they*) serve as the **subject** in a sentence: You *and* I *go to college;* She *should study hard;* It *needs paint.* You will notice that each of these sentences should be preceded by a reference that indicates the noun being replaced by a pronoun. *Objective pronouns* (*me, you, him, her, it, us, them*) serve as the objects in a sentence, that is, what the subject is acting on: *Life has given* you *and* me *much pleasure; Maria hid* it *from* her; *Roller coasters thrill* them. *Objects* are the receivers of the action of the subject and verb.

Because *it* and *you* (and all nouns) have the same form in both subjective and objective pronouns, many people confuse them by using the objective pronoun for the subjective pronoun. They will say, "Me and him saw a film" instead of "He and I saw a film." People may, of course, speak as they wish, but others might consider these choices poor grammar, especially in writing.

Possessive Case Pronouns

Possessive pronouns (*mine, yours, his, hers, its, ours, theirs, whose*) occur frequently and help for efficiency in writing and speaking: *This book is* mine; yours *is over there;* his *isn't here;* theirs *is lost.* Notice that only *his, its,* and *whose* may also be used as adjectives (*his book, its cover, whose book*).

7. Plenty of _____ like _____. They get _____ for _____ and for _____. The _____ does not develop _____.

8. _____ has a _____. If _____ get(s) one, _____ will both have _____. Why do _____ both want to own a _____?

9. The _____ has not stopped; _____ has continued for _____. If _____ doesn't stop soon, _____ will have to call _____ and _____.

10. _____ plays (the) _____ very well. _____ participates in (the) _____ and _____. _____ practices often, but _____ enjoys it.

Exercise 1.4   Changing Nouns and Pronouns

Change as many nouns to pronouns as possible so that the following paragraphs still make sense.

Example   Mary likes skating. ~~Mary~~ *She* often goes to the rink.

1. Amy Beach, the first famous American female composer, lived from 1867 to 1944. Although females were accepted into music conservatories by the latter part of the nineteenth century, females still could not study composition until the twentieth century. Females were rarely accepted as instrumentalists by orchestras, and females were considered unladylike if females gave recitals. Nevertheless, Amy persevered. At age eighteen, Amy was on the way to a very promising career as a performer when Amy married Dr. Henry Harris Aubrey Beach. Dr. Beach did not allow Amy to perform in public except once a year for charity, so Amy stayed home composing music.

2. Amy's husband, Henry Beach, and Amy's mother, Mrs. Cheney, both valued Amy's immense talent and encouraged Amy's work. Henry Beach and Mrs. Cheney, however, felt bound by tradition, taste, and reputation, so Henry Beach and Mrs. Cheney imposed restrictions on Amy in order to protect Amy. However, after the deaths of Henry Beach and Mrs. Cheney in 1910 and 1909, Amy embarked on a performing career that took Amy to many parts of Europe and all over the United States. Strangely enough, the early restrictions imposed on Amy forced Amy to concentrate on composing music rather than playing music, thus establishing Amy's reputation for all time.

Exercise 1.5   Using Nouns and Pronouns

Use the following nouns and pronouns in short paragraphs of two to three sentences. Use the nouns and pronouns in any order you wish.

1. university, University, New Jersey, new jersey, dawn, Dawn

2. avenue, Avenue, park, Park, building, Building

3. me, myself, I, themselves, ourselves, himself or herself

4. each, few, many, all, whichever, whatever

5. mine, yours, ours, theirs, whose, hers

6. him, her, us, them, who, what

7. everyone, nobody, anybody, anything, whoever, whichever

8. that, whomever, itself, myself, ourselves, himself

9. bridge, Bridge, city, City, main street, Main Street

10. sue, Sue, dodge, Dodge, hospital, Hospital

Exercise 1.6   Using Nouns and Pronouns

Use the noun indicated to write a paragraph that will contain pronouns that relate to the noun.

Example   (dog) ____Karl likes dogs, but they don't like him. They usually growl when he____

____comes near them. They also run away from him.____

1. (telephone) _____

_____

_____

2. (computer) _____

_____

_____

3. (refrigerator) _____

_____

_____

4. (horse) _____

_____

_____

5. (cow) _____

_____

_____

6. (mother) _____

_____

_____

7. (father) _____

_____

_____

8. (uncle) _____

_____

_____

9. (aunt) _____

_____

_____

10. (cousin) _____

_____

_____

11. (sibling) _____

_____

_____

12. (brothers) _____

_____

_____

13. (sisters) _____

_____

_____

14. (children) _____

_____

_____

15. (pets) _____

_____

_____

16. (cars) _____

_____

_____

17. (trains) _____

_____

_____

18. (houses) _____

_____

_____

19. (tree) _____

_____

_____

20. (flower) _____

_____

_____

Exercise 1.7   Proofreading

*Correct the **ten** errors involving proper and common nouns. Correct the **five** nouns that should or could be pronouns.*

Better Late Than Never

Bill went to a famous High School in California, but Bill will be the first to admit that he did not study very hard. He floated through english class by copying Jane's paper and using Mischa's notes. Jane and Mischa didn't even know he was doing it. In biology, he copied reports and said someone's experiment was his experiment. His Sister was a year ahead of him so he was able to use many of his sister's reports and tests. He failed spanish 1 twice before he cheated and finally passed. Only in math did he have to apply himself because he couldn't fake math. He didn't do wonderfully, but he did manage to graduate.

Bill really wanted a good job and no more school, but all his friends were going to college, so he decided to go also. What a shock he got when he signed up and found out that he would have to take two remedial courses: developmental english 1 and reading 01! Only his Math class would not be remedial.

Summary

   I. Nouns
      A. Definition: **Nouns** are words for persons, places, things, ideas, and concepts.
         Examples: *professor, Iowa, chair, happiness, honesty*

and common nouns

roper nouns** refer to people and animal names, places, titles, and brands and are written with a capital letter at the beginning.
   Examples: *Stephen, Spot, Grand Canyon, Doctor Jones, Toyota*
2. **Common nouns** are all other nouns not referring to a particular person, place, or thing.
   Examples: *inventor, the bridge, my book*

C. Concrete and abstract nouns
   1. **Concrete nouns** refer to things that can be seen, heard, touched, smelled, or tasted.
      Examples: *table, music, computer, odor, meatloaf*
   2. **Abstract nouns** refer to things that cannot be seen, heard, touched, smelled, or tasted
      Examples: *trust, evil, love, sadness*

II. Pronouns
   A. Definition: **Pronouns** take the place of nouns when the reference is clear.
   B. Pronoun cases: Subjective, objective, possessive
      1. The **subjective case** pronouns are *I, you, she, he, it, we, they, who(ever).*
         Examples: ***I** like pizza.* ***You** look hungry.* ***Who** wants a slice?*
      2. The **objective case** pronouns are *me, you, her, him, it, us, them, whom(ever).*
         Examples: *Give **it** to **me,** not to **him.** Give **them** to **whomever.***
      3. The **possessive case** pronouns are *mine, yours, his, hers, its, ours, theirs, whose.*
         Example: *The pizza is **yours** and **hers.***
   C. Other types of pronouns
      1. The **indefinite pronouns** are *anybody, anyone, anything, each, everybody, everything, either, neither, none, nothing, nobody, some, somebody, someone, something, one, other(s), thing(s), all, few, many.*
         Example: ***Somebody** ate the pie, but **nobody** is here.*
      2. The **demonstrative pronouns** are *this, that, these, those.*
         Example: ***This** will replace the lost pie.*
      3. The **relative pronouns** are *that, what(ever), whichever, who(ever), whom(ever), whose.*
         Example: *The pie **that** was eaten was Bill's.*
      4. The **reflexive** and **intensive pronouns** are *myself, yourself, himself, herself, itself, ourselves, yourselves, themselves.*
         Examples: *He hurt **himself.*** (reflexive)
                   *We **ourselves** are to blame.* (intensive)

III. Person in Pronouns
   A. Definition: **Person** refers to the person(s) speaking (**first person**), spoken to (**second person**), and spoken about (**third person**). Third person can refer to things as well as persons.
   B. Types of person
      1. Person can be singular or plural.
      2. Person can be first person, second person, or third person.

Person in Pronouns

	Singular	Plural
First person		
Subjective	*I*	*we*
Objective	*me*	*us*
Possessive	*my, mine*	*our, ours*
Second person		
Subjective	*you*	*you*
Objective	*you*	*you*
Possessive	*your, yours*	*your, yours*
Third person		
Subjective	*he, she, it*	*they*
Objective	*him, her, it*	*them*
Possessive	*his, her, hers, its*	*their, theirs*

(*Note: Who* is subjective for all persons.
Whom is objective for all persons.
Whose is possessive for all persons.)

Chapter 2

Verbs

Read the following paragraph and underline the **verbs** in it.

Our beginnings do not foreshadow our ends if one judges by the Hudson River. A few miles east of the Bad Luck Ponds, the Hudson came down between the ridges to race alongside route 28; it was a mountain stream: clear, cold, shallow, noisy. A few miles from its source in Lake Tear-in-the-Clouds a mile up on Mount Marcy (the Indian name for the mountain is better: Tahawus, "Cloud-Splitter") and three hundred river miles from the thousand oily piers of Hoboken, Weehawken, and Manhattan, here it was a canoer's watercourse. Above the little Hudson, spumes of mist rose from the mountains like campfire smoke. (William Least Heat Moon, *Blue Highways: A Journey into America*)

Verbs make up the very heart of any sentence. The nouns and pronouns tell what the sentence will be about, but the verbs tell what the nouns and pronouns are doing, whether they simply exist (state of being verbs) or have action.

Not only do the verbs tell us the action in a sentence, but they also tell us *when* the action took place. To do this, verbs change tense (time) to past, present, or future. No other parts of speech change tense, so finding the verb in a sentence can be accomplished by changing the time of the sentence. For example, notice that only the verb change indicates the time or duration in these sentences:

The cat walked on the fence.
The cat will walk on the fence.
The cat is walking on the fence.
The cat walks on the fence.

You will notice that other words, such as *will* and *is*, go along with the main part of the verb—called the ***base form***—and become a part of the complete verb in the sentence.

Verb Tenses

Basically, verbs may be divided into ***past, present***, and ***future*** tenses, but within each of these tenses exist several refinements that give a more precise meaning to the verb.

Past tense (completed condition or action)

Simple past	The cat **walked** on the fence.
Past progressive	The cat **was walking** on the fence.
Past perfect	The cat **had walked** on the fence.
Past perfect progressive	The cat **had been walking** on the fence.

Present tense (conditions or actions now)

Simple present	The cat **walks** on the fence.
(Simple present also means repeated or habitual action.)	
Present progressive	The cat **is walking** on the fence.
Present perfect	The cat **has walked** on the fence.
Present perfect progressive	The cat **has been walking** on the fence.

Future tense (conditions or actions later)

Simple Future	The cat **will walk** on the fence.
	The cat **is going to** walk on the fence.
Future progressive	The cat **will be walking** on the fence.
Future perfect	The cat **will have walked** on the fence.
Future perfect progressive	The cat **will have been walking** on the fence.

Each tense indicates something different:

> *simple (past, present, future):* when an action occurred
> *progressive:* an ongoing duration of an action
> *perfect:* a single action that has ended
> *perfect progressive:* an ongoing duration of an action that has ended

Main Verbs and Helping Verbs

Main verbs indicate the action or the state of being in the sentence. Some sentences have only a main verb, as, for example, *The cat walks on the fence* and *The cat walked on the fence.*

Helping (or **auxiliary**) **verbs,** such as *has, been,* and *will,* become part of the complete verb phrase in a sentence. Some helping verbs may sometimes be main verbs, as in *The cat has fur.* Some modifying words, such as *not, only,* and *always,* are not part of the verb; they are adverbs that modify the verb.

These are the most common helping verbs:

be (am, is, are, was, were, been, being)
do (does, did, done, doing)
have (has, had, having)
will (shall)

Modal Auxiliary Verbs

Modal auxiliary verbs, such as *needing, permitting,* or *wanting,* give further meaning to main verbs. These are the modal auxiliary verbs:

can	may	should	must	have to
could	might	would	ought to	

Notice that modal auxiliary verbs change form for tense but not for person:

> The cat could walk on the fence.
>
> The cats could walk on the fence.

Linking Verbs

Linking verbs connect a subject (a noun or pronoun) with its complement, that is, a word (adjective, noun, or pronoun) that modifies, renames, or means the same as the subject. These are the most common linking verbs:

> be (is, are, was, were, been)
> feel, look, smell, sound, taste (the five senses)
> appear, become, grow, prove, remain, seem, turn (conditions)

The cat is gray, The cat looks gray, and *The cat appears gray* use the linking verbs *is, looks,* and *appears. Gray* is an adjective that modifies *cat. The cat is a terror* and *The cat becomes a friend* use the linking verbs *is* and *becomes* and rename the cat *a terror* and *a friend,* both nouns. Because the complement renames or means the same as the subject, it is also in the subjective case if it is a pronoun. For that reason *It is I, The thief is she,* and *The enemies are they* are correct.

Most linking verbs, however, can also be nonlinking verbs. Notice the difference between *The cat smells bad* and *The cat smells a fish* or *The cat grew hungry* and *The cat grew long whiskers.*

Intransitive and Transitive Verbs

Intransitive verbs do not have a direct object, that is, a receiver of the action of the subject and verb. For example, in *The cat walks and jumps on the fence,* there is no direct object. *Walks* and *jumps* are intransitive verbs in this sentence.

Transitive verbs take a direct object. For example, in *The cat smells a fish, fish* is the direct object because it is the receiver of the action of the subject and verb. Ask who or what the cat smells, and the answer will be the direct object, *fish.*

Many verbs can be both intransitive and transitive in their use. For example, in *The cat walks,* the verb *walks* is intransitive because it does not have a direct object. But in *The man walks his cat,* if we ask "The man walks whom or what?" the answer is *cat.* So *walks* is a transitive verb in this sentence.

Be careful of considering other words and phrases as direct objects. They will not answer the question "Who or what?" with the subject and verb.

Regular and Irregular Verbs

Regular verbs, most of the verbs we use, follow a set pattern in forming tenses:

Present	Past	Past Participle	Present Participle
walk(s)	walked	have(has) walked	are(is) walking

Our third person singular verbs add *-s* (she talks); all others are the same. Notice that adding *-ed* to the base form of the verb changes it both to the past tense and the past participle. Adding *-ing* changes it to the present participle.

However, many verbs, including some of our most common ones, are ***irregular***; that is, they change their past tense and their past participles in various ways. Only the present participle has very little change in form.

List of Irregular Verbs

	Present	*Past*	*Past Participle*	*Present Participle*
Type 1	burst(s)	burst	burst	bursting
	knit(s)	knit	knit	knitting
	set(s)	set	set	setting
Type 2	come(s)	came	come	coming
	run(s)	ran	run	running
Type 3	bring(s)	brought	brought	bringing
	catch(es)	caught	caught	catching
	dig(s)	dug	dug	digging
	dive(s)	dived (dove)	dived	diving
	drag(s)	dragged	dragged	dragging
	fight(s)	fought	fought	fighting
	hang(s) (*person*)	hanged	hanged	hanging
	hang(s) (*thing*)	hung	hung	hanging
	lay(s)	laid	laid	laying
	lead(s)	led	led	leading
	lie(s) (*untrue*)	lied	lied	lying
	lose(s)	lost	lost	losing
	raise(s)	raised	raised	raising
	read(s)	read (say *red*)	read (say *red*)	reading
	sit(s)	sat	sat	sitting
Type 4	begin(s)	began	begun	beginning
	drink(s)	drank	drunk	drinking
	ring(s)	rang	rung	ringing
	shrink(s)	shrank	shrunk	shrinking
	sing(s)	sang	sung	singing

	sink(s)	sank	sunk	sinking
	spring(s)	sprang	sprung	springing
	swim(s)	swam	swum	swimming
Type 5	blow(s)	blew	blown	blowing
	do(es)	did	done	doing
	draw(s)	drew	drawn	drawing
	fly (flies)	flew	flown	flying
	grow(s)	grew	grown	growing
	know(s)	knew	known	knowing
	lie(s) (*recline*)	lay	lain	lying
	swear(s)	swore	sworn	swearing
	tear(s)	tore	torn	tearing
	wear(s)	wore	worn	wearing
Type 6	arise(s)	arose	arisen	arising
	bite(s)	bit	bitten	biting
	break(s)	broke	broken	breaking
	choose(s)	chose	chosen	choosing
	drive(s)	drove	driven	driving
	eat(s)	ate	eaten	eating
	fall(s)	fell	fallen	falling
	forget(s)	forgot	forgotten	forgetting
	freeze(s)	froze	frozen	freezing
	get(s)	got	gotten	getting
	give(s)	gave	given	giving
	hide(s)	hid	hidden	hiding
	ride(s)	rode	ridden	riding
	shake(s)	shook	shaken	shaking
	speak(s)	spoke	spoken	speaking
	steal(s)	stole	stolen	stealing
	take(s)	took	taken	taking
	write(s)	wrote	written	writing
Type 7	am (is, are)	was (were)	been	being
	go(es)	went	gone	going

Since regular verbs have the same form for both past tense and the past participle, people sometimes use the wrong form with irregular verbs. Often people use *should have went* and *might have ran* when they should use *should have gone* and *might have run*. We may speak the way that suits us and our audience, but we should write with attention to grammatical rules, so choose the precise verb form.

Exercise 2.1   Finding Verbs

Underline the **complete verbs** *in these paragraphs.*

Example   Her car <u>might</u> not <u>have been</u> new.

1. Tomatoes have become a part of almost every cuisine in the world although they entered the human diet inauspiciously. When native South Americans first found these plants, they thought the tomatoes were poisonous. But some brave person tried one, and then word of mouth traveled. Spanish explorers took them back to Europe; Portuguese explorers carried them to Asia. Malaysians made ketchup and the world loved it.

2. One of the basic foods of the world is the casava, although it can also be called *manioc* or *yuca* (sometimes spelled *yucca*). Casava may be eaten mashed, boiled, fried, or steamed. In Nigeria, for example, it is pounded into a flour and then cooked with water and eaten with meat stews. In Cuba, it is cut into chunks and steamed or fried with garlic. In Brazil, it is ground into a powder, toasted, and sprinkled on vegetables or beans.

3. Harvesting seaweed may be the next frontier for feeding a hungry world. Seaweed is rich in vitamins and protein, and it is also fat free, though rather high in sodium. People in the Canadian coastal provinces have long been eating what they call dulce while the Japanese have had many forms of seaweed for centuries. More recently, Americans have been introduced to seaweed in Japanese restaurants.

4. Fish may seem like an ordinary food, but to many Americans it is not. They eat mainly canned fish, such as tuna or salmon, and sometimes frozen fish sticks or fish filets. But many Japanese restaurants have opened in recent years; they serve raw fish on top of rice or rolled up in the rice. Many people thought they would never develop a taste for raw fish, but they find that with a little soy sauce and a touch of wasabe, it is quite tasty.

5. Australians use the term *bush tucker* for various foods from the outback introduced by aborigines to the European settlers. Bush tucker is comprised of many berries and various herbs that most people would find very good to eat. Also various flowers, flower petals, and leaves can be delicious raw or cooked. However, bush tucker also includes some insects and larvae, which may be tasty but may sound unappetizing to most people.

Exercise 2.2   Finding Verbs

Underline the **complete verbs** *in this essay.*

Money Madness

My friend Suzanne is such an impractical person. She has enough money to support herself and her three children, but she is always strapped anyway. She just doesn't know how to budget and to spend wisely within her means. Her attempt at clothes shopping is a good example.

Suzanne lost quite a lot of weight a couple of years ago and decided to buy a whole new wardrobe. She could have altered her present wardrobe, but she had been wanting some new clothes, so she threw all her old clothes out. During an all-day blitz, she went to almost all the clothes stores in the mall and bought six new blouses, six new skirts, three sweaters, and two pairs of pants.

When she dressed the next morning, she discovered her big mistake. The flowered blouses did not go with the polka-dotted and plaid skirts, the embroidered sweaters clashed with the striped pants and the skirts. She didn't have anything to wear. Luckily, she had the black sweatsuit she wore to the stores. Now she wears all the tops with the black sweatpants and all the bottoms with the black sweatshirt.

As soon as she gets more money, Suzanne is going to buy even more clothes. This time she will stick strictly to solid colors. She certainly has wasted a lot of time and effort on her wardrobe.

Exercise 2.3   Changing Verb Tenses

*Using **past, present,** and **future tenses,** change whatever tense you find to one of the other two tenses.*

Example   My dog ~~was~~ a dachshund.
                       is

1. Maria is an architect. She works in a firm that has a good reputation among the social elite. She builds houses for clients who have a lot of money to spend. Even though her clients want to hire her and give her free rein to do what she wants, she knows she has to please them. So Maria feels a lot of pressure to be flexible and to do good work.

2. Jamie was a *barrista,* a person who knew all about coffee and how to make different coffee drinks. He practiced all the special techniques. He knew how to use an espresso machine; he could add just the right amount of milk, or *latte;* he was perfect at making cappuccino. His efficiency was beautiful to watch. He hoped one day to have his own coffee lounge.

3. Tokyo will be an almost earthquake-proof city. Old buildings will be retrofitted so that they will withstand shaking; they will have reinforced understructures

built on to the old structures. New buildings will adhere to a strict code of construction. Tall buildings especially will be built with an underground "cradle" that will rock with a quake, so the building will not fall down.

4. Soccer was the most popular sport in the world. It was played in all the countries of Central and South America, Africa, and Asia. In North America, especially Canada and Mexico, people have played soccer for years, and the United States has played recently in two World Cups. Sometimes players have become rowdy, but mostly fans, not players, from various countries have caused trouble.

5. Michael's dream was to win a million dollars in the lottery. He thought that if he just bought enough tickets, he would win the whole amount some day. So he spent about twenty dollars a week only on tickets. If he had saved that money over ten years, he would have had a nice nest egg. But he thought the enjoyment of buying the tickets and dreaming about winning gave him more pleasure.

Exercise 2.4   Using Irregular Verbs

*Fill in the blanks with the correct form of the **irregular verb** whose base form has been indicated in parentheses.*

Example   Yesterday the cat (swim) __swam__ in the pool.

1. What's better than a swimming pool on a hot day? I hadn't (go) _____ to the pool or (swim) _____ for over a year. I (dive) _____ into that refreshing water, (sink) _____ to the bottom, (spring) _____ up to the surface, (shake) _____ the water off, and then (lie) _____ on a deck chair for hours. When I (leave) _____, the sun had already (set) _____. A perfect day had (draw) _____ to a close.

2. People can be very inconsiderate at the movies. One couple had already (come) _____ late and then (get) _____ up to buy popcorn. Then they (fight) _____ with each other about who had (forget) _____ the drinks. When they (bring)

_____ their drinks in, they (see) _____ they had (lose) _____ their seats, so they (choose) _____ others by going up and down the aisle looking and asking. Then they made so much noise with their food you'd think they hadn't (eat) _____ or (drink) _____ anything for days.

3. My son (swear) _____ he would keep his new clothes clean and nice. But one day I (can) _____ see that he had (tear) _____ his pants on purpose. He (lie) _____ by saying he had (fall) _____ down and (rip) _____ both knees. The next day I (catch) _____ him with scissors and another pair of new pants. He had already (cut) _____ a hole in one knee. I have (give) _____ up hope. I (buy) _____ his latest pair of pants at the Salvation Army.

4. Years ago Los Angeles had plans for a subway system to help connect this vast city. Although construction had (begin) _____ and huge holes had been (dig) _____, further plans have (break) _____ down. Delays and changes have (drive) _____ up the price, further negotiations have (get) _____ nowhere, and things have (go) _____ from bad to worse. The city may have (bite) _____ off more than it can chew. Even though it has (take) _____ much longer than anyone ever (think) _____, it still might be (build) _____ one day.

5. I (be) _____ very thankful for e-mail. I never (think) _____ I would like it, but now I have (write) _____ to friends and relatives I haven't (catch) _____ up with in years. Some of their jokes have (drag) _____ out for pages, but somehow I haven't (grow) _____ tired of them. And I have never (choose) _____ to just delete the jokes without reading them. Maybe I have (lead) _____ a dull life, but I have (get)

_____ so involved with e-mail that I have even (arise)
_____ early to look at it.

Exercise 2.5   Using Verb Tenses

Write paragraphs using the following **verbs.** *Add adverbs, such as* not, only, *and* always, *if you wish.*

1. swear(s)   has sworn   will have sworn   will have been swearing

2. ride(s)   rode   has (have) ridden   has (have) been riding

3. freeze(s)   will freeze   will have frozen   has (have) frozen

4. drink(s)   drank   has (have) drunk   will have been drinking

5. break(s)   broke   has (have) broken   had been broken

6. blow(s)   blew   has (have) been blown   will have blown

7. hang(s)   hung   has (have) hung   had been hung

8. knit(s)   knit   has (have) been knit   will knit

9. hide(s)   hid   has (have) hidden   had been hidden

10. take(s)   took   has (have) taken   will have taken

Exercise 2.6   Using Irregular Verb Tenses

Write paragraphs using the following **irregular verbs.** *Add adverbs, such as* not, only, *and* always, *if you wish.*

1. speak(s)   spoke   has (have) spoken   will have been speaking

2. lie(s) (*recline*)   lay   has (have) lain   would have been lying

3. spring(s)   sprang   has (have) sprung   should have been sprung

4. shake(s)   shook   has (have) been shaken   could have been shaken

5. give(s)   gave   has (have) been given   might have been given

6. go(es)   went   should have gone   would have gone

7. arise(s)   arose   could have arisen   may have arisen

8. drive(s)   drove   would have driven   should have been driven

9. bring(s)   brought   could have brought   might have brought

10. bite(s)   bit   may have been bitten   should have been bitten

Exercise 2.7   Proofreading

Find the verbs and change some of them to keep consistent verb tenses in each paragraph.

1. Sumo wrestling is highly popular in Japan, where the champion wrestlers will be treated like movie stars. However, they follow very strict rules in their lives. They have eaten very carefully and will practice many hours every day.

2. Tossing the caber is a popular sport in Scotland. It consisted of a man's lifting a fir tree pole (the caber) about seventeen feet long and weighing about ninety pounds and throwing it. The person who will throw it the farthest wins the game.

3. Although mountain biking probably started with a bicyclist's enjoying a little recreation and exercise, it has now become a sport with events, sponsors, and even admission fees to watch racers. It will seem that no recreation has escaped competition and commercialism.

4. One of the new sports in the Winter Olympics is curling, a game that uses granite rocks, ice, and brooms. It originated in Scotland, where ice was plentiful in winter, granite rocks will not be hard to find, and where, probably, every household has a collection of various brooms.

5. Bungee jumping has become a popular pastime in the past several years. People climb to a high platform usually attached to a crane. They will strap themselves into a harness and then, with the help of bungee cords, jumped off the platform, nearly hit the ground, and then sprang back up again several times.

Summary

I. Definition: **Verbs** present the action or state of being in sentences.
II. Tenses of Verbs
    A. The **past tense** of verbs consists of the simple past, past progressive, past perfect, past perfect progressive.
        Examples: *He swam.* (past)
                  He was swimming. (past progressive)
                  He had swum. (past perfect)
                  He had been swimming. (past perfect progressive)

B. The **present tense** of verbs consists of the simple present, present progressive, present perfect, present perfect progressive.

Examples: *He swims.* (simple present)

He is swimming. (present progressive)

He has swum. (present perfect)

He has been swimming. (present perfect progressive)

C. The **future tense** of verbs consists of the simple future, future progressive, future perfect, future perfect progressive.

Examples: *He will swim.* (simple future)

He is going to swim. (also simple future)

He will be swimming. (future progressive)

He will have swum. (future perfect)

He will have been swimming. (future perfect progressive)

III. Main Verbs and Helping Verbs

A. The **main verbs** (the base form) are the most important part of the verb.

Example: *He swims.*

B. The **helping verbs** consist of auxiliary (helping) verbs, modal auxiliary verbs, and linking verbs.

1. Auxiliary (helping) verbs complete the main verb and become part of the complete verb phrase.

Example: *He **has** swum.*

2. Modal auxiliary verbs give further meaning to main verbs.

Example: *He **can** swim, so he **should** swim.*

3. Linking verbs connect the subject with a word that modifies, renames, or means the same as the subject.

Examples: *She looks happy.* (modifies)

She became a nurse. (renames)

She is a nurse. (means the same as subject)

IV. Regular and Irregular Verbs

A. **Regular verbs** form past tense and past participles by adding *-ed.*

Examples: *They **danced**.* (past tense)

*They have **danced**.* (past participle)

B. **Irregular verbs** form past tense and past participles in a variety of ways that must be memorized.

Examples: *They **hid**.* (past tense)

*They have **hidden**.* (past participle)

*He **flew**.* (past tense)

*He has **flown**.* (past participle)

Chapter 3

Adjectives and Adverbs

Read the following paragraph and underline the words that modify (describe) other words, that is, the **adjectives** and **adverbs.** Don't worry if you don't get all of them.

I feel like a brown bag of miscellany propped against a wall. Against a wall in company with other bags, white, red and yellow. Pour out the contents, and there is discovered a jumble of small things priceless and worthless. A first-water diamond, an empty spool, bits of broken glass, lengths of string, a key to a door long since crumbled away, a rusty knife-blade, old shoes saved for a road that never was and never will be, a nail bent under the weight of things too heavy for any nail, a dried flower or two still a little fragrant. In your hand is the brown bag. On the ground before you is the jumble it held—so much like the jumble in the bags could they be emptied, that all might be dumped in a single heap and the bags refilled without altering the contents of any greatly. A bit of colored glass more or less would not matter. Perhaps that is how the Great Stuffer of Bags filled them in the first place—who knows? (Zora Neale Hurston, "How It Feels to Be Colored Me," from *I Love Myself When I Am Laughing*)

Adjectives and adverbs are not strictly necessary for complete sentences in the way that nouns and verbs are, but they add meaning, interest, specifics, and details. Adjectives and adverbs differ in the words they *modify* (describe).

Adjectives and Adjectivals

Adjectives and adjectivals (words used as adjectives) describe nouns and pronouns. *Adjectives* tell the number (three, some), size (large), shape (oval), quality (happy), color (blue), and ethnic or religious quality (Jewish) of a noun or pronoun.

Adjectivals are words from various parts of speech used as adjectives to modify a noun or pronoun. Adjectivals include:

The *definite article:* the
The *indefinite articles:* a, an
The *demonstratives when used with a noun:* this, that, these, those

The ***possessive adjectives:*** *my, your, his, her, its, our, their, whose*
The ***possessive nouns and pronouns:*** *Michael's, today's, nobody's*
The ***past and present participles of verbs:*** *broken* wheel, *dancing* bears
Other nouns themselves: *spider plant, soccer ball, oak tree.*

Adjectives usually follow this order:

Article, demonstrative, or possessive	Number	Size	Shape	Quality	Color	Ethnic or religious designation	Noun used as adjective	
the	three	large	round	flowery	red	American	cowboy	hats
these	few		fat	happy	white	Persian	house	cats
Susan's	one	small	square		grayish	Catholic		church
	some	tiny	thin	crushed	blue		river	stones

Adjectives sometimes come later in a sentence and are called ***predicate adjectives*** or ***complements:***

Her three favorite dresses are **large** and **flowery.**

The blue house looks **small.**

Another useful way to look at these modifying words is through the system of determiners. ***Determiners*** include indefinite articles (*a, an*), the definite article (*the*), demonstratives (*this, those*), possessive adjectives (*my, her, their*), possessive nouns and pronouns (*Alice's, her dog's, everyone's, anybody's*), quantity words (*a lot of, every, some*), and numbers (*two, fourteen*).

Adverbs

Adverbs describe verbs, adjectives, and other adverbs:

Describing verbs: drive **slowly,** eat **fast**
Describing adjectives: **very** large dresses, **too** much food
Describing adverbs: drive **very** slowly, **much** too much food

Many adverbs end in *-ly,* but a few common adjectives also end in *-ly* (*friendly, gingerly, leisurely, miserly*). A number of common words can be both adjectives and adverbs (*fast, much*).

Good *and* Well, Bad *and* Badly

When to use *good* versus *well* and *bad* versus *badly* can be tricky. *Good* is an adjective and is used, as all adjectives are, to describe a noun (a good *book,* The *book* is good). *Well* is an adverb and is used, like all adverbs, to describe a verb, adjective, or adverb (*He speaks* well, *a* well-*rounded education*), but is also an adjective (*a* well *person*). In *The athlete looks good, good* (an adjective) describes the *athlete's* physique. In *The athlete looks well, well* (an adjective used with the linking verb *looks*) can describe the athlete's health, OR *well* (an adverb describing the verb *looks*) can tell how the athlete is able to observe. In the case of *bad* and *badly*, we can use *bad* only when describing a person, thing, or idea (a noun or pronoun) because it is an adjective (*a bad dog, The tree looks bad.*). *Badly* is an adverb and describes a verb, adjective, or adverb. So *I feel badly* would describe the numbness of my fingertips or my poor ability to feel emotions.

Comparatives and Superlatives

In using adjectives in comparisons, you should add *-er* to one- and some two-syllable words (*taller, happier*) and *more* or *less* to some two- and all three- or more syllable words (*more frequent, less intelligent*). For superlatives, adjectives add *-est* to one- and some two-syllable words (*tallest, happiest*) and *most* or *least* to most two- and all three- or more syllable words (*our most frequent, least intelligent*). Whether two-syllable adjectives are used one way or the other is a matter of regional differences. (Some people use *stupidest* and some *most stupid*, for example.)

Adjectivals—articles, demonstratives, possessives, and nouns—cannot be used in the comparative or superlative. Neither can numbers themselves, although some quantities can (*the fewest, the most, the least*). Determiners also cannot become comparative or superlative except for some quantities.

Adverbs add *-er* to one-syllable words (rare since so many adverbs end in *-ly*) and *more* or *less* for the comparative (*more quickly, less intelligently*). For the superlative, you add *-est* for one-syllable words (rare) and *most* or *least* to all other adverbs (*the most slowly, least intelligently*). Only adverbs that modify verbs can be used in the comparative and the superlative.

Some of our most common adjectives, however, are exceptions:

	Comparative	Superlative
good	better	best
bad	worse	worst

A few adjectives, such as *unique, perfect,* and *favorite,* are already superlative in meaning, so they cannot be made comparative or superlative. Something cannot be "more unique" or "the most perfect," or "my most favorite."

Grammar is changing, however. Since such a common word as *fast* is both an adjective and adverb, many people think that all the comparative and superlative forms of the adjective and the adverb are the same. So instead of using, for example, *more quickly,* as in *The plane gets you there more quickly* (the correct form), they write or say, "The plane gets you there quicker," using the adjective form instead of the adverb form. Also *the most unique, my most favorite,* and *more perfect* have become common phrases. Sometimes using a popular expression seems preferable to using the grammatically correct form, especially in speaking, but for writing you should stay with the correct forms.

Punctuating Adjectives and Adverbs

Coordinate adjectives should have a comma after each adjective EXCEPT the final one before the noun or pronoun they modify. Test for coordinate adjectives by adding *and* between each adjective; if adding *and* sounds all right, then replace the *and* with a comma:

the big and bad wolf = the big, bad wolf

some small and sweet and ripe berries = some small, sweet, ripe berries

my tired and aching and blistered feet = my tired, aching, blistered feet

Adjectivals (EXCEPT for past and present participles), numbers, nouns, and the final adjective do not take commas after them:

some maple leaves

a soccer ball

these nine vacation spots

When you mix coordinate adjectives, adjectivals, numbers, and nouns, be sure to put the commas where they belong:

possessive adjective	number	quality	present participle	color		
her	three	beautiful,	flowing,	red		dresses

possessive noun	size	quality	ethnic		
Joe's	big,	flowery	Hawaiian		shirt

number	quality	quality		color	noun	
two	blooming,	luxuriant,		green	spider	plants

Adverbs also take commas after each one except the last one (*my very, very old sweater; driving quickly, recklessly, and dangerously*). If you add *and* in a series of three or more adjectives or adverbs, use a comma before the *and* unless the last two items are linked (*My car is large, clumsy, and old; I eat apples, pears, and peaches and cream*). Journalists generally omit the comma before *and* in a series.

Exercise 3.1 Finding Adjectives, Adjectivals, and Adverbs

*Underline the **adjectives**, **adjectivals**, and **adverbs** in these paragraphs. Notice the punctuation.*

Example True contentment is extremely rare.

1. This old classroom barely deserves its name. Some walk-in closets are probably larger and neater, although the bright lights glow garishly. Bits of paper held by staples, tape, and glue dot the drab green walls, reminding students of missed events. Wooden desks are mutilated with graffiti. The scuffed, gouged, brownish floor tiles sit loosely, posing hazards for the inattentive walker. The ceiling tiles are studded with dried wads of gum, a reminder of childish, bored students.

2. My English professor is small, round, and gray. She is short, probably not much over five feet tall, and wears flat shoes, so she doesn't help matters. At least, when she stands in front of our class she seems pretty much the same height as all the seated students. Her shortness is emphasized by her roundness. Her nonexistent waist is the largest part of her round body. Her gray hair is matched usually by gray clothes. Even when she wears other colors like navy blue or black, she still looks gray.

3. The cherry blossoms in Washington, D.C., are beautiful. There are hundreds of pink and white trees lining the Tidal Basin and along Haines Point. Around mid-April most of the cherry blossoms bloom, so tourists come for the festival. Mostly though, people just like to stroll slowly among the blooming trees enjoying the delicate blossoms, sometimes picking up a fallen bloom to wear in a buttonhole.

4. My brother's house is full of funny things that he has collected. He has slimy-looking plastic slugs lying around the kitchen; they look so real that people are startled. Also he has a coffee cup on its side with fake coffee flowing out on the dining table. On a side table he has some real-looking fake food, like bagels and sushi, lying around. He changes things around often, so I never know what to expect when I visit.

5. When I lived in the tropics, postage stamps did not have glue on the back. The weather was so humid and steamy that even dry glue would melt and stick to anything. I always had a bottle of glue next to my small supply of stamps. I would put a dab of glue on a piece of scrap paper; then I would rub the back of the stamp in the glue and quickly stick it on my envelope. In modern times, self-stick stamps that come in big sheets or little rolls have really revolution-ized postage stamps.

Exercise 3.2   Finding Adjectives and Adverbs

*Underline the **five comparative** and **superlative adjectives** and **adverbs** in each of these paragraphs. Write **ADJ** for adjectives and **ADV** for adverbs above the examples.*

Example   She won the contest for the <u>loudest</u> shirt.

ADJ

1. When I was young, I wanted the biggest and most luxurious house of all. I thought I would make friends more quickly, and they would like me the most if I seemed richer.

2. In high school, I wanted the newest, fastest, and brightest car so everyone would be impressed. But the most popular kids seemed to have more important things on their minds.

3. At work, my colleagues thought I was the laziest person. I was the latest to arrive and the earliest to leave, and I had the weakest bladder. They all said my jokes were the funniest, but the boss didn't laugh and fired me.

4. In college, I have decided to be the most intellectual and the most studious. Now other students telephone me more often and sit more closely to me in class. But are they being friendlier, or do they just want to copy my notes?

5. I have decided to be the best student in my classes. The professors think I am the smartest student, so they give me the most attention and feel the most satisfied with me. When I do well, the professors feel better.

6. Of course, I am not the smartest person in any of my classes. However, I am the hardest-working one. I take the most notes in class, I take the longest on exams, and I start my term papers the earliest of anyone.

7. In class I raise my hand more often than anyone and ask the most questions. I like to get the best information from my professors; they really have to work harder when I'm there. I want to make sure that I have the most complete information on a topic.

8. I also answer the most questions in class. When we have group discussions, I am always the best leader. I get better discussions from all the other students by probing them more deeply even when they make the stupidest statements.

9. Sometimes I think I am the most hated student in class. I make the other students look bad, especially the worst students who are the least involved. I do my best to help everyone, but if others don't make the slightest effort, my time is wasted.

10. Since I have resolved to do better in life, I have been much happier. Concentrating harder on my work has made me more efficient, so I now have time for leisurely pursuits. I hope to become more proficient at skiing.

Exercise 3.3   Filling in Adjectives and Adverbs

*In the following paragraphs, fill in appropriate **adjectives** and **adverbs**. Add other words if necessary.*

Example   Contentment is a ___rare___ trait.

1. Swimming is _____ sport. All you need is _____ pool. The water is _____, _____, and _____. Swimming laps feels _____ and _____.

2. His _____ car was _____ I had ever seen. The _____ body had _____ paint and _____ chrome. The _____ seats looked _____.

3. Venice, Italy, is possibly _____ city in the world. The freedom from cars makes the city feel _____ and _____. The _____ canals crisscross between _____ buildings, making travel by boat _____ way to go. Gondolas are for tourists but still _____ and _____.

4. My _____ sister is _____ girl. She plays _____ sports and has _____ been on a team. She _____ takes _____ lessons and competes in _____ contests. She has _____ won _____ medals.

5. The _____ sycamore trees along my _____ street have very _____ leaves and particularly _____ bark. Unlike other trees, the bark on the sycamore is _____ and _____. In the autumn, the leaves _____ cover the ground, so I have to rake them. But during the rest of the year, I have to rake the _____ bark because it looks _____ and _____ lying on the ground.

Exercise 3.4   Writing with Adjectives and Adverbs

A. *Use the indicated **adjectives** to write sentences.*

Example   (tiny, small) ___I have a small car with a tiny stereo.___

1. (monstrous, enormous) _____

   _____

2. (gigantic, immense) _____

   _____

3. (gargantuan, colossal) _____

   _____

4. (minuscule, puny) _____

   _____

5. (infinitesimal, wee) _____

   _____

6. (lilliputian, petite) _____

   _____

7. (fiery, scalding) _____

   _____

8. (sweltering, torrid) _____

   _____

9. (frigid, icy) _____

   _____

10. (nippy, chilly) _____

    _____

11. (sensitive, touchy) _____

    _____

12. (leisurely, friendly) _____

    _____

B. *Use the indicated* **adverbs** *to write sentences.*

Example   (quickly, rapidly) __I can run rapidly but become tired quickly.__

1. (monstrously, enormously) _____

   _____

2. (hugely, immensely) _____

   _____

3. (colossally, widely) _____

   _____

4. (microscopically, minutely) _____

   _____

5. (infinitesimally, diminutively) _____

   _____

6. (heatedly, torridly) _____

   _____

7. (feverishly, hotly) _____

   _____

8. (frigidly, icily) _____

   _____

9. (frostily, chillingly) _____

   _____

10. (inconsequentially, oddly) _____

    _____

11. (subtly, elusively) _____

    _____

12. (surreptitiously, obscurely) _____

    _____

Exercise 3.5   Writing with Adjectives and Adverbs

Use the indicated **adjectives** *and* **adverbs** *to write sentences.*

Example   (quick, quickly) __I need a quick haircut; I can do the job quickly with your__
   __help.__

1. (legal, legally) _____

_____

2. (honest, honestly) _____

_____

3. (free, freely) _____

_____

4. (simple, simply) _____

_____

5. (candid, candidly) _____

_____

6. (soft, loudly) _____

_____

7. (loud, softly) _____

_____

8. (peaceful, angrily) _____

_____

9. (angry, peacefully) _____

_____

10. (rash, cautiously) _____

_____

11. (cautious, rashly) _____

_____

12. (foolhardy, timidly) _____

_____

Exercise 3.6   Writing with Adjectives and Adverbs

*A. Write a paragraph using **adjectives** and **adverbs** to describe:*

1. Your textbook _____

_____

_____

_____

_____

2. Used socks _____

_____

_____

_____

3. A perfect tomato _____

_____

_____

_____

4. Your favorite singer, actor, or athlete _____

_____

_____

_____

_____

5. A classmate _____

_____

_____

_____

_____

B. *Write sentences using a **comparative adjective**, a **superlative adjective**, or an **adverb**, for each of these adjectives.*

Example   (good) ___*She is a better student than I am.*_____

1. (bad) _____

2. (clean) _____

3. (dirty) _____

4. (wild) _____

5. (silly) _____

6. (casual) _____

7. (beautiful) _____

8. (friendly) _____

9. (mean) _____

10. (ugly) _____

Exercise 3.7   Proofreading

A. Add **commas** *after the adjectives and adverbs where needed.*
B. *Change* **comparative adjectives, superlative adjectives,** *and* **adverbs** *to their correct form.*

The Politics of Earthquakes

Our world is constantly changing its form, but an earthquake is a definite dramatic reminder that our world is not a very stable place in more ways than one.

Earthquakes cause more or less damage depending on their location, first of all. The damagingest earthquakes occur in very populated areas. If the construction of buildings has been done bad, many will topple, often killing or wounding the inhabitants. So earthquakes are often the problem of the most poor people.

For the relative few more rich industrial areas, houses built good can withstand much of an earthquake. Even if cracks occur, ceilings and floors do not collapse and kill inhabitants.

So earthquakes, while certain an act of nature, are also a political issue, just as many, many other issues are.

Summary

  I. Adjectives and Adjectivals
    A. Definition: **Adjectives** and **adjectivals** describe nouns and pronouns.
    B. Types and uses of adjectives
      1. Adjectives tell the number.
        Examples: *six, several, some, a few*
      2. Adjectives describe size.
        Examples: *huge, gigantic, tiny*
      3. Adjectives describe shape.
        Examples: *square, flat, rounded*

4. Adjectives describe a quality of the noun or pronoun.
   Examples: *decorated, sad, enthusiastic*
5. Adjectives describe color.
   Examples: *reddish, blue, scarlet*
6. Adjectives give an ethnic or religious designation.
   Examples: *Asian, Irish, Jewish, Catholic*
7. Nouns are used as adjectives to describe.
   Examples: *brick* (house), *cargo* (ship)

C. Types of adjectivals
   1. Articles
      a. The definite article is *the.*
         Examples: *the house, the tree*
      b. The indefinite articles are *a* and *an.*
         Examples: *a person, an apple, an hour*
   2. Demonstratives are adjectivals when used with a noun (*this, that, these, those*).
      Examples: *this pig, those pigs*
   3. Possessives are adjectivals that show ownership (*my, your, his, her, its, our, their, whose*).
      Examples: *my dog, your pig, our stable*
   4. Possessive nouns and pronouns show ownership.
      Examples: *Pete's place, yesterday's news, nobody's business*
   5. Past and present participles are used to modify.
      Examples: *the **crooked** path* (past participle)
                *a **flowing** brook* (present participle)
   6. Nouns themselves can modify.
      *Examples: **mountain** caves, **lion** cubs, **field** mice*

D. Order of adjectives and adjectivals
   1. First come articles, demonstratives, or possessives.
   2. Number comes next.
   3. Size, shape, quality, and color usually follow.
   4. Ethnic or religious designation comes next.
   5. Last comes any noun used as an adjective.
      Example: *The two huge, ugly, gray Chinese lap dogs.*

II. Adverbs
   A. Definition: *Adverbs* describe verbs, adjectives, and other adverbs.
      1. Adverbs describe verbs.
         Examples: *drink **quickly**, run **smoothly***
      2. Adverbs describe adjectives.
         Examples: ***hardly** enough food, **too** many people*
      3. Adverbs describe other adverbs.
         Examples: *drink **too** quickly, walk **very** rapidly*

III. *Good* and *Well, Bad* and *Badly*
   A. *Good* is an adjective.
      Example: *good dogs*

B. *Well* is an adjective and adverb.
    Examples: *a well body* (adjective)
                  She runs well. (adverb)
C. *Bad* is an adjective.
    Examples: *a bad habit, bad attitudes*
D. *Badly* is an adverb.
    Example: *He sings badly.*
IV. Comparatives and Superlatives
    A. Adjectives
        1. Add *-er* for **comparative** and *-est* for **superlative** of one- and some two-syllable adjectives.
            Examples: *taller person, craziest experience*
        2. Add *more* or *less* for comparative and *most* or *least* for some two- and all three- or more syllable words.
            Examples: *more intelligent child, less trustworthy agent, most persistent person, least attentive audience*
        3. Adjectivals, numbers, noun modifiers, and determiners do not have comparative and superlative forms.
            Examples: *these three plastic cups, two cats*
    B. Adverbs
        1. Add *more* for comparative and *most* for superlative.
            Examples: *more quickly, most quickly*
        2. Only adverbs modifying verbs have comparative and superlative forms.
    C. Exceptions of comparative and superlative forms
        1. *Good* takes the forms *good, better, best.*
            Examples: *my good hat, my better hat, my best hat*
        2. *Bad* takes the forms *bad, worse, worst.*
            Examples: *my bad book, my worse book, my worst book*
    D. Words already superlative: *favorite, perfect, unique*
        Example: *my favorite hat* (NOT *most favorite hat*)
V. Punctuating Adjectives and Adverbs
    A. Place a comma after each adjective EXCEPT for articles, demonstratives, possessives, numbers, and the last one.
    B. Place a comma after each adverb except the last one.
    C. Place a comma before *and* in a series of three or more adjectives or adverbs with commas.

Chapter 4

Prepositions, Conjunctions, and Interjections

Read the following paragraph and underline the **prepositions,** double underline the **conjunctions,** and circle the **interjections.** Don't worry if you don't get all of them.

Indeed, the facts and consequences of auto congestion are greatly exaggerated in most large cities. During rush hour, I have driven into and out of Dallas, Kansas City, Phoenix, St. Louis, and San Diego without much more than an occasional slowdown. Moreover, despite the massive reliance on cars and a short-term decline in the economic vitality of their downtown areas, most of these cities have restored their central areas. Kansas City is bleak in the old downtown, but the shopping area (built 75 years ago!) called Country Club Plaza is filled with people, stores, and restaurants. San Diego and San Francisco have lively downtowns. Los Angeles even managed to acquire a downtown (actually, several downtowns) after it grew up without much of one—and this in a city allegedly "built around the car." Phoenix is restoring its downtown and San Diego never really lost its center. (James Q. Wilson, "Cars and Their Enemies," *Commentary*)

Prepositions

Like conjunctions, ***prepositions*** are connecting words and appear frequently in our sentences. We have hundreds of prepositions, but here are some of the common ones:

about	among	below	during	in place of
above	around	beneath	except	in regard to
according to	as	beside	except for	inside
across	as for	between	for	in spite of
after	at	beyond	from	instead of
against	because of	by	in	into
along	before	despite	in addition to	like
along with	behind	down	in front of	near

of	outside	throughout	underneath	within
off	over	till	until	without
on	past	to	up	
out	since	toward	upon	
out of	through	under	with	

To picture a preposition, imagine it as what a squirrel can do to a tree or trees; for example, a squirrel can go *in* a tree, *near* a tree, *up* a tree. Of course, some prepositions such as *like* or *until* will not work.

Most frequently, prepositions are used to begin prepositional phrases: *to* the beach, *with* singing and dancing, *for* whatever you want. These prepositional phrases may be used as adjectives and adverbs. If the preposition *to* is followed by a verb, *to* is not a preposition but forms the **infinitive**—that is, the base form—of the verb (*to be, to see, to walk*).

A frequent use of prepositions occurs in **two-part verbs.** Verbs already often have more than one part since a base verb may have a helping verb. But some verbs also have a preposition (also called a **particle**) at the end that changes the meaning of the verb. Notice the difference between these two sentences:

The injured person **came to** in five minutes.

The injured person **came to** the emergency ward.

In the first sentence, *came to* means "regained consciousness." *To* is a preposition that is part of the verb, and *in five minutes* is a prepositional phrase. In the second sentence, *came* is simply the past tense of *come*, and *to the emergency ward* is a prepositional phrase.

Among the many two-part verbs, here are a few:

catch up	put over	stand up	tune down	turn out
come to	run into	take in	tune in	walk on
drop in	see about	take on	tune off	walk up
drop out	see to	take to	tune out	watch for
follow up	sit down	think of	turn down	watch out
look after	sit up	think over	turn in	win over
look in	stand for	think up	turn off	

(We even have some three-part verbs, such as *feel up to* and *look in on*.) Most can be used either as a two-part verb or as a verb plus the preposition of a prepositional phrase. To tell the difference between these forms, see if another entirely different verb can replace the verb, such as *tend* for "look after," *ponder* for "think over," and *pass* for "walk on." See if the verb without the preposition has an entirely different meaning: *stand* and *stand for* have very different meanings. See if a prepositional phrase follows the verb; for example, *She looks out for her mother* has *looks out* as a two-part verb and *for her mother* as a prepositional phrase. See if the two parts of the two-part verb can be separated and still mean the same; for instance, *turn down the offer* may also be *turn the offer down*. Figuring out these forms is not always easy, however, and it takes some practice.

Conjunctions

Conjunctions connect words, phrases, and whole sentences to each other. These are some common conjunctions:

after	either . . . or	or	when
although	even though	provided	where
and	for	since	whereas
because	if	so	while
before	neither . . . nor	though	yet
both . . . and	nor	unless	
but	not only . . . but (also)	until	

Notice that some conjunctions have more than one part, so that the parts occur in earlier and then later parts of a sentence. Use these *correlative conjunctions* as follows:

Neither an ATM **nor** the post office has travelers' checks.

You must go **either** to your bank **or** to American Express.

You should have **both** travelers' checks **and** foreign currency.

Not only will you have immediate cash **but also** you will feel safe with checks.

Correlatives have the same structure after each part, whether they are nouns, prepositional phrases, or complete sentences.

As is true of most words, many conjunctions also serve as other parts of speech. Fortunately, our most common ones, *and* and *or*, are always conjunctions and nothing else.

Interjections

Interjections include those mild or strong words we use at the beginning of a sentence usually to express some emotion: "*Oh*, I forgot my camera. *My goodness*! I'm so forgetful." Sometimes the interjection can appear in mid-sentence: *He had, well, deviated from the truth.* Although *well* may appear occasionally, interjections rarely appear in most formal writing, except for dialogue. Obscene interjections should never be used unless they are quoted directly from others when exact wording is necessary.

Some interjections do not come from other parts of speech: *amen, egad, gosh, golly, gee, heck, hey, oh, wow, yikes.* But many words are used as interjections (or *exclamations*) while also being other parts of speech: *boy, cool, damn, God, great, heavens, hell, incredible, indeed, Jesus Christ, no kidding, really, swell, well.* Many other words are also used with emphasis enough to sound like an exclamation.

Exercise 4.1   Finding Prepositions, Conjunctions, and Interjections

A. Underline the **twelve prepositions** *in this paragraph. Be careful not to confuse the* to *in infinitive verbs (for example,* to live*) with prepositions.*

Let us imagine what life would be like in a carless nation. People would have to live very close together so they could walk or, for healthy people living in sunny climes, bicycle to mass-transit stops. Living in close quarters would mean life as it is now lived in Manhattan. There would be few freestanding homes, many row houses, and lots of apartment buildings. There would be few private gardens except for flowerpots on balconies. The streets would be congested by pedestrians, trucks, and buses, as they were at the turn of the century before automobiles became common. (James Q. Wilson, "Cars and Their Enemies," *Commentary*)

B. Underline the **nine conjunctions** *in this paragraph:*

Marriage arrangements are usually described from the man's point of view, not because the desires of women are irrelevant but because powerful men have usually gotten their way. Men are bigger and stronger because they have been selected to fight one another, and they can form powerful clans because in traditional societies sons stay near their families and daughters move away. The most florid polygynists are always despots, men who could kill without fear of retribution. The hyperpolygynist not only must fend off the hundreds of men he has deprived of wives, but must oppress his harem. (Steven Pinker, *How the Mind Works*)

C. Underline the **interjections** *in this paragraph.*

A perfect marriage requires, well, two perfect people. They must agree on the small issues (vacations, cleaning, friends and relatives), the medium issues (location, working, children), and the big issues (ethics, morality, political stance, lifestyle). Oh, let's not forget the most important issue of all: spending money. If all these factors come together for two people, *voilà*, they have the perfect marriage.

D. Underline the **eighteen prepositions** *in this paragraph.*

Cars have made suburban life possible. Before cars, people lived in cities, where they were very close to each other; they used trams for transportation. In the country, people relied on horses and buggies for transportation. They were isolated and rarely went into the city. Cars allowed people to live farther away from their jobs, so that they could commute to and from the city. With improved roads, highways, and suburban trains, people could live even farther from the city and still commute. A normal commute might entail an hour on the train, then a half hour in the car. In many ways, it meant a better life for the family.

*E. Underline the **thirteen conjunctions** in this paragraph.*

Because suburban life was supposed to be better than urban life, many people aspired to buy that little house with a garden and a picket fence. Yet many found that suburban life either isolating or expensive or both. The family stayed away from the city, and the breadwinner spent too much time commuting. Children could run and play outdoors, but they did not go to museums, zoos, or cultural events. When large shopping malls began to open, families and groups of teenagers congregated in them to visit and shop. But often they stayed home and watched television since they had nothing else to do.

*F. Underline the **six two-part verbs** in the following paragraph.*

The suburban lifestyle has its benefits. Many people bring up children in a pleasant environment supposedly free of crime and big-city worries. They look after each other in the neighborhood also, unlike in the alienated urban setting. The suburbs stand for the simple life where people watch out for each other and care for everyone's children, not just their own. Not everyone will take to living in the suburbs, but the benefits are many.

Exercise 4.2   Filling in Prepositions and Conjunctions

*A. Fill in **prepositions** in the following paragraph.*

Changes _____ our environment have brought many consequences, some of which are still unknown. _____ example, coral is dying _____ enormous rates _____ the world _____ a result _____ rising ocean temperatures possibly caused _____ global warming. As much as 80 percent _____ the corals _____ the Seychelles and 90 percent _____ those _____ Indonesia have already died although the consequences are still uncertain.

B. *Fill in* **conjunctions** *in the following paragraph.*

_____ sea temperatures probably will soar to record highs as global warming continues, worse occurrences might ensue. The death of the corals could have serious consequences for the food chain _____ the environment. Few fish feed on corals, _____ many fish feed on worms, clams, _____ crabs in the corals _____ use the reefs for shelter. _____ there are no viable corals reefs, then fish will not have food _____ shelter, _____ they will go elsewhere _____ die. The implications for the fishing _____ tourism industries will be devastating, _____ the economy of these countries will also suffer.

C. *Fill in* **prepositions** *in the following paragraph.*

The normal sea temperature _____ the Indian Ocean _____ the Seychelles had been regularly _____ 84 degrees Fahrenheit. But more recently the temperature _____ the water has been measured to be _____ high _____ 91 degrees. This higher temperature is a result _____ a bleaching _____ the coral _____ a scale that has never before occurred. This bleaching has occurred _____ a number of reasons.

D. *Fill in* **conjunctions** *in the following paragraph.*

_____ the corals have lost their color _____ are bleached, they are not dead yet, _____ they are starving _____ don't reproduce. Obviously, this condition will be followed by death _____ the conditions continue. In the Seychelles, corals that survive the best were found in the murky _____ heavily polluted water at the mouth of the harbor, probably _____ the cloudiness of the water protected the reefs from the bleaching _____ heating of the sun.

E. *Fill in* **prepositions** *and* **conjunctions** *in the following paragraph.*

Many countries _____ the south Pacific Ocean _____ the Indian Ocean have established protections _____ further damage _____ the corals. _____ a number of difficulties continue. Higher temperatures _____ global warming cannot be stopped _____ we do not know how to stop rising temperatures. _____ pollution _____ the water usually harms the corals, sometimes, as _____ the Seychelles, pollution has helped. Finally, humans have damaged much _____ the coral reefs _____ fishing _____ tourism. The solutions will be hard to find.

Exercise 4.3   Filling in Prepositions, Conjunctions, and Interjections

Fill in prepositions, conjunctions, and interjections in the blanks.

Dolphins are often referred to _____ porpoises, _____ there are no porpoises inhabiting the seas _____ Australia, just the fourteen species _____ dolphins. Dolphins may have various shades _____ grey _____ the back _____ may be white _____ the belly. The short, stout beak has twenty-three to twenty-five pairs _____ teeth _____ the jaws _____ the lower jaw tends to jut out farther than the upper.

Dolphins are social mammals _____ are generally seen _____ large herds _____ _____ smaller family units known _____ pods. Being mammals, dolphins must breathe air. _____ _____ this they swim close _____ the surface. Food is mainly schooling pelagic fishes which are found _____ echo-locating. Dolphins are protected _____ Australian waters _____ many accidental kills occur _____ shark nets _____ fishing nets. (Neville Coleman, *Australia's Great Barrier Reef*)

Exercise 4.4   Using Prepositions and Two-Part Verbs

*A. Use the following **prepositions** in sentences.*

Example   (over) ___I won't cry over you._____

1. (according to) _____

   _____

2. (instead of) _____

   _____

3. (along with) _____

   _____

4. (in spite of) _____

   _____

5. (as for) _____

   _____

6. (in regard to) _____

   _____

7. (except for) _____

_____

8. (in place of) _____

_____

9. (because of) _____

_____

10. (in addition to) _____

_____

*B. Use the following **two-part verbs** in sentences. Change the tense or the person if you want.*

1. (turn over) _____

_____

2. (look into) _____

_____

3. (see about) _____

_____

4. (ask after) _____

_____

5. (watch for) _____

_____

6. (turn into) _____

_____

7. (have at) _____

_____

8. (think up) _____

_____

9. (win over) _____

_____

10. (drop over) _____

_____

Exercise 4.5   Using Conjunctions

Use the following conjunctions in sentences.

Example   (unless) _____ I'll go unless I have too much work. _____

1. (nor) _____

_____

2. (both . . . and) _____

_____

3. (either . . . or) _____

_____

4. (neither . . . nor) _____

_____

5. (not only . . . but also) _____

_____

6. (yet) _____

_____

7. (whereas) _____

_____

8. (provided) _____

_____

9. (even though) _____

_____

10. (for) _____

_____

Exercise 4.6   Using Prepositions, Conjunctions, and Interjections

1. Write a paragraph about the cover of a textbook using some or all of these **prepositions:** *at, below, beside, next to, on*

2. Write a paragraph about a sibling using some or all of these **conjunctions:** *both . . . and, but, until, where, when*

3. Write a paragraph to a friend about a great party using some of your favorite **interjections:**

4. Write a paragraph giving directions to your home from your school using some or all of these **prepositions:** *behind, between, near, past, through*

5. Write a paragraph telling why you are going to the movies using some or all of these **conjunctions:** *although, if, so, until, while*

6. Write a paragraph about your bedroom using some or all of these **prepositions:** *in front of, inside, underneath, throughout, between*

7. Write a paragraph imagining your dream vacation using some or all of these **conjunctions:** *neither . . . nor, both . . . and, but, so, whereas*

8. Write a paragraph describing an accident using these **prepositions** and **interjections:** *beneath, near, without, Oh, no! Please, God!*

9. Write a paragraph describing an argument using these **conjunctions** and **two-part verbs:** *either . . . or, not only . . . but (also), since, take on, turn down*

10. Write a paragraph describing an animal using these **prepositions** and **conjunctions:** *between, instead of, along with, while, when*

Exercise 4.7 Proofreading

*Correct the **four preposition errors** and the **four conjunction errors**. Eliminate **four** of the **five interjections**.*

Wow! Snorkeling in the Great Barrier Reef at the northeast coast of Australia was the adventure of a lifetime for me. A motorboat took a group of us from the shore to deep water, during the way either supplying us with wetsuits and instructing us to the use of face masks and fins. In the open sea, we slipped into the water from a platform and swam away down the boat. Peering into the depths, I saw miles of coral formations, six-foot-long clams, monstrous groupers, and even a shark. God Almighty! A clam closed up whereas my shadow passed over it; yikes, I thought it had grabbed my foot since our guide said it would not do that. Yeah, right! Luckily, he also said the shark was friendly, or else I really would have panicked. Well, I guess I'm ready to go back, but I'll watch out for those clams.

Summary

I. Prepositions
   A. Definition: **Prepositions** are connecting words.
   B. Uses
      1. Prepositions connect prepositional phrases to nouns, pronouns, verbs, and adjectives.
         Examples: *the house **on the street,** to run **to the store,** the blue **of the gown***
      2. Prepositions form a part of two-part verbs (and sometimes three-part verbs).
         Examples: *walk into, keep out, want in on*
II. Conjunctions
   A. Definition: **Conjunctions** connect words, phrases, and sentences.
   B. Types of Conjunctions
      1. One-word conjunctions
         Examples: *although, if, unless, until, while*
      2. Correlative conjunctions
         Examples: *both . . . and, not only . . . but (also)*
III. Interjections (or Exclamations)
   A. Definition: **Interjections** are words or phrases used to express mild or strong emotion.
   B. Types of interjections
      1. Some words are only interjections and no other part of speech.
         Examples: *amen, gosh, heck, wow*
      2. Some words used as interjections come from other parts of speech.
         Examples: *boy, God, heavens, hell* (nouns)
                cool, great, swell (adjectives)
                indeed, really, well (adverbs)
      3. Some phrases and clauses are used with enough emphasis to become interjections.
         Examples: *for heaven's sake, if only I could!*

Chapter 5

Subjects and Objects

Underline the **subjects** in the following paragraph. Don't worry if you can't find all of them.

Plant communities are not static but are continually modifying their own environment. The accumulation of decaying organic material builds up the soil and increases its ability to support plant life. Gradually dry land is created out of wet land, and sterile soil becomes enriched with humus. For example, a pond will evolve into a swamp, and an open field will eventually become a forest. As each successive plant community gives way to the next, the habitat becomes more stable, and in time supports a climax community, such as a beech-hemlock forest. If there are no major disturbances (natural or manmade), the climax community will remain essentially unchanged. (Lee Peterson, *A Field Guide to Edible Wild Plants*)

Subjects

All sentences must have at least one ***subject*** indicating who or what the sentence is about. The subject may be a single word that is a noun or pronoun, a *phrase* (a group of words that go together), or a *clause* (a group of words that go together and has its own subject and verb):

Noun: This **book** seems very interesting.
Pronoun: **It** is about recognizing edible plants.
Phrase: **Learning about plants** has many benefits.
Clause: **Whoever likes plants** should read this book.

Finding the Subject

To find the subject, ask, "Who or what?" and add the verb and the rest of the sentence. For example, ask, "Who or what seems very interesting?" The answer is, "This book," the subject. Or ask, "Who or what should read this book?" The answer is, "Whoever likes plants." Notice that the answer is *not* "whoever," since the meaning of the sentence would be entirely changed.

Be careful of phrases and clauses that may come between the subject and the verb. In the sentence *The plants in my garden are aloes*, ask, "Who or what are aloes?" The answer is, "The plants," the subject. The phrase *in my garden* modifies (describes) *plants* but is not the subject. When the subject is a pronoun, be especially careful. In the sentence *Some of my plants have blooms*, notice that *some* is the subject. *Of my plants* is a phrase modifying *some*. In answering the question "Who or what have blooms?" you might think that *plants* is the right answer, but notice that the sentence does not say that plants have blooms, but rather that *some* plants have blooms. To find the subject, try crossing out phrases first. Then see what is left.

Location of Subjects

Although subjects often come at or near the beginning of a sentence, they may come anywhere:

> On the shelf is **a plant.**
>
> There is **a plant** on the shelf.
>
> It is **a beautiful day** for walking in the garden.

With the constructions *there is/are, here is/are,* and *it is* (when the *it* does not refer to a specific person or thing), the subject is ***delayed.*** The verb must be singular for a singular subject and plural for a plural subject:

> There **is** (There's) a plant on the shelf. (singular verb)
>
> There **are** (There're) plants on the shelf. (plural verb)

Multiple Subjects

Subjects may be plural, but they also may be multiple. If the subjects are connected by ***and,*** treat them as plural:

> **The cactus** and **the aloe** are healthy. (both singular)
>
> **The cacti** and **the aloes** are healthy. (both plural)
>
> **The cacti** and **the aloe** are healthy. (one plural, one singular)

If they are connected by ***or,*** treat them individually whether they are singular or plural:

> **The cactus** or **the aloe** is healthy.
>
> **The cacti** or **the aloes** are healthy.

If one subject is singular and one plural, make the verb agree with the closer subject. If you don't like the sound of it, change the subjects around:

> **The cacti** or **the aloe** is healthy.
>
> **The aloe** or **the cacti** are healthy.

Be careful of intervening phrases (usually prepositional phrases) that are not part of the subject:

The aloe, as well as the cacti, is healthy.

The cacti in the garden are healthy.

Understood Subject

When you use the **imperative** (command), since the sentence is giving instructions or orders, the subject *you* is understood, that is, implied and not spoken or written:

(You) Please water the plants.

(You) Stop walking in the flower beds.

(You) Help!

Since commands can only be given to *you* (singular or plural), only *you* is an understood subject.

Subject-Verb Agreement

The verb *agrees* with the subject; that is, a singular subject takes the singular of the verb and a plural subject takes the plural of the verb. Normally this problem is not difficult if you can locate the subject and verb in a sentence.

Objects

Nouns, pronouns, phrases, and clauses may be used as **objects,** the *who* or *what* that is acted upon. They take the form of direct objects, indirect objects, and objects of the preposition. Not all sentences have objects.

While nouns have the same form in both subjective and objective forms, pronouns change form, so be sure to use the pronoun objective form (*me, you, him, her, it, us, them, whom*) for direct objects, indirect objects, and objects of the preposition.

Direct Objects

In *The plant has blooms, plant* is the subject and answers the question "Who or what has blooms?" For the **direct object,** turn the question around to "The plant has whom or what?" The answer is "blooms," the direct object. Here are other examples:

The plant has **a flower.** (single direct object)

The plant has **leaves** and **thorns.** (multiple direct object)

The plant has **them.** (pronoun direct object in objective form)

Indirect Objects

In the sentence "The cactus gave me a prick on the finger," *me* is the indirect object and answers the question "Gave to or for whom or what?" In this sentence, *cactus* is the subject, *gave* is the verb, and *prick* is the direct object.

A word may serve sometimes as an indirect object and sometimes as a direct object. To determine which is which, consider the meaning of the sentence and ask "(Verb) what?" for the direct object and "(Verb) to or for whom or what?" for the indirect object.

		indirect object		*direct object*
I fed	the	pumpkins	some	fertilizer.

		indirect object		*direct object*
I fed	the	guests	the	pumpkins.

	indirect object		*direct object*
I fed	them	the	pumpkins.

		direct object	*prepositional phrase*
I fed	the	pumpkins	to them.

Objects of Prepositions

A preposition is followed by its **object,** which can be a word, a phrase, or a clause:

by the beautiful **garden** (a noun or pronoun)
by **getting a garden** (a phrase)
by **whatever is available** (a clause)

The object of the preposition should be in the objective case, so use objective case when using pronouns with prepositions: *for him* (not *for he*), *to her and me* (not *to she and I*), *between you and me* (not *between you and I*).

Exercise 5.1   Finding Subjects, Direct Objects, Indirect Objects, and Objects of Prepositions

*A. Underline the **subject(s)** in the following sentences.*

1. Many plants in the world climb up and cling to things.
2. Vines, such as ivy, may take over vast tracts of land.
3. Kudzu also grows rapidly and takes over everything.
4. There are vines all over buildings sometimes.
5. Peas, snow peas, and green beans grow as vines.

6. Some roses are also the climbing kind.
7. If not cut back, vines can destroy some buildings.
8. Succumbing almost entirely to plant growth is the ruin of Angkor Wat in Cambodia.
9. Completely entombed in vines was the mythical castle of Sleeping Beauty.
10. The Ivy League schools got their nickname because of vines growing on their buildings.

B. Underline the **subjects** *in the following paragraph. They may appear at the beginning, middle, or end of a sentence. They also may be multiple. If the subject is* you *understood, add* you.

Many wild plants can be made into tea, and most of them will be caffeine free. The plants need to be dried and then stored properly to keep their flavor. With long-stemmed plants, tie the stems together and hang them upside down in a warm, well-ventilated place. Otherwise, the leaves may be spread on a slightly raised screen so that air circulates around them. This is the method for large quantities of leaves. For small quantities, there is also a simple procedure. Spread the leaves on half a newspaper and fold it over. It is direct sunlight that should be avoided. Sun and heat will destroy the flavoring oils. After thoroughly drying the leaves, place them in airtight jars. They may be kept for months this way. Brew the leaves as with any tea.

C. Underline the **direct objects** *in the following sentences. Remember that the direct object may be a single noun or pronoun or multiple nouns and pronouns.*

1. My aunt and uncle have really beautiful roses.
2. They have planted rows of various kinds of roses all along a fence.
3. The space along the fence has sunlight for most of the day and protection from the wind.
4. Some of the roses have big, multipetaled blooms; others have small, delicate flowers.
5. My uncle prunes the rosebushes carefully, but he leaves the petals on the ground.
6. Pruning takes practice, but he really understands roses.
7. My aunt plants garlic around the bushes.
8. The garlic keeps away insects, she says.
9. Insects do not like the smell of garlic, I guess.
10. But my aunt and uncle's hard work, not garlic, keeps the roses beautiful.

*D. Underline the **indirect objects** in the following sentences. Remember that the indirect object may be a single noun or pronoun or multiple nouns and pronouns. Ask yourself, "(Verb) to or for whom or what?"*

1. My uncle presented my mother with a small rosebush to plant in our yard.
2. He told her to plant it in a protected, sunny spot.
3. And he advised her to plant it at night so the bush would not get too much sun all at once.
4. My mother gave the advice and the problem some thought and planted it next to the driveway in the sun.
5. She fed the rosebush some fertilizer to make it stronger.
6. She told my uncle that she forgot to plant it at night.
7. The next day my mother asked my brother to take the car for an oil change.
8. Later, my mother gave my uncle a call because the rosebush looked terrible.
9. He had advised her to plant it at night and she didn't, he said.
10. Secretly, my brother showed me the tire marks where he had run over the rosebush both going to and coming from the mechanic's.

*E. Underline the **objects of the preposition** in the following sentences. A sentence may contain more than one prepositional phrase.*

1. My uncle was mad at my mother about the rosebush.
2. Both my aunt and uncle really take pride in their roses.
3. They don't like for their roses to be damaged or for other people to neglect the roses.
4. My mother felt bad about the dead rosebush for a long time.
5. She went to a nursery to ask for advice.
6. She brought back lots of fertilizers from the nursery.
7. My brother felt guilty about the rosebush and about his secret.
8. Finally, I went to my mother and revealed the secret to her.
9. At first, my brother was angry at me for telling.
10. But my mother felt much better and is off the hook with my uncle.

Exercise 5.2   Filling in the Subject

*Fill in appropriate **subjects** in the blanks; some may be nouns and some may be pronouns. Try to make sense!*

1. _____ decided to plant a vegetable garden this year. The _____ had to be chosen; then _____ had to be

weeded and the _____ had to be turned and fertilized. After two weeks, _____ planted rows of carrots, leeks, and turnips. Also _____ put in three tomato bushes. Every three days, except for rainy days, _____ would water all the plants. Once a week _____ pulled weeds. Finally, after an eternity, the _____ started to grow. _____ saw little shoots poking out of the soil.

2. First, the _____ came out; then the _____ and _____ also did. Luckily, _____ had marked each row with a picture of the plant, or else _____ wouldn't know them. The _____ had nice pale green feathery leaves; the _____ had flat and wide, but also pale green, leaves; the _____ had the dark green, wide, flat leaves. After another month, _____ should have been ready, so _____ dug up a carrot. What a pitiful thing!

3. The _____ had been sitting there all along not doing anything, but finally _____ started getting taller. _____ tied the stalks to sticks to hold them up. These _____ will also keep the leaves off the ground. In July, the _____ started coming out and got larger and redder. One morning, to my horror, the _____ had almost no leaves on it. _____ had been eaten by tomato worms, those big green and black ugly things. _____ made a mixture of pepper, garlic, and cayenne in water and sprayed it on the tomatoes. The _____ didn't like that and left. Will my _____ recover?

4. One day _____ of the carrot stalks was shaking; the _____ were still. That _____ just jerked back and forth. Finally, _____ pulled the stalk out of the ground. _____ came out very easily. _____ had no body to it, just top leaves. _____ told me that gophers probably had burrowed underground and were eating the carrots from underneath, certainly one

of the hazards of root vegetables. _____ could kill the gophers by
drowning them or poisoning them. But _____ have decided on
peaceful coexistence. The _____ can have the root vegetables.

Exercise 5.3   Identifying Direct Objects, Indirect Objects, and Objects of Prepositions

In this essay underline the **direct objects;** *double underline the* **indirect objects;** *and circle the* **objects of prepositions.**

All about Eggplant

If you know eggplants, you probably give them the highest praise. If you don't know eggplants, you should learn about them. They can be grown easily and have great versatility in the kitchen.

Most people buy sets and transplant them in the early spring. Provide them with space and sunlight. You should water them regularly and pinch off some of the blossoms. Pinching helps to increase the size of each eggplant on the plant. They do, however, take a long time to grow, almost three months. Pick them early; do not allow the eggplants to grow too large. If they lose their gloss and deep purple color, they may develop a bitter taste. Really large eggplants have passed their peak.

You can make eggplant relish, eggplant salad, eggplant parmigiana, stuffed eggplant, sauteed eggplant, stewed eggplant, and several other preparations. You will surely like all of these dishes. Serve your friends a moussaka, and you will hear raves.

Exercise 5.4   Writing with Direct Objects, Indirect Objects, and Objects of Prepositions

Fill in **direct objects, indirect objects,** *and* **objects of prepositions.**

1. Because Carl asked _____, I sent _____ a(n)
   _____ for the _____ . It cost _____ ,
   but Carl would not pay _____ for _____ . He
   brought _____ with _____ too. I kicked
   _____ out.

2. Learning grammar takes _____ and _____ but has many _____ . Just knowing the parts of speech helps _____ (to) _____ and (to) _____ better. It also helps _____ have more _____ in their _____ . Everyone should learn _____ .

3. Joey enjoys _____ because he likes _____ . He goes to _____ often and practices _____ for _____ . Once, he spent _____ at _____ and continued _____ almost all day. He wants _____ to go with _____ .

4. Going to college requires _____ and _____ . Students want the _____ even though it is so inconvenient and costly. Will they get _____? Do they find _____? Can they make _____? How will they see _____ in _____? Will they like _____? They can only know _____ later.

5. When I go in _____ , I have to think about _____ . Should I take _____ or should I walk to _____ . I need _____ , but I don't like _____ . If I carry _____ , I can't take _____ because I don't have _____ . I hate _____ .

Exercise 5.5   Writing with Subjects and Objects

*Use the words indicated as **subjects** and **objects** to write sentences as directed.*

Example   (*plant* as subject) ___A plant needs water and sun.___

1. (*telephone* as subject) _____

   _____

2. (*telephone* as direct object) _____

   _____

3. (*telephone* as indirect object) _____

_____

4. (*telephone* as object of a preposition) _____

_____

5. (*Fluffy* as subject) _____

_____

6. (*Fluffy* as direct object) _____

_____

7. (*Fluffy* as indirect object) _____

_____

8. (*Fluffy* as object of a preposition) _____

_____

9. (*cousin* as subject) _____

_____

10. (*cousin* as direct object) _____

_____

11. (*cousin* as indirect object) _____

_____

12. (*cousin* as object of a preposition) _____

_____

13. (*airplane* as subject) _____

_____

14. (*airplane* as direct object) _____

_____

15. (*airplane* as indirect object) _____

_____

16. (*airplane* as object of a preposition) _____

_____

17. (*honesty* as subject) _____

_____

18. (*honesty* as direct object) _____

_____

19. (*honesty* as indirect object) _____

    _____

20. (*honesty* as object of a preposition) _____

    _____

Exercise 5.6   Writing with Subjects and Objects

1. Write a paragraph about your left hand using nouns and pronouns as **subjects.**

2. Write a paragraph using these phrases and clauses as **subjects:** *whoever is the designated driver, (not) paying attention, having a good time, (not) to be cautious, (not) taking responsibility*

3. Write a paragraph using some or all of these nouns and pronouns as **direct objects:** *car, freedom, expense, gas, license, responsibility, driver's ed, safety record, driving lessons, driving test.*

4. Write a paragraph with **indirect objects** using some or all of these verbs: *allow, assign, ask, give, bring, pay, show, send, throw, write*

5. Write a paragraph with **objects of prepositions** using some or all of these prepositions: *according to, around, at, by, down, for, in, of, up, with*

Exercise 5.7   Proofreading

*In the following paragraph, find a total of **five errors of subject-verb agreement** and **objective case**.*

My daffodils and crocuses are the first flowers to appear in the spring. Sometimes spring has not really even arrived, and the flowers are already there. I have even seen them poking out of the snow. What a lovely, yet pitiful, sight! But what a pleasure it is to see the colors that they displays in the drabness of winter's end. Daffodils that I have forgotten about appears in a nice line along the fence. It seems a miracle that I put those bulbs in the ground so long ago. After all this time, they have survived the cold, the snow, and the appetites of squirrels and other predators. The crocuses sometimes are hardly noticed in the shade of branches. The yellows and bluish purple goes so nicely together. They disappear so quickly, just a few short days and they are gone. But they are gifts to my neighbors and I. The best part are that they don't need to be planted every year, and they don't need tending at all. For we lazy flower lovers, they are faithful friends. If only more people were like flowers.

Summary

I. Subjects
   A. Definition: The **subject** is *who* or *what* the sentence is about.
   B. Identifying the subject
     1. Ask, "Who or what [fill in the verb]?" to find the subject.
       Example: *The tree is tall.* (Ask, "Who or what is tall?" Answer, "the tree," the subject)
     2. Eliminate phrases that come between the subject and verb.
       Example: *The tree in the yard is tall.* (Eliminate the prepositional phrase *in the yard.*)
   C. Location of subject
     1. The subject may be at the beginning of the sentence.
       Example: ***Flowers*** *are nice.*
     2. The subject can be in the middle of the sentence.
       Example: *Here is a **flower** for you.*
     3. The subject may be at the end of the sentence.
       Example: *In my garden are many **flowers.***
   D. Multiple subjects
     1. Subjects connected with *and* are plural.
       Example: *Flowers and trees are nice to look at.*
     2. Subjects connected with *or* are treated individually.
       Example: *My flowers or my trees need water.*
     3. If one subject is singular and one plural, make the verb match the subject nearer to the verb.
       Examples: *My flowers or my tree is blooming.* (singular)
               My tree or my flowers are blooming. (plural)
   E. Understood subjects
     1. *You* is implied in commands and need not be written.
       Example: *(You) Give me the book.*
     2. No other person except *you* can be an understood subject.
   F. Subject-verb agreement
     1. Singular subjects take singular verbs.
       Example: *The **flower has** petals.*
     2. Plural subjects take plural verbs.
       Example: *The **flowers have** petals.*
II. Objects
   A. Definition: **Objects** are the *who* or *what* that is acted upon.
   B. Forms of objects
     1. Nouns have the same form in both subjects and objects.
       Examples: *The **table** is here.* (subjective form)
              *I like the **table.*** (objective form)
     2. Pronouns change forms for subjects and objects.
       Examples: ***I*** *like the table.* (subjective form)
              *The table suits **me.*** (objective form)

C. Types of objects
1. Direct objects are who or what receives the action of the verb.
Example: *The child threw the **ball**.*
2. Indirect objects are to or for whom or what the action of the verb is intended.
Example: *The child gave **me** the ball.*
3. Objects of prepositions come after a preposition in a prepositional phrase.
Example: *The child threw the ball to the **dog**.*

Chapter 6

Other Complements

Read the following sentences and underline the words you think are the **complements.** Don't worry if you are not sure.

1. My brother always meant to be a surfer in Hawaii.
2. But he got tired of the "endless summer" lifestyle.
3. He became an astrophysicist.
4. But he grew weary of staring into the vast emptiness of space.
5. He did not remain an astrophysicist for very long.
6. Returning to Hawaii, he became an oceanographer.
7. This change might prove difficult for him.
8. But the salt water and waves taste good to him.
9. This move seems right, so the future looks bright.
10. My brother appears to be happy.

A **complement** means a *completer,* a word or words that complete a thought or idea. But many words could fall into this category, such as direct objects and indirect objects, which both complete a thought or idea. So we will limit what we call complements to subjective complements and objective complements because both of these forms rename or describe another word in the sentence. **Appositives** also rename nouns and pronouns.

Subjective Complements

Subjective complements are sometimes called predicate nouns and predicate adjectives, *predicate* meaning the word or words that say something about the subject.

If we consider complements as renamers and describers, we will find them easier to understand. The **renamer** is a noun that means the same as the subject; the **describer** is an adjective that describes the subject. The subject and the subjective complement are connected by a linking verb:

		linking verb	*subjective complement*	
That	surfer	is	my	friend.

		linking verb	*subjective complement*
The	surfer	looks	good.

Although there are many linking verbs, here are some common ones that may be used in all tenses, starting with the most common in its less obvious tenses:

be *(am, is, are, was, were, will be, could be, should be, would be, must be, may be, might be, am being, is being, are being, was being, were being, has been, have been, will have been, could have been, should have been, would have been, must have been, may have been, might have been)*

appear
become
continue *(The winter continues cold.)*
emerge *(The senator emerged the leader.)*
feel
get *(They have not gotten angry.)*
grow
look
mean
prove *(The meetings have proven useful over time.)*
remain
seem
smell *(The air will smell fresh after the rain.)*
sound
taste
turn

Many verbs can sometimes be linking verbs, sometimes intransitive verbs (no direct object), and sometimes transitive verbs (having a direct object). To tell the difference, ask yourself whether the subject is renamed or described by the complement. If so, that word is a subjective complement; if not, it is something else. The complement must be either a noun or adjective. Notice these differences:

		subjective complement	
	linking verb	*describes* she	
She	felt	good.	

			direct object
	transitive verb		
She	felt	the	water.

	intransitive verb	*prepositional phrase*
She	felt	for her seat.

Sometimes *to be* may be added between the linking verb and the subjective complement:

She proved to be a candidate.

She appears to be right.

Objective Complements

Objective complements are also renamers and describers but rename or describe the direct object in a sentence. The verb in the sentence, of course, must be transitive (having a direct object). Notice how the objective complement renames or describes the direct object:

	direct object	*objective complement*	
He finds	surfing	challenging.	

	direct object	*objective complement*	
He made his	children	surfers,	too.

These are some of the common verbs in their various tenses that often take objective complements:

appoint
assign
call (*The team called her the best surfer.*)
consider
declare
elect
find (*You will find the movie interesting.*)
make
name (*We named Jamie our new president.*)
paint
set (*They set the pigeons loose.*)
think
want (*I want you quiet.*)

These verbs most often are used simply as transitive verbs and sometimes have an indirect object. So be sure that what you think is the objective complement renames or describes the direct object. Notice the difference here:

	direct object	*objective complement*
They found that	man	crazy.

	indirect object	*direct object*
They found that	man	a seat.

	direct object	*adverb*
They found that	man	soon.

Only in the first sentences does one word (*crazy*) rename or describe the direct object (*man*).

Sometimes *as* is used before the objective complement: *We named Jamie as our president.* Also, *to be* may be inserted between the direct object and the objective complement: *We declared Jamie to be our president.* Once in a while the order of the direct object and the objective complement may also be reversed:

They set the pigeons loose.

They set loose the pigeons.

Appositives

Another renamer is the ***appositive,*** defined as a noun, a pronoun, or a group of words that means the same as the noun right before it:

My brother, **the surfer,** lives in Hawaii. (renames *brother*)

She bought a new car, **an Italian import.** (renames *car*)

Use commas around the appositive (unless the second comma is superseded by other punctuation) if the appositive is not crucial for identifying the noun in question. If the information is necessary for identification, then do not surround the appositive with commas:

My best friend, **Susan,** is visiting. (appositive is not crucial for identifying *best friend*)

My friend **Susan** is visiting. (appositive is crucial for identifying a particular friend among other friends)

My neighbor, **an oceanographer,** is very interesting. (appositive is not crucial for identifying *neighbor*)

My neighbor **the oceanographer** is very interesting. (appositive is crucial for identifying a particular neighbor among other neighbors)

Sometimes the commas are eliminated for proper names used as appositives in all cases.

Exercise 6.1   Identifying Subjective Complements

*A. In the following sentences, underline the **subjective complement** and draw a line to the subject that it renames or describes. Some sentences have more than one subjective complement.*

Example   Mary grew angry.

1. Jacques Cousteau (1910–1997) was a great oceanographer.
2. At a young age, he became a naval officer.
3. At sea, he grew intrigued by the ocean.
4. He was tireless in his fascination with the sea and continued faithful to its exploration.

5. Cousteau also proved a talented and adept filmmaker.
6. He seemed comfortable both in front of and behind the camera.
7. He emerged the winner of two Academy Awards for best documentary films, *The Silent World* and *World without Sun*.
8. He remained an oceanographer and underwater explorer for the rest of his life.
9. In 1943, Cousteau, along with Emile Gagnan, was the inventor of the aqualung.
10. This aqualung, a compressed-air cylinder attached to a face mask, became our present-day scuba gear.

*B. In the following sentences, underline the **subjective complement** and draw a line to the subject that it renames or describes. Some sentences have more than one part with subjective complements.*

1. Underwater travel and exploration always seemed intriguing to humans.
2. In seventeenth-century England, a leather-enclosed boat was the first submersible and traveled under the Thames.
3. Later, in the 1920s, Charles William Beebe and Otis Barton became the developers of the "bathysphere."
4. The bathysphere looked strange; it was a large steel vessel attached to a cable and lowered from a ship.
5. It proved somewhat dangerous because the cable could break and lose the sphere.
6. With the invention of the aqualung by Jacques Cousteau, a diver could remain submerged for several hours at a time.
7. Then in the 1950s, Auguste Piccard was the inventor of the bathyscaph, a self-propelling underwater vessel.
8. His son Jacques became the record holder for plunging to a depth of 35,810 feet in a bathyscaph.
9. Currently, occupied submersibles for underwater exploration seem useful since they have lots of equipment on them.
10. Some robot submersibles also appear promising for extremely deep water exploration, one of them exploring the *Titanic*.

*C. In the following paragraph, underline the **five subjective complements** and draw a line to the subject that it renames or describes. Not all sentences have subjective complements.*

Scuba diving has become a popular sport but should be learned with an instructor. First, you must be a good swimmer. Then you should take lessons at a certified school that has an underwater facility. Before you dive, you will learn how to operate the scuba gear. When you appear ready, the instructor will take you underwater. After practicing for some time, you will get comfortable with the process. The final step will be scuba diving in the open sea.

D. In the following paragraph, underline the **five subjective complements** *and draw a line to the subjects that they rename or describe.*

If you remain enthusiastic and adventurous, you will continue scuba diving whenever you get the chance. Northeast Australia, Hawaii, the Caribbean, and Florida are just some of the places for great scuba diving. Other places far and near will also prove acceptable for viewing coral and fish. The sport will seem rather expensive, but once you taste the joys of scuba, you will not care about the cost.

Exercise 6.2   Filling in Subjective Complements and Appositives

A. Add a **subjective complement** *to the following sentences. Try both noun and adjective subjective complements.*

1. Swimming is _____.
2. Many people appear _____ with (by, in) swimming.
3. It has continued _____ for many years.
4. I remain _____ about swimming.
5. At first I liked it; then I grew _____ of (by, with) it.
6. The water sounded _____ to me.
7. The chlorine in the pool smelled _____ to me.
8. The water also tasted _____ to me.
9. Each day, swimming did not look _____ to me.
10. Finally, I grew _____ of it and had to quit swimming.

B. Combine each pair of sentences into one sentence with an **appositive** *in it. An appositive renames the noun or pronoun that comes before it. Add commas if they are necessary.*

Example   My brother's name is Robert. He likes to surf.

_____My brother Robert likes to surf._____

1. Max is my friend. She swims every day.

_____

2. Her pool is 50 meters long. Fifty meters is regulation size.

3. Max is a serious swimmer. She goes early in the morning.

4. Other people go early. They are also serious swimmers.

5. A lap is 100 meters. A lap is two lengths of the pool.

6. Max does twenty laps. She does 2,000 meters.

7. Other people do 100 laps. They are really dedicated swimmers.

8. Max's sister is named Sam. Sam never goes swimming with her.

9. Sam likes to play in the water. She is not a good swimmer.

10. Sam prefers the Jacuzzi. The Jacuzzi is a large tub with swirling water.

Exercise 6.3   Writing with Appositives

*In the following sentences, add an **appositive** at an appropriate place. More than one place may be appropriate.*

Example   My dog is hungry.   My dog, Spot, is hungry.

1. Kathy is always late when she meets me.

2. We had a date for a movie at the multiplex last Saturday.

3. I had a coupon for tickets and waited outside for her.

4. Finally, the usher said my movie was about to start.

5. Luckily, the usher knew Kathy, so he held the ticket for her.

    _____

6. Kathy arrived at 8:30 saying the usher would not let her in.

    _____

7. Another time, she came to dinner at my house over an hour late.

    _____

8. I was really angry because Brenda and Stephen were also there.

    _____

9. I had made hot appetizers and a special recipe.

    _____

10. The vegetables got really overcooked, and the dessert had to wait too long.

    _____

11. Kathy said her car was not running, and she had a last-minute phone call from Eloise.

    _____

12. Yesterday she was late for a celebration; I can hardly forgive her because Tom, Jane, and Cassie were all on time.

    _____

13. She said her father had to repair his car in order to drive her over to my place.

    _____

14. She is never late for our class or for her job.

    _____

15. Is she late for me because she knows I will wait, or is she just a procrastinator?

    _____

Exercise 6.4   Writing with Subjective Complements

*Write sentences using the verb indicated and adding a **subjective complement**. Change the tense and the person of the verb if you wish.*

Example   (feel) ___He feels nervous about the test.___

1. (should have been) _____

_____

2. (continue) _____

_____

3. (must be) _____

_____

4. (turn) _____

_____

5. (might have been) _____

_____

6. (sound) _____

_____

7. (have been) _____

_____

8. (mean) _____

_____

9. (remain) _____

_____

10. (get) _____

_____

11. (grow) _____

_____

12. (smell) _____

_____

13. (should be) _____

_____

14. (emerge) _____

_____

15. (prove) _____

_____

Exercise 6.5   Writing with Subjective Complements

1. Use the following verbs about how you feel in the morning to write sentences with **subjective complements:** *feel, get, remain, seem, taste*

2. Use the following verbs about an election to write sentences with **subjective complements:** *appear, became, emerge, remain, seem*

3. Use the following verbs about eating spinach to write sentences with **subjective complements:** *feel, look, smell, sound, taste*

4. Use the following verbs about playing tennis to write sentences with **subjective complements:** *be* (any form), *appear, grow, prove, remain*

5. Use the following verbs about doing homework assignments to write sentences with **subjective complements:** *become, continue, feel, get, mean*

Exercise 6.6   Identifying Objective Complements

*In the following sentences, underline the **objective complement** and draw an arrow to the direct object that it renames or describes. Some sentences have more than one objective complement.*

Example   The sycamore leaves made the patio <u>messy</u>.

1. The club elected Sami president.
2. Thrilled, Sami declared herself ready and able.
3. She considered several members as vice-president.
4. But among them she found only one person happy to work.
5. Only Paula thought herself capable and willing.
6. Sami assigned Paula to be vice-president and entertainment chair.
7. Sami did not want Paula as secretary or treasurer.
8. She called Paula organized and hard working.

9. But she did not think Paula sociable or good with money.

10. A little insulted, Paula made Sami mad by planning a disco party without consulting her.

Exercise 6.7   Writing with Objective Complements

*A. Add **objective complements** in the following sentences. Other words will also fit, but try to use objective complements instead.*

1. We considered the house _____.

2. Dad declared it _____; he decided to redo it.

3. So we could start right away, we set the clock _____.

4. I thought Dad _____ for doing that.

5. We painted the house _____ with white window trim.

6. But we found the paint _____ and _____, so painting took a long time.

7. We called Mom _____ because she would not help us.

8. She made Dad _____ when she splashed paint on him.

9. Dad called the paint job _____ when the neighbors praised the beauty of the house.

10. We all considered the house _____ after this.

*B. Write sentences using **objective complements** with the following verbs. Remember to add a direct object and then the objective complement.*

1. (appoint, call, consider, elect) _____

_____

_____

2. (assign, make, name, think) _____

_____

_____

3. (declare, find, paint, want) _____

_____

_____

Summary

I. Complements
   A. Definition: **Complements** are noun and adjective "completers" that re-name or describe the subject.
   B. Types of complements
      1. **Subjective complements**
         a. Words renaming a subject are nouns.
            Example: *She was a mechanic.*
         b. Words describing the subject are adjectives.
            Example: *She is skillful.*
      2. **Objective complements**
         a. Words renaming the object are nouns.
            Example: *He nominated Shirley president.*
         b. Words describing the object are adjectives.
            Example: *He found his job challenging.*
      3. **Appositives**
         a. Appositives rename nouns or pronouns that precede them.
            Example: *Their dog* **Spotty** *is black and white.*
         b. Appositives can be nouns, pronouns, or groups of words.
            Examples: *My friend,* **a lawyer,** *is smart.*
            The owner, **somebody rich,** *will take responsibility.*
            Mr. Jones, **my next-door neighbor,** *is here.*

Phrases

Chapter 7

Prepositional Phrases

Read the following paragraph and underline the **prepositional phrases.** Don't worry if you can't find all of them.

While taking a walk in my neighborhood on an early summer evening at twilight, I stopped to chat with a neighbor who was walking his dogs. As we stood, I noticed that the large expanse of yard in front of which we were standing was aglitter with the intermittent flickering of fireflies. I called attention to the sight, remarking on how magical it looked. "It's like the Fourth of July," I said. He agreed, and then told me he had read that the lights of fireflies are mating signals. He then explained to me details of how these signals work—for example, groups of fireflies fly at different elevations and could be seen to cluster in different parts of the yard. (Deborah Tannen, *You Just Don't Understand*)

Certainly the most common type of *phrase* (a group of words that go together but do not have their own subject and verb) is the ***prepositional phrase.*** It begins with a preposition (such as *at, in, with*) and ends with the object of the preposition (usually a noun or pronoun), along with any modifiers of the object:

preposition	*article*	*adjective*	*object of preposition (OP)*
after	the	green	house

Prepositions

There are hundreds of prepositions, and they may be used in various ways, but you most frequently encounter them at the beginning of prepositional phrases. To test for prepositional phrases, see if the preposition seems to have an object. Ask yourself, "What?" after the preposition. For example, in the sentence *She ran to the station*, *to* is the preposition, so ask, "To what?" The answer is, "To the station."

If the preposition does not have a logical answer to the preposition + what question, it might be a ***particle,*** a part of a verb. For example, in *He will* sit out *this dance,* notice that *out* goes with *sit* to form the verb *sit out*, which has a different meaning from *sit*. It does not form a prepositional phrase with *this dance*. If you ask, "Out what?" the answer is *not* "out the dance"; that does not make sense. Prepositions also function as adverbs modifying the verb, as in *He sat out in the cold*, where *out* modifies the verb *sat*. Remember that only nouns (and phrases and clauses used as nouns) and pronouns help form prepositional phrases. The *to* that is part of the infinitive of a verb does not start a prepositional phrase: *He wants* to sit *in a chair* (to sit is the infinitive of the verb).

Objects of Prepositions

As is obvious, the **object** of a preposition should take objective case nouns and pronouns. Nouns in both subjective and objective case are the same, but pronouns have different forms for subjects (*I, you, he, she, it, we, they*) and objects (*me, you, him, her, it, us, them*), except for *you* and *it*, as you can see. Thus you should write *at him, between her and me, to them.*

You may use these prepositional phrases as modifiers of nouns (*the house* in the woods), verbs (*He ran* to a tree), adjectives (. . . *happy* with the dog). Each of the objects of the prepositions may in turn be modified by other prepositional phrases or other words. For *the house in the woods*, you might modify *woods* with *near the lake* to make *the house in the woods near the lake,* and even further modify *lake: the house in the woods near the lake by the highway.*

The object of the preposition may also be a kind of noun called a **gerund** (the -*ing* form of a verb that is used as a noun). These gerunds always end in -*ing* and act the same as nouns:

He changed the will **by attaching a codicil.**

Next to rewriting the will, this was the most drastic.

The will, **without being witnessed,** was invalid.

Witnesses attest to the will **by signing it.**

You can find the prepositional phrase by looking for the preposition and then by examining the words that follow. (Notice the prepositional phrases in the preceding sentence.)

Instead of having just one noun or pronoun as the object of the preposition, sometimes a prepositional phrase will include a clause (a group of words with its own subject and verb) as the object of the preposition. For example, in the sentence *She will give the book to whoever wants it, to* is a preposition and *whoever wants it,* a clause, is the object of the preposition. Notice the prepositional phrases in these examples:

We will allocate the funds **for whichever project is best.**

The project should be completed **by whoever is most able.**

It may seem difficult to find these longer prepositional phrases, but simply finding the preposition and then looking at the words that follow it will help in identifying them.

Punctuating Prepositional Phrases

Usually prepositional phrases do not take commas before or after, unless there is punctuation for some other reason. But sometimes they are set off by commas when they express a thought that is emphatic, separate, or contrary.

This pizza is large, **even for me.** (emphatic)
This pizza, **by my estimation,** weighs five pounds. (separate)
This pizza, **despite your criticism,** is excellent. (contrary)

These sentences could also dispense with the commas.

Exercise 7.1   Finding Prepositional Phrases

*A. Underline the **ten prepositional phrases** in this paragraph.*

I have no sense of direction. I have to memorize how to go to wherever I need to go. For example, I can drive easily to the building where I work, but if someone asks me how to get to the train station from that building, I don't know how. I only know how to get there from my home. It can be very embarrassing because I don't seem to know my own town even though I have lived there for many years. I memorize appearances and go from these familiar landmarks. Other people more easily follow a little compass in their heads, so they automatically know which direction they should take.

*B. Underline the **ten prepositional phrases** in this paragraph.*

I have learned to take certain precautions because of my bad sense of direction. Some of them are easy to follow. When I go into a large building—a train station, department store, or office—that is unfamiliar to me, I turn around and look at the entrance so I'll know what it looks like. If the entrance has a sign or marker, I'll try to remember what it says. I make a big effort to look at landmarks from both sides, so I'll recognize them from the other direction. In that way I can more easily retrace my steps.

*C. Underline the **ten prepositional phrases** in this paragraph.*

I have also learned to avoid some dangerous situations because of my poor directional sense. When I go swimming, I do not dive underwater. A few times I have done that and tried to swim back up to the surface but was actually trying to go in the wrong direction. I bumped my head on the bottom of the swimming pool. When I went scuba diving to impress friends, I got really lost underwater. In the murky water, I could not tell which way was up, down, or sideways. I started to panic. Then I stopped swimming and watched the direction of my bubbles. Luckily, my diving partner also came to my rescue and led me back to the surface. I am not ready to scuba dive again soon, but in a sense I've learned how to avoid danger.

*D. Underline the **ten prepositional phrases** in this paragraph.*

Why one person has a good sense of direction while another person has a poor one is not really clear. It is possible the right side of the brain (the right hemisphere) controls our spatial orientation. So people with right-hemisphere dominance, a trait found more often in men, are better at directions. Left-hemisphere dominance, more often found in women, means better verbal ability. For these reasons, more men go into aviation and architecture. But many women also fly planes and design buildings. Possibly some girls and boys are just not brought up in the same way, and they develop differently from each other.

*E. Underline the **ten prepositional phrases** in this paragraph.*

People can probably improve their spatial orientation through a little effort. They can look carefully at the sun's position to see if the sun is to the east, in the middle of the sky, or to the west. Then they can be aware of their direction according to the sun. With practice, they will get a feel for their direction.

Exercise 7.2   Completing Prepositional Phrases

*A. In the blanks fill in **prepositions** that will make sense in these paragraphs. Use some of these prepositions or find your own: about, above, across, around, at, because of, before, beneath, beside, by, for, from, of, in, in front of, into, near, on, through, to, toward, under, upon, until, with*

1. _____ the cover _____ my textbook is a sketch _____ a wooden door _____ a small paned window _____ the top half. _____ the window appears an oak tree _____ thick green leaves waving _____ the breeze. The sky _____ the tree is pale blue _____ big cumulus clouds obscuring most _____ it. _____ the window is a small wooden desk _____ an open book. A pen and a notebook lie _____ it. A chair sits _____ the desk.

2. The chair invites me to sit _____ it. I am also supposed to look _____ the book and write _____ the notebook. The window shows me the world outside. The blue sky and fluffy clouds represent _____ me a world _____ possibilities. Some parts _____ the world will be happy and other parts sad. _____ the window, the door is still closed _____ me. It shows that I am not yet ready to go out _____ the world, so it must remain closed. But only I can open that door _____ the outside. _____ me lies the power to open it. But I must be prepared _____ the situations there. The oak tree is me _____ the future when I am _____ the world. I was a small acorn full _____ potential and someday will be a mighty oak facing the world.

B. *In the blanks, fill in* **objects of the preposition** *that will make sense.*

1. The professor distributed to _____ a copy of _____. She told everyone to study hard for _____. She also said that 50 percent of _____ would be based on _____. She is our hardest professor, so we are all worried about _____.

2. Looking at _____ helped my studying for _____. It was comforting to see the nice picture of _____ and of _____. But reading in _____ was another matter. Concentrating on _____ is very difficult.

3. Learning correct grammar is difficult for _____. There are so many terms for _____ and for _____. People have to learn about _____. Also they have to know about _____ at _____.

4. Going to _____ means taking him in _____ for _____. If we go to _____, we will take the car to _____ and ask for _____.

5. When you cross the street, wait for _____. Because of _____, you should look to _____ and then to _____ so no cars are coming toward _____. Cross the street only at _____.

6. Never go to _____ with _____. That place is not for _____, and you will do bad things to _____. Instead of _____, go home despite _____.

7. Around _____, you may find me in back of _____ looking for _____. Wait for _____ if I am late. I might come along with _____ or with _____.

8. In addition to _____, he goes to _____ and to _____. In place of _____, he has other opportunities for _____. Sometimes he goes without _____.

9. According to _____, the time for _____ is now, but the time for _____ is later. To _____ go the rewards. Because of _____, all things will happen for _____.

10. Near _____, behind _____, next to _____, inside _____, you will find it. Bring it to _____ in _____.

Exercise 7.3   Writing with Prepositional Phrases

*Use the indicated **prepositional phrase** in a sentence.*

Example   (on the train) __I took a nap on the train.__

1. (despite the weather) _____

2. (according to plan) _____

3. (in regard to your health) _____

4. (in place of this event) _____

5. (in spite of your problems) _____

6. (off the subject) _____

_____

7. (out the window) _____

_____

8. (in addition to the forecast) _____

_____

9. (along with the family) _____

_____

10. (instead of the dog) _____

_____

Exercise 7.4   Writing with Prepositional Phrases

*Combine each group of sentences into one sentence, being sure to include the information in the **prepositional phrases** in the final sentence.*

Example   He went to the store. He went to the bank.

He went to the store and the bank. _____

1. In the future, I want to live in the country. I also want to be far from the city.

_____

2. Being on a farm would be idyllic. Being away from the hustle of the city would also be wonderful.

_____

3. I would walk down the country lanes. I would go up the rolling hills. I would go by the river.

_____

4. In the summer, I could go swimming in the river. I could pick flowers in the meadows. I could listen to songbirds.

_____

5. I would pick berries for my friends. I would also pick berries for selling by the road. I would also pick berries for myself to eat.

_____

6. I could use the berries for pies. I could sell them to customers. I could sell them by the roadside.

   _____

7. I could drive to town every week. I would have a list of chores. I would bring my list with me.

   _____

8. I could buy food in the grocery store. I could pick up supplies at the hardware store. I could withdraw money from the bank.

   _____

9. Maybe I would go to a coffee shop. I would go for lunch. I could chat with the other friendly country people.

   _____

10. People in small towns are friendly. People on farms like to talk. People in the country have more time.

    _____

_____

Exercise 7.5   Filling in Prepositional Phrases

*Fill in the blanks with entire **prepositional phrases** so that the paragraphs make sense.*

1. Making a trip _____ takes much planning. You must decide where to go _____. Then you must consider applying _____. You must pack _____ and be prepared _____.

2. Reading a book _____ will help me understand more. Asking people _____ is also helpful. The customs _____ will be interesting and will make me aware _____. I hope I don't insult people _____.

3. People should have a map _____ so they can find their way _____. If they get lost, they can show the map _____. Even if they don't speak the same language, they can find their way _____. This method _____ may not help make friends, but it is very efficient.

4. Learning some words _____ certainly will make a tourist more welcome _____. Saying "Hello," "Goodbye," "Please," and "Thank you" _____ pleases the local people. If tourists take an interest _____, the local people will also be interested _____.

5. Every city _____ has some historical sights _____, but just walking _____ is lots of fun. Seeing how people _____ go _____ is fascinating.

Exercise 7.6   Using Prepositional Phrases

*Use the following **prepositional phrases** to write paragraphs of two or three sentences. Change parts of them if you need to.*

1. about six hours, around 6:00, before dark, after rush hour

2. by taking another route, for asking directions, of losing our way, despite wanting to stop

3. about whatever you want, instead of whenever you go, with anyone you like, except for everyone I dislike

4. according to the time, on account of rain, because of the schedule, in spite of the delay

5. in front of the big clock, beside the jewelry store, near the train station, with a box of chocolates

6. for whatever she needs, to whomever she accepts, toward whichever she wishes, by whatever means she wants

7. across the river, under the highway, beneath the bridge, through the woods

8. in regard to the weather, in place of the umbrella, along with a raincoat, in addition to boots

9. in spite of studying so hard, because of sleeping through class, in addition to skipping class, except for writing a term paper

10. within the time limit, outside the rules, in place of the exam, beyond the limits of the law

Exercise 7.7   Proofreading

Find and correct the **one error in a prepositional phrase** *in each of these paragraphs.*

1. In America, receiving compliments causes conflict. A received compliment must be acknowledged; that is a social convention. We could accept the compliment to saying "Thank you," but we usually don't. It seems like boasting if we just accept it, so most people make a disparaging remark. For example, if a person were complimented on a sweater, the person might respond, "This old rag? I bought it ten years ago in a thrift shop for a dollar."

2. Isn't a negative response to a compliment really an insult to whoever made the compliment? It tells the complimenter that he or she has terrible taste by liking an old, cheap sweater. Even more illogical is why the person is wearing this sweater. Is the occasion so unimportant that it doesn't deserve anything better than one's worst clothing? Yet we persist at responding this way because of our embarrassment about compliments.

3. When we refuse to accept a compliment gracefully, we are being very negative to ourselves and about other people. It is surprising that people still give compliments when so many problems ensue. But perhaps knowing when and when not to give compliments is more important than what we say about something. If we made no compliments at all, we would save ourselves lots of trouble. But there are exceptions.

4. We make an exception on dressy occasions. Then we expect compliments from everyone. If someone does not adequately compliment us, we are hurt for the omission. Many spouses and significant others have been bewildered by a change in mood when they didn't say anything. Obviously, giving and receiving compliments is fraught with complications and difficulties, causing social and linguistic nightmares.

5. The best way to accept compliments probably is simply to accept them and acknowledge them. If someone tells you you are wearing a nice sweater, you might simply say, "Thank you. I like it, too." Or if you think the compliment is untrue, as when someone says you have lost weight, you could say, "Oh, I hope you are right," or "Thanks by saying that, but I don't think I have recently."

Summary

I. Prepositional Phrases
  A. Definition: A **prepositional phrase** is a group of words that begins with a preposition and ends with the object of the preposition.
  B. Parts of prepositional phrases
    1. Prepositions usually begin a prepositional phrase.
        Examples: *in, of, to, through*
    2. Object(s) of a preposition usually end a prepositional phrase.
        a. A word can be the object of a preposition.
            Examples: *in the **house**, to **him**, through **it***
        b. A gerund or gerund phrase can be an object of the preposition.
            Examples: *for **walking**, by **going to the beach***
        c. A clause can be the object of a preposition.
            Examples: *at **whenever you want**, for **whoever pays the most***
    3. Modifiers of objects of prepositions can be used.
        Examples: *to **the long** beach, in **two green** bags*
  C. Uses
    1. Prepositional phrases can modify nouns.
        Examples: *a path **to the beach**, the truth **about her***
    2. Prepositional phrases can modify verbs.
        Examples: *He walks **in the rain**. He sings **to them**.*
    3. Prepositional phrases can modify adjectives.
        Example: *They are content **in their house**.*
  D. Punctuation of prepositional phrases
    1. Prepositional phrases usually are not set off with commas.
        Example: *We ran **to the house by the water**.*
    2. Prepositional phrases can sometimes be set off with commas.
        a. Prepositional phrases can be set off to be emphatic.
            Example: *This dress is for me, **not for you**.*
        b. Prepositional phrases can be set off to separate.
            Example: This dress, ***for whatever reason**, is really ugly.*
        c. Prepositional phrases can be set off to be contrary.
            Examples: *I think, **to the contrary**, it is very attractive. **Despite your opinion**, I'm going to buy it.*

Chapter 8

Verbal Phrases: Adjective

Underline the one **adjective verbal phrase** in each of the following sentences. Don't worry if you can't find them.

1. In the Greek myth of *Pygmalion and Galatea,* King Pygmalion makes a statue of a woman possessing ideal qualities.
2. Pygmalion falls madly in love with the statue representing perfection in his eyes.
3. Completely taken with the statue, Pygmalion pines away with unrequited love.
4. The goddess of love, Aphrodite, feeling sorry for him, makes the statue come alive; thus Galatea is born.
5. In modern times, George Bernard Shaw wrote *Pygmalion,* a play based on the same story.
6. His Pygmalion is Henry Higgins, known as a linguist.
7. He finds a poor young woman selling violets outdoors.
8. Using all the "modern" methods, Higgins teaches Eliza correct language and proper manners.
9. Once taught proper English, Eliza passes as a high-class lady, even a princess.
10. But Eliza hates the hypocrisy of the upper class; not wanting any part of it, she returns to her old life.

Verbal phrases, as the name indicates, are phrases (a group of words that go together) that start with the participial form of a verb, such as the -*ing,* the -*ed,* and the -*en* forms of verbs: *dancing, walked, taken.* The -*ing* form is called the **present participle;** the -*ed* and -*en* forms are called **past participles.** These participles (sometimes called **adjectivals**) may be used as one-word adjectives: *his* growing *child, an* exhausting *time, the* fabled *Nile, her* limited *budget, my* broken *door, Eliza's* spoken *words.* In **adjective verbal phrases** (also called **participial phrases**), the verbal phrase includes more words and the whole phrase acts as an adjective—that is, it modifies a noun or a pronoun. Notice what each adjective verbal phrase modifies here:

(the adjective verbal phrase modifies play)
This play, **based on a Greek myth,** had the same title.

(the adjective verbal phrase modifies play*)*

Everyone liked this play **based on a Greek myth.**

(the adjective verbal phrase modifies Pygmalion*)*

Appearing to be a Cinderella story, *Pygmalion* has a twist.

(the adjective verbal phrase modifies play*)*

Written in 1914, Shaw's play probably upset many people.

The adjective verbal phrase may have more than one part to the verb (**Being asked** to dance at the ball, *Eliza felt elated*). And sometimes adverbs modifying the adjective will precede the verbal itself (**Very much** taken by surprise, *Eliza danced all night*).

Nonrestrictive Adjective Verbal Phrases

Nonrestictive adjective verbal phrases are set off by commas and add information that is not crucial to the meaning. In the sentence *Eliza, dancing all night, felt elated*, notice that the basic sentence is *Eliza felt elated.* The adjective verbal phrase, *dancing all night*, adds more information, but it is not crucial. The same is true when the adjective verbal phrase is placed elsewhere: Dancing all night, *Eliza felt elated.*

Usually the nonrestrictive adjective verbal phrase comes immediately before or immediately after what it modifies, as in the previous example. But it can also come later in the sentence if the meaning is clear: *Eliza felt elated*, having danced all night.

Make sure that the adjective verbal phrase has something appropriate to modify. For example, in *Trying her best, the hat would not fit*, the adjective verbal phrase, *Trying her best* cannot modify *hat* since a hat cannot try her best. Either the adjective verbal phrase or the word modified must be changed:

Although Sally tried her best, the hat would not fit.

Trying her best, Sally could not make the hat fit.

Restrictive Adjective Verbal Phrases

Restrictive adjective verbal phrases are *not* set off by commas and *do* change the meaning of the sentence. They identify and restrict the meaning of the nouns they modify. If the adjective verbal phrase were omitted, the entire sentence would not have the same meaning or would have no meaning. For example, in *The man dancing with Eliza is a count*, the adjective verbal phrase is crucial in identifying a particular man among the very general category of men. It cannot be omitted and retain the same meaning. Or in *People invited to the party were very well dressed*, the adjective verbal phrase restricts the noun *people*. Notice also that it cannot be placed elsewhere in the sentence and retain the same meaning.

Parts of Adjective Verbal Phrases

As a kind of verbal phrase, the adjective verbal phrase in itself may have direct and indirect objects, various modifiers, and complements:

	participles	*direct object*	*prepositional phrase modifying* having taken	
	Having taken	**her**	**to the ball,**	he left.

adverb	*participle*	*adjective*	*direct object*	
Soon	**wanting**	**a pleasant**	**nap,**	he left.

	participle	*subjective complement*	*prepositional phrase modifying* happy	
	Looking	**happy**	**about the dance,**	he stayed.

adverb	*participle*	*direct object*	*objective complement*	
Not	**finding**	**the music**	**pleasant,**	he left.

Since phrases do not have subjects, the subjective complement in the adjective verbal phrase refers to the subject of the whole sentence. However, the objective complement in the adjective verbal phrase refers to the direct object in the adjective verbal phrase.

Absolute Phrases

A type of phrase related to the adjective verbal phrase is the ***absolute phrase,*** so called because it gives added information but does not modify anything the way an adjective verbal phrase does. The absolute phrase is made up of a noun or pronoun subject and a participle along with any modifiers or complements. It may appear at the beginning, middle, or end of a sentence and is always followed, surrounded, or preceded by a comma or commas:

> **All things considered,** I'd prefer a hat as a gift.
>
> I need a hat, **the sun being so strong,** but I hate straw hats.
>
> I don't need a hat, **the rain having stopped.**

Variations in absolute phrases include beginning with *with* and sometimes omitting the participle *being:*

> **With the brim (being) so large,** this hat shades my face well.
>
> I like these hats, **the colors (being) varied.**

Absolute phrases add variety to sentences, as well as often being the most economical way to express a thought.

Exercise 8.1   Finding Adjective Verbal Phrases and Absolute Phrases

*A. Underline the **nonrestrictive adjective verbal phrases** (with commas) in the following sentences. Be careful of other uses for commas.*

Example   Oleander, <u>needing little care</u>, grows abundantly.

1. *My Fair Lady,* based on Shaw's play, is a musical comedy.
2. Written by Lerner and Loewe, it became a huge success.
3. It ran for years on Broadway, breaking all records.
4. The story is basically the same as Shaw's, making just one big change at the end.
5. Blessed with good songs, the show became the hit of the season.
6. Imitating Eliza's way of speaking, "Wouldn't It Be Loverly," one of the most popular songs, tells of her longing for a better life.
7. "I Could Have Danced All Night," sung by Eliza, lets her recall her triumph at the ball.
8. Captivated by Eliza, Freddy, a handsome young socialite, wants to marry her.
9. Knowing him all too well, Eliza won't marry a rich but silly and irresponsible man even if he loves her.
10. Feeling used and discarded by Higgins, Eliza nevertheless returns to him at the end.

*B. Underline the one **restrictive adjective verbal phrase** in each of the following sentences. Remember that they will* not *be set off with commas.*

Example   Corn <u>planted in one row</u> will not grow.

1. Many of the songs written for the show tell of the delights of high society.
2. The clothes worn by the society women were truly beautiful.
3. The show was enhanced by sets creating the era.
4. Henry Higgins leads a life devoted to his hobby of linguistics.
5. The people making up high society seem to have everything.
6. But Shaw showed upper-class people imprisoned by wealth.
7. The snobs cared only for money inherited from ancestors.
8. People inheriting money dominated high society.
9. Wealth should not be the force driving us to work.
10. Eliza becomes a Cinderella marrying her prince.

C. Underline the **one absolute phrase** in each of these sentences. The first one is done for you.

1. <u>The storm coming in the morning</u>, the commute was disrupted.
2. Cars were stopped, the rain having flooded the streets.
3. The street being flooded, no one went anywhere.
4. Many cars, their engines flooded, would not move.
5. Buses having stopped, passengers were either left in the rain or trapped inside.
6. Streets were clogged with vehicles, no one going anywhere, but all were trying.
7. No one predicted such a heavy downpour, rain usually being light in this season.
8. Two inches an hour being normal, this storm dumped two inches in half an hour and continued for another hour.
9. Nothing could be done, this having been a once-in-a-hundred-years occurrence.
10. All things considered, no wonder my roof leaked.

Exercise 8.2 Finding Adjective Verbal Phrases

Underline the **one** or **two adjective verbal phrases** in the following paragraphs.

1. Red maples have become more abundant, especially in recent years. Formerly rather scarce, they now grow from Canada to the south and west to the Great Lakes. Being adaptable to different climates and terrains, the red maple is winning out.
2. Dominating forests for thousands of years, oaks have slowly declined. They succumbed to attacks by gypsy moths, but animals and birds also like to eat acorns, so propagation of oaks becomes slower.
3. Forest fires helped the sturdy oaks to stay alive; other trees died. But now we have very few forest fires, so other trees previously destroyed by frequent fires have taken root. The oak must compete with them for light, water, and space.
4. If oaks decrease in an area, the whole forest will change. The deer and many birds feeding on acorns will also desert the area. In addition, the birds feed on the many insects living in the rough bark of the oaks.
5. Elms and hickories have also been vastly reduced by disease, along with many other types of trees. They also provide food and shelter for birds and insects. If the animals and birds cannot feed or live with a different type of tree growing in the area, they will leave or die.
6. Chestnut and walnut trees, providing valuable nuts for many nut-eating animals, have also declined. Some pests, such as squirrels and deer, sometimes

need reduction, but such changes affect the entire ecosystem and bring about profound alterations. Unwelcome surprises might occur.

7. The colors have also changed. In the fall, the oak yellows, having long dominated the New England countryside, have been replaced by the reds of the red maple. In the spring, the light and dark green hues of oaks, hickories, and pines have lost out to the rosy look of the red maple's buds and flowers.

8. The timber industry must take some responsibility for the changes in the forests. Hardwoods, being stronger for building, are the preferred harvest, not the heavy but weaker red maples. However, timber cutters take away oaks and hickories and then leave an abundance of red maple saplings. Spurred by additional sunlight and rain, the red maples soon dominate the forest.

9. Formerly thought to be extremely destructive, forest fires were always avoided. However, limiting and controlling them carefully, conservationists have deliberately set forest fires to regulate growths. If we want certain trees to return, we can make them come back.

10. Over the millions of years that forests have dominated the world, they have changed repeatedly. Previously encircling the world, they were almost destroyed by ice ages and human needs. As settlers leaving for more open land left the forests alone, the trees again regenerated in area after area.

Exercise 8.3 Finding Adjective Verbal Phrases and Absolute Phrases

A. The following essay has **ten adjective verbal phrases.** *Underline the nonrestrictive adjective verbal phrases, and double underline the restrictive adjective verbal phrases.*

Polite Parisians

Many American tourists visiting Paris for the first time have come back with tales of rude French people. The tourists say that they couldn't understand anyone and that French people had no patience with them. Sometimes they were even given false information or told to go away.

Wrongly stereotyped, Parisians suffer from a bad reputation. Forming their views on too little information, Americans reinforce the idea. Parisians enhancing that reputation are rare but do exist. Many tourists visiting Paris first encounter a taxi driver. Harassed by traffic, taxi drivers sometimes seem ill humored and impatient with non-French speakers. Their job is to get people to their destination, but sometimes the people don't know their destination or don't know how to tell the driver their destination. Having wasted a lot of time, the driver responds rudely. It's frustrating all around.

Sometimes, tourists wanting a typical French meal don't like brains or pâté or kidneys. They send back perfectly good meals and demand something more like what they are used to eating. Then they can't get what they want. It can be upsetting for everyone.

Parisians are proud of their language. They feel hurt by tourists who slaughter French or ignore its existence altogether. They may want to help a tourist lost in the city, but the tourist has to make some efforts to come halfway. After all, the tourist is in a French-speaking country.

Practically all Parisians speak some English and usually want to be of assistance. They often go out of their way to help; being rather reserved, however, they also are careful not to intrude. Perhaps their reserve is misinterpreted as aloofness or arrogance.

If American tourists would learn some phrases in French and then make some attempt at speaking French, they would find many kind, friendly, helpful Parisians.

B. *Underline the **five absolute phrases** in this paragraph.*

Her mind made up, Caitlin refused to cook Thanksgiving dinner for her whole family, they wanting her special turkey. She had too much work at school and, being swamped at work, she could not take the time. Caitlin, with her family being so large, had always cooked in the past. But this year, Thanksgiving coming at midterm time, just seemed impossible. Her brother, saying he had new clients, would not host the event. Finally, Caitlin said she would make the turkey and bring it to someone else's house. This compromise seeming to be the only solution, everyone agreed and went to her parents' place.

Exercise 8.4   Filling in Adjective Verbal Phrases

A. *Using a participial form of the listed verbs, write **adjective verbal phrases** that suit these sentences.*

Example   (give) Mindy arrived on time, ___given the heavy traffic___ .

1. (consider) _____, many people came for the picnic on the beach.

2. (come) People _____ took the longest to arrive.

3. (bring) People _____ had a lot to carry.

4. (weigh) _____, the volleyball equipment was very welcome.

5. (prefer) Most families brought food _____.

6. (drag) Teenagers, _____, sat sullenly with their families.

7. (run) Small children, _____, bothered everyone.

8. (complain) _____, the women had to prepare all the food.

9. (try) The men, _____, had to compete at building fires, playing volleyball, and running races.

10. (find) Everyone went home happy, _____.

B. *Using a participial form of the listed verbs, write* **adjective verbal phrases** *that suit these sentences. Add* not *or* never *if you want.*

1. (be) Walter, _____, decided to return to college after spending ten years away from school.

2. (want) _____, he looked for a college with a night school.

3. (offer) He decided on a good college _____.

4. (complete) He had a hard time _____ for two courses because of working full time.

5. (decide) _____, he quit his job and found a part-time job with flexible hours.

6. (give) He applied for financial aid, _____.

7. (deal) Then he registered as a full-time student for four courses _____.

8. (teach) Walter hopes some day to work in an elementary school _____.

9. (start) _____, he needs to catch up by taking extra courses in the summer.

10. (know) _____, Walter is happy with his life and the future he has planned.

Exercise 8.5   Using Adjective Verbal Phrases and Absolute Phrases

*A. The following phrases may be used in different ways, but try using them as **adjective verbal phrases.** Add* not *or* never *if you want. Be sure to add commas for nonrestrictive adjective verbal phrases.*

Example   (eating an apple) ___That horse eating an apple is ours.___

1. (taking a bath) _____

2. (injured on the ice) _____

3. (taken by surprise) _____

4. (fallen out of favor) _____

5. (considering the consequences) _____

6. (selling all the tickets) _____

7. (sensing our discomfort) _____

8. (studied thoroughly) _____

9. (pining away with love) _____

10. (excelling at all things) _____

11. (pleasing to all) _____

12. (unnoticed by everyone) _____

13. (hoping for a treat) _____

_____

14. (set for dinner) _____

_____

15. (kept away secretly) _____

_____

B. *Try using the following* **absolute phrases** *in sentences.*

1. (all things being equal) _____

_____

2. (I being the best) _____

_____

3. (no one else having my good qualities) _____

_____

4. (my professor knowing high quality) _____

_____

5. (everyone singing my praises) _____

_____

6. (my talents being natural) _____

_____

7. (my boss discerning true quality) _____

_____

8. (my parents having seen my abilities) _____

_____

9. (my classmates being impressed with my astuteness) _____

_____

10. (all things considered) _____

_____

Exercise 8.6   Writing Adjective Verbal Phrases and Absolute Phrases

*A. Use the indicated word as a participal to make an **adjective verbal phrase,** and then complete the sentence. Make sure to put in commas with nonrestrictive adjective verbal phrases.*

Example   (look) ___Looking around the room, she found a chair.___

1. (have) _____

   _____

2. (be) _____

   _____

3. (write) _____

   _____

4. (sing) _____

   _____

5. (eat) _____

   _____

6. (stand) _____

   _____

7. (sit) _____

   _____

8. (bend) _____

   _____

9. (hit) _____

   _____

10. (toss) _____

   _____

*B. Use the indicated word to form an **absolute phrase;** then complete the sentence.*

Example   (cat) ___The mice will play, the cat being away.___

1. (book) _____

   _____

2. (library) _____

_____

3. (librarian) _____

_____

4. (stacks) _____

_____

5. (encyclopedia) _____

_____

6. (dictionary) _____

_____

7. (journals) _____

_____

8. (carrels) _____

_____

9. (talking) _____

_____

10. (silence) _____

_____

Exercise 8.7 Proofreading

*Correct the **five errors in adjective verbal phrases** in the following paragraph. Some have been erroneously punctuated as nonrestrictive or restrictive.*

Most people should improve their muscle tone by doing exercises. Having conditioned muscles you will feel better, move more easily, have less joint pain, and decrease risk of injury. Muscles, stretched before exercising, will be less likely to pull. Muscles, stretched after a workout, will be less sore. Muscles, strengthened with resistance exercises, improve endurance and efficiency. For a simple stretch, touch your toes while either standing or sitting. For resistance exercises, use either your own body weight or weight apparatus. Push-ups, done on the floor or against a wall, strengthen arms and shoulders. Free weights or various weight machines can also be helpful. Your muscles, strengthened through exercise, will be more flexible and make you feel better.

Summary

I. Adjective Verbal Phrases
   A. Definition: **Adjective verbal phrases** are phrases made up of the participial forms of a verb (*-ed, -en, -ing*), along with other words that go with them, and modify nouns and sometimes pronouns.
   B. Types of adjective verbal phrases
      1. **Nonrestrictive adjective verbal phrases** (set off with commas)
         a. Add information not crucial to the meaning.
            Example: *The cat,* **leaping in the air,** *caught the fly in its mouth.*
         b. May be placed before or after the modified word.
            Examples: **Taken by surprise,** *the cat jumped.*
            The cat, **taken by surprise,** *jumped.*
         c. May be placed elsewhere only if the meaning is clear.
            Example: *The cat jumped,* **having been taken by surprise.**
      2. **Restrictive adjective verbal phrases** (no commas)
         a. Give crucial information that changes the meaning.
            Example: *The cat* **leaping in the air** *is agile.*
         b. Must be placed immediately after the noun or pronoun that they modify.
            Example: *The steak* **eaten last night** *was bad.*
II. Absolute Phrases
   A. Definition: **Absolute phrases** give added information but do not modify anything.
   B. Parts of absolute phrases
      1. Absolute phrases are made up of a noun or pronoun plus a participle and usually modifiers.
         Examples: *the news being good, someone having a cold*
      2. Absolute phrases are set off from the rest of the sentence with commas.
         Examples: *This time,* **all things considered,** *I'm happy.*
         All things considered, *this time I'm happy.*
         This time I'm happy, **all things considered.**

Chapter 9

Verbal Phrases: Infinitive

Underline the **infinitive verbal phrases** in each of these sentences:

1. Canada geese seem to live all year round in the park nearby.
2. They appear to be very happy in this environment.
3. Everyone likes to see them walking around and eating the grass.
4. They don't mean to ruin the park, but they do.
5. They have managed to leave their droppings all over the ground.
6. People can't find a place to walk or to sit on the grass.
7. The town does not have the funds to clean up this mess.
8. To shoot the geese would be a terrible shame.
9. The mayor decided to post two dogs for eight-hour shifts.
10. The geese will learn to avoid the dogs somehow.

A verbal phrase is made of a verb form plus the words that go with it. *Infinitive verbal phrases* are made up of the infinitive form of the verb (*to* plus the verb) along with modifiers or complements: to see *Canada geese,* to enjoy *nature.* Auxiliary verbs in their infinitive form may also make up infinitive verbal phrases: to have seen *Paris,* to be walking *in the field,* to have been freed *of sorrow.* Infinitive verbal phrases are used as nouns, as adjectives, and as adverbs.

Infinitive Verbal Phrases as Nouns

Infinitive verbal phrases as nouns serve as subject (and delayed subject), direct object, and subjective complement:

To kill the geese would be unthinkable. (subject)

It would be unthinkable **to kill the geese.** (delayed subject; *it* has no meaning; the real subject is *to kill the geese*)

The geese wanted **to eat the grass.** (direct object)

The mayor's plan is **to chase away the geese.** (subjective complement)

Some verbs often (but not always) take an infinitive verbal phrase after them. Here are a few common ones:

I **agreed** to wait for him.

We **appear** to be waiting for her.

I **claimed** to want a job.

We **consent** to see him.

I **decided** to go with her.

We **deserve** to have the prize.

I **forgot** to take it with me.

We **learn** to play the piano.

I **meant** to mail the letter.

We **promise** to be true.

I **regret** to inform you of this news.

We **remembered** to sign the card.

I **seem** to be pleased.

We **swear** to tell the truth.

I **wish** to visit you.

Some verbs very often (but not always) have an indirect object (either noun or pronoun) and an infinitive verbal phrase. Here are a few frequently used ones:

He **advises** her to help people

She **allowed** him to take the seat.

They **asked** Tony to be at home.

He **begged** her to attend the party.

She **convinced** him to avoid math.

They **dared** Maria to tell the truth.

He **encouraged** her to study harder.

She **expected** him to arrive on time.

They **forced** Tony to clean the kitchen.

He **hired** her to fix the computer.

She **needed** him to wait for her.

They **ordered** Maria to pay the fine.

He **permitted** her to stay up later.

She **persuaded** him to write a letter.

They **reminded** Tony to wake up the guests.

He **requires** her to drive the car.

She **taught** him to use the computer.

They **told** Maria to buy a bicycle.
He **urged** her to major in accounting.
She **wants** him to have a nice trip.

Infinitive Verbal Phrases as Adjectives

Infinitive verbal phrases may act as adjectives by modifying nouns and pronouns:

The mayor's idea **to rid the park of geese** was simple. (modifies *plan*)
He wanted dogs **to chase the geese.** (modifies *dogs*)
The ones **to do the job** came from the pound. (modifies *ones*)

Infinitive Verbal Phrases as Adverbs

Infinitive verbal phrases serve as adverbs by modifying verbs and adjectives (but not other adverbs):

We abolished the geese **to provide a cleaner park.** (modifies verb *abolished*)
The dogs were eager **to chase the geese.** (modifies adjective *eager*)

Omission of **to** *in the Infinitive*

A few verbs omit the *to* in the infinitive that follows them: *help, hear, let, make, see, watch.* These verbs almost always have an indirect object, and the infinitive (even without the *to*) serves as the direct object:

He **helped** her remove the paint. (OR *to remove the paint;* infinitive *to remove*)
She **hears** him recite the poem. (infinitive *to recite*)
They **let** Tony sing the song. (infinitive *to sing*)
He **made** her read the book. (infinitive *to read*)
She **saw** him eat the apple. (infinitive *to eat*)
They **watch** Maria make a goal. (infinitive *to make*)

Infinitive Verbal Phrases as Objects of Prepositions

The prepositions *besides, but,* and *except,* when followed by a verb, also sometimes omit the *to* of the infinitive, which serves as the object of the preposition:

He did nothing besides return the money.
She had no choice but take the gift. (OR *to take the gift*)
They did little except dig the holes. (OR *to dig the holes*)

Parts of Infinitive Verbal Phrases

Infinitive verbal phrases not only serve as parts of sentences but also have their own parts. Since the infinitive is basically a verb form, it takes direct and indirect objects, adjectives, adverbs, prepositional phrases, and complements:

	infinitive	*direct object*
They did not wish	**to take**	**the gift.**

	infinitive	*adverb*	*prepositional phrase modifying infinitive*
Adel hoped	**to swim**	**rapidly**	**in the meet.**

	infinitive	*subjective complement*
She wanted	**to seem**	**grateful.**

The indirect object of the sentence becomes the subject of the infinitive verbal phrase:

	indirect object as subject of infinitive phrase	*infinitive*	*direct object of infinitive phrase*
He expected	**them**	**to take**	**the lead.**

To *as Preposition and as Infinitive Marker*

Be careful not to confuse the preposition *to* with the *to* of the infinitive. The preposition is not followed by a base verb, while the infinitive is made up of the *to* plus the base form:

He needs **to take an exam.** (infinitive verbal phrase)

She is resistant **to taking an exam.** (prepositional phrase)

They walked **to the park.** (prepositional phrase)

Exercise 9.1   Finding Infinitive Verbal Phrases

*A. Underline the **one infinitive verbal phrase** in each of the following sentences.*

Example   She asked me <u>to take flowers</u> to the patients.

1. Mohandas and Kasturbai agreed to marry each other at age thirteen at the insistence of their parents.
2. Then Mohandas Gandhi went to study law in England in 1888.

3. Returning to India, he started to practice law in Bombay.

4. Next he went to live in South Africa as a legal consultant.

5. Racial discrimination in South Africa caused him to want changes.

6. Gandhi returned to India to organize a movement fighting discrimination against Indians in South Africa.

7. He and his family were called back to South Africa and traveled between these two countries to fight against prejudice.

8. In addition, Gandhi petitioned to the British to keep India an undivided integral country.

9. He also urged Indians to favor Indian Home Rule while still belonging to the British Empire.

10. Gandhi also vowed to renounce all worldly goods to the consternation of his family and friends.

B. *Underline the* **one** *or* **two infinitive verbal phrases** *in each of the following sentences.*

1. While in South Africa, Gandhi convinced Indians to take a vow of passive resistance and to fight against discrimination.

2. Gandhi used the word *Satyagraha* to mean passive resistance, the concept of resistance to authorities without using violence.

3. The vow of passive resistance forbids resisters to retaliate or to react even if force is used on them.

4. Gandhi refused to leave South Africa when ordered to and therefore went to prison for a few months.

5. Gandhi volunteered to help many causes and urged others to engage in these causes also.

6. His family allowed him to continue his fight and even struggled to support the same causes.

7. Kasturbai also went to prison when she dared to resist authority.

8. After many years in South Africa, Gandhi and his family returned to India to establish his Satyagraha ashram.

9. In India, he lent his support to textile workers and to other causes while managing to found the all-India Satyagraha movement.

10. As an ascetic, Gandhi did little for himself except work for the cause of the common person.

*C. Underline the **infinitive verbal phrases** in the sentences in the following paragraphs. Not all sentences have infinitive verbal phrases, but some may have more than one.*

1. Gandhi went to prison many times during his career. He perpetually challenged the authorities to arrest him and so they did, quite often. He often expected to be imprisoned. Sometimes he spent only a few days in prison, but once he was forced to spend two years there under harsh conditions.

2. Another method Gandhi used to attract people to his cause was fasting. He fasted sometimes to rid himself of the enjoyment of food, to do penance, and to protest against wrongs. Usually he vowed to fast for twenty-one days but sometimes pledged to fast to death unless his demands were met. He often started to fast while he was in prison.

3. Writing was a third method Gandhi used to influence people to join his cause. He wrote a number of guides to healthful living, to proper diet, to religious faith, and to moral education. He also wrote many political tracts to explain his principles of Satyagraha and civil disobedience. In addition, he wrote about his own experiences but always with an eye to improving the lives of others.

4. Satyagraha, to resist authority passively, was Gandhi's great belief. To underscore his desire for peace, he demanded that his followers not fight back when they were struck. He adhered to this policy all his life, but he permitted his followers to abandon it once or twice in the face of strong opposition. Gandhi always believed that violence only led to more violence.

5. Near the end of his life, after his retirement from politics, Gandhi returned to the fray by fighting for India's independence from British rule. He wanted to keep India whole and was opposed to dividing up the country into parts. But even as he sought to resolve differences peacefully, he was assassinated on his way to his evening prayers.

Exercise 9.2   Finding Infinitive Verbal Phrases

*Underline the **fifteen infinitive verbal phrases** in the following essay.*

Gandhi's Legacy

Mahatma Gandhi barely lived long enough to see Indian independence from British rule, but he knew he was instrumental in bringing it about. Long after his death, his influence continues to be felt. His gift to the people of the world is his love of peace and harmony.

The familiar statue of Gandhi can be seen in many parks and open spaces around the world. It shows him walking with his familiar long strides. He carries a pole to help steady himself. His rail-thin body is draped with his familiar *dhoti*, a loincloth wrapped around his waist, between his legs, and over his shoulder. To see the statue is to feel peace and love.

In a more practical sense, Gandhi also influenced the great hippie movement of the 1960s and 1970s. Some hippies only received the message to use drugs and to drop out of society, not Gandhian ideas. But many others received the message to simplify their lives, to be self-sufficient, to respect the environment, to stop polluting our land and sea, and to use natural products. They also received Gandhi's spiritual message to seek enlightenment and to promote peace among the peoples of the world.

The most obvious influence was on Martin Luther King, Jr. King put Gandhi's precepts into action during his march on Selma, Alabama, where he advocated a peaceful demonstration. King abhorred violence of any kind, even if others were willing to fight for their cause. He was successful in maintaining this stance to the end of his life. Like Gandhi, King was assassinated for his beliefs.

In the new millennium, peace in the world has not been achieved, but Gandhi's influence lives on. Maybe someday his message will be heard and embraced by all.

Exercise 9.3   Identifying the Use of Infinitive Verbal Phrases

*A. Underline the **infinitive verbal phrases** and then write in the blank which **noun** form it is, using these abbreviations:*

S *subject*
DS *delayed subject*
DO *direct object*
SC *subjective complement*

Example   Poinsettias fail <u>to rebloom without total darkness</u>. <u>DO</u>

1. To become a bird watcher means engaging in a passionate sport. _____
2. First, it is necessary to buy the best binoculars you can afford. _____
3. To be a good birder takes knowledge, so pick up the latest and best field guide to birds in your area. _____
4. If you want to be independent, go birdwatching alone. _____
5. Most people prefer to join a group of dedicated birders. _____
6. You might wish to find an expert for instruction. _____
7. It takes time to learn the identification of birds. _____

8. You will need to rise very early in the morning. _____
9. And don't forget to bring the binoculars, a hat, and water. _____
10. You also need to wait a long time. _____
11. You should let others find the birds in the trees. _____
12. Other people will help you identify any birds you see. _____
13. If you see the bird land on a branch, observe it carefully. _____
14. Then watch the bird fly away and note the flight pattern. _____
15. If you can hear the bird sing, you should connect the song and the bird. _____
16. Make the other people help you identify what you have seen. _____
17. Then remember to check off the bird in your field guide. _____
18. At home, you should plan to study your field guide carefully. _____
19. To become an expert takes time and patience. _____
20. It will reward you greatly to go bird watching often. _____

B. Underline the **infinitive verbal phrases** and then write in the blank which **modifier** it is, using these abbreviations:
   ADJ *adjective*
   ADV *adverb*

1. The field guide to be carried with you should be studied thoroughly. _____
2. Before a field trip, take time to study the likely birds in the area. _____
3. The day to visit a birdwatching area should be bright and clear. _____
4. Don't be too quick to identify a bird immediately. _____
5. Watch a distant bird carefully and wait to identify it. _____
6. The birds to watch carefully are flying ones. _____
7. Don't be too eager to find new birds in an area. _____
8. Avoid annual competitions to spot at least one hundred different birds in a day until you are more sure of yourself. _____
9. Sites to see a variety of birds include the seashore, lakes, swamps, and fields. _____
10. Most people are able to distinguish ducks, geese, and swans, so starting at a lake is a good idea. _____

Exercise 9.4   Using Infinitive Verbal Phrases

*Add **infinitive verbal phrases** to complete the following sentences.*

Example   Crocuses are the first flowers __to bloom in the spring__.

1. He threatened _____.

2. She will urge him _____.

3. They prefer not _____.

4. He waited _____.

5. She forbids him _____.

6. They need encouragement _____.

7. He wanted time _____.

8. She hopes for high grades _____.

9. They expect the party _____.

10. He permitted the dog _____.

11. She felt happy _____.

12. They were eager _____.

13. He did not feel pleased _____.

14. She seems happy _____.

15. They appear willing _____.

16. _____ is the best policy.

17. _____ takes courage.

18. _____ should not be strange.

19. _____ might not be bad.

20. _____ ought to be all right.

Exercise 9.5   Writing with Infinitive Verbal Phrases

*Make up sentences using the following **infinitive verbal phrases.***

Example   (to tell the truth) __He is willing to tell the truth.__

1. (to play the lottery) _____

    _____

2. (to gamble in a casino) _____

    _____

3. (to bet in football pools) _____

    _____

4. (to visit Las Vegas) _____

_____

5. (to frequent the racetrack) _____

_____

6. (to wager at dog races) _____

_____

7. (to see a cockfight) _____

_____

8. (to shoot craps) _____

_____

9. (to toss dice) _____

_____

10. (to speculate on real estate) _____

_____

11. (to travel to Morocco) _____

_____

12. (to visit Marrakech, Casablanca, and Fez) _____

_____

13. (to shop in a souk) _____

_____

14. (to eat couscous and tagines) _____

_____

15. (to ride a camel) _____

_____

16. (to see the Sahara Desert) _____

_____

17. (to ride across sand dunes) _____

_____

18. (to wear a turban) _____

_____

19. (to get lost in a casbah) ————————————————

————————————————

20. (to make the trip of a lifetime) ————————————

————————————————

Exercise 9.6   Using Infinitive Verbal Phrases

*Use the following **infinitive verbal phrases** as subject, delayed subject, direct object, adjective, adverb, or subjective complement, as indicated.*

Example   to tell the story (as direct object)
              The child wanted to tell the story.

1. to tell the story well (as subject) ————————————

————————————————

2. to tell the story well (as delayed subject) ——————————

————————————————

3. to be pleased (as direct object) ——————————————

————————————————

4. to be pleased (as adverb) ————————————————

————————————————

5. to be pleased (as adjective) ————————————————

————————————————

6. to be pleased (as subjective complement) ——————————

————————————————

7. to want a house (as subject) ————————————————

————————————————

8. to want a horse (as delayed subject) ————————————

————————————————

9. to want a dog (as direct object) ——————————————

————————————————

10. to want a computer (as adjective or adverb) ——————————

————————————————

11. to bake potatoes (as subject) _____

    _____

12. to bake potatoes (as delayed subject) _____

    _____

13. to bake potatoes (as direct object) _____

    _____

14. to bake potatoes (as subjective complement) _____

    _____

15. to bake potatoes (as adjective) _____

    _____

16. to bake potatoes (as adverb) _____

    _____

17. to gladden her heart (as subject) _____

    _____

18. to gladden her heart (as direct object) _____

    _____

19. to gladden her heart (as subjective complement) _____

    _____

20. to gladden her heart (as adverb) _____

    _____

Exercise 9.7   Using Infinitive Verbal Phrases

Write paragraphs using the following **infinitive verbal phrases.** *You may have more than one infinitive verbal phrase in a sentence, but you don't need an infinitive verbal phrase in each sentence.*

1. to be rich, to have lots of money, to buy happiness, to feel secure, to need wealth

2. to read a good book, to see action movies, to walk in the park, to loll on the beach, to watch television

3. to lift weights, to jog for miles, to swim in the pool, to hike in the mountains, to row for hours

4. to get married, to have children, to own a house, to find a good career, to take vacations

5. to hear good music, to attend the ballet, to appreciate opera, to read literature, to see plays

6. to work on Wall Street, to know important people, to attend important meetings, to earn and spend millions, to have power

7. to throw a party, to invite my best friends, to eat and drink, to dance the tango, to talk with interesting people

8. to be busy, to feel harried, to run late, to rush through everything, to have insomnia

9. to raise children, to see them learn, to take them with me, to tell them stories, to watch them grow up

10. to vacuum the carpets, to dust the shelves, to clean the bathrooms, to mop the kitchen floor, to change the beds

Summary

I. Infinitive Verbal Phrases
 A. Definition: **Infinitive verbal phrases** serve as nouns, adjectives, adverbs, and objects of a preposition.
 B. Parts of infinitive verbal phrases
  1. The **infinitive form of the verb** (*to* plus the verb form) is the major part.
   Examples: *to eat, to sleep, to study, to run*
  2. Modifiers or complements are added to make a phrase.
   Examples: *to run a race, to sleep soundly*
 C. Uses
  1. Infinitive verbal phrases can be used as nouns.
   a. They can be a subject (including a delayed subject).
    Examples: ***To be happy*** *is difficult.*
    It is difficult ***to be happy.***
   b. They can be a direct object.
    Example: *I want* ***to have a good life.***
   c. They can be a subjective complement.
    Example: *She appears* ***to have everything.***
  2. Infinitive verbal phrases can be used as adjectives.
   a. They can modify nouns.
    Example: *His goal* ***to earn a degree*** *is possible.*
   b. They can modify pronouns.
    Example: *They asked her* ***to make a speech.***
  3. Infinitive verbal phrases can be used as adverbs.
   a. They can modify verbs.
    Example: *He resigned* ***to have peace of mind.***
   b. They can modify adjectives (but not adverbs).
    Example: *He was glad* ***to receive a diploma.***

D. Omission of the *to* of the infinitive
    1. *To* is often omitted in the verb after *hear, help, let, make, see, watch.*
        Examples: *We helped Tom **study** math.* (to study)
                   *Tom let them **ask** questions.* (to ask)
    2. *To* is often omitted in the verb after *besides, but, except.*
        Example: *He did nothing except **listen** at the door.* (to listen)
E. Avoiding confusing different uses of *to*
    1. The preposition *to* is followed by an object.
        Examples: *to the house, to Shelly, to them*
    2. The infinitive *to* is followed by a verb form.
        Examples: *to worry, to walk, to have, to be*

Chapter 10

Verbal Phrases: Noun

Underline the one **noun verbal phrase** in each of these sentences.

1. Smoking any substance should be banned in public and in places where the public may go.
2. Harming others either outdoors or indoors is against the law.
3. Passive smoke is a known carcinogen that contributes to hurting people, especially children.
4. We have banned smoking in workplaces because nonsmokers should not be subjected to a smoker.
5. Why should there be an exception for working in restaurants and bars?
6. Letting people indulge in dangerous behavior appears to be a basic human right, but not if it involves others.
7. However, behaving dangerously may land a person in the hospital for costly care that he or she cannot afford.
8. Seeking reimbursement for medical costs has forced states to sue tobacco companies.
9. The equivalent is requiring people to use seatbelts in cars.
10. Although we are allowed to hurt ourselves, putting on seatbelts is required so that we will not cost the state a lot of money.

Noun Verbal Phrases (Gerund Phrases)

Verbal phrases are made up of a verb form plus the words that go with it. **Noun verbal phrases** (also called **gerund phrases**) always use a **gerund**, the present participle of a verb used as a noun. So the *-ing* form of verbs, such as *dancing, eating, looking,* and *making,* combine the function of nouns (naming things) and the form of verbs (expressing action). Adding modifying words either before or after the gerund makes them into **noun verbal phrases.** Noun verbal phrases are used the same way as nouns are used in sentences: as subjects, indirect objects, direct objects,

objects of the preposition, subjective complements (but not objective complements), and appositives:

> **Going to the movies** is fun. (subject)
> I'll give **going to the movies** a chance. (indirect object)
> I like **going to the movies.** (direct object)
> I kill time by **going to the movies.** (object of preposition)
> My hobby is **going to the movies.** (subjective complement)
> My hobby, **going to the movies,** is fun. (appositive)

Remember that *-ing* forms of verbs can also be part of the complete verb and not a gerund. In *My son is going to the movies*, the complete verb is *is going*, and tells what the subject (*my son*) is doing. In *My hobby is going to the movies*, the complete verb is *is. Going to the movies* is the subjective complement; it is not my hobby that is going.

In addition to the *-ing* form of main verbs serving as gerunds, auxiliary verbs and linking verbs may also be used:

> **Having finished the exam** was a relief.
> **Having given the professor my test** made me nervous.
> **Being tired of studying** didn't help.

Parts of Noun Verbal Phrases

These noun verbal phrases have various noun uses, but unlike regular nouns, gerunds are verb forms and will have the attributes of verbs, so the noun verbal phrase may have an indirect object, direct object, or, in the case of linking verbs, a subjective complement. For example, notice how these noun verbal phrases have their own parts in addition to whatever the whole sentence contains.

gerund	direct object	
Having finished	**the exam**	was a relief.

gerund	indirect object	direct object	
Having given	**the professor**	**my test**	made me nervous.

gerund	subjective complement	prepositional phrase	
Being	**tired**	**of studying**	didn't help.

gerund	direct object	objective complement	
Keeping	**my grades**	**high**	is a priority.

Notice that the subjective complement (the renamer or describer of the subject) actually does not have a subject to rename. It is a subjective complement because it comes after a form of a linking verb, such as ***being, looking, seeming, tasting.***

Whether the noun verbal phrase is being used in the whole sentence as the subject, indirect object, direct object, subjective complement, object of the preposition, or appositive, it still may have these various parts within the noun verbal phrase.

Since noun verbal phrases are nouns, modifiers should be appropriate for nouns:

His going to the movies took time. (NOT *Him going . . .*)

Our being tired didn't help. (NOT *Us being . . .*)

My having finished the exam was a relief. (NOT *Me having . . .*)

But the same gerund also functions as a verb form, so adverbs, rather than adjectives, modify the gerund:

Going **frequently** to the movies is fun.

Our being **silently** at home didn't help.

My having finished the exam **rapidly** was a relief.

Some writers use noun verbal phrases in prepositional phrases that have nothing to modify. For example, in *By getting good grades, it would help me,* the noun verbal phrase (*getting good grades*) is used as the object of the preposition **by,** but then the prepositional phrase must modify *it,* which cannot get good grades. Changing the sentence to *I would be helped* is possible, but simply omitting **by** and the comma will make a clear sentence: *Getting good grades would help me.* Now the noun verbal phrase is the subject of the sentence. Of course, using a noun verbal phrase as the object of the preposition **by** is fine as long as it has something to modify:

By getting good grades, she won an award. (modifies *she*)

Exercise 10.1   Finding Noun Verbal Phrases

*A. Underline the **one noun verbal phrase** in each of the following sentences.*

Example   <u>Reading a book every week</u> sounds difficult.

1. Learning English pronunciation can be very difficult.
2. As with most other languages, one starts to learn English by memorizing words.
3. Pronouncing English words requires a lot of memorization.
4. For example, rhyming *bone, cone,* and *lone* is easy, but why don't *done* and *none* also rhyme, to say nothing of *gone?*
5. These nonrhyming words make speaking English complicated.
6. Changing the pronunciation for no reason at all also makes for complications.

7. Saying *greasy* with an **s** sound is standard, although some people use a **z** sound.
8. Pronouncing *easy* with an **s** sound should be normal, but it is not.
9. Making the **th** sound is hard enough in English, but we actually have two sounds, voiced and voiceless.
10. The **th** in *these, this,* and *that* is made by vibrating the sound, while *thank, thought,* and *thrill* are not vibrated.

B. *Underline the **one noun verbal phrase** in each of the following sentences.*

1. Learning English verbs also has its problems.
2. The problem is not in conjugating verbs.
3. Using almost the same form for first, second, and third person in both singular and plural is easy.
4. Having an **s** on third person singular verbs is the only change.
5. Future tense is formed by adding *will* to the main verb.
6. But stringing together all those auxiliary verbs to the main verb, such as *will have been going,* can get complicated.
7. Figuring out the past and the progressive tenses poses the most problems.
8. You cannot avoid memorizing irregular verb forms.
9. Using these verb forms frequently with friends can help if they will take the time to correct you.
10. The best method must be reading newspapers and books.

C. *Underline the **noun verbal phrases** in the following paragraphs. Each paragraph has two or three noun verbal phrases.*

1. When it comes to choosing a mate, a female penguin knows better than to fall for the first creep who pulls up and honks. She holds out for the fittest suitor available—which in Antarctica means one chubby enough to spend several weeks sitting on newly hatched eggs without starving to death.
2. The Asian jungle bird *Gallus gallus* is just as choosy. Males in that species sport gaily colored head combs and feathers, which lose their luster if the bird is invaded by parasites. By favoring males with bright ornaments, a hen improves her odds of securing a mate (and bearing offspring) with strong resistance to disease.
3. For female scorpion flies, beauty is less about size or color than about symmetry. Females favor suitors who have well-matched wings—and with good reason. Studies show they're the most adept at killing prey and at defending

their catch from competitors. (Geoffrey Cowley, "The Biology of Beauty," *Newsweek*)

D. *Underline the **noun verbal phrases** in the following paragraphs. Each paragraph has two or three noun verbal phrases.*

1. Franklin Delano Roosevelt was one of the most vigorous presidents the United States ever had. Becoming president in 1933 at the height of the Depression would be a challenge for anyone. Roosevelt started by introducing a number of bills for improving the welfare of the populace.

2. Creating public works jobs helped thousands of unemployed people. Young men were recruited by the Civilian Conservation Corps (CCC) for planting trees and building dams. The Works Progress Administration (WPA) employed millions of people to build roads, bridges, and structures.

3. Artists started painting pictures and murals in different cities while writers traveled widely within the country, producing folklore, guidebooks, and histories. Putting on shows across the nation was the job of theater companies. All this was done under the auspices of government programs.

4. Roosevelt did not think only of helping the victims of the Depression. He also wanted to prevent future stock market crashes by introducing bills regulating financial transactions on Wall Street. Helping farmers stay on their farms was the goal of another bill passed. A repetition of the 1929 crash had to be prevented.

5. A controversial plan, Social Security, caused much debate but also passed Congress. Securing every employee's future through payroll deductions and employers' contributions sounded too much like socialism to some people. Indeed, having the word *social* in both Social Security and socialism made people uncomfortable.

Exercise 10.2   Finding Noun Verbal Phrases

*Underline the **ten noun verbal phrases** in the following essay.*

Selling, Skiing, and Smiling

What life will be like in the year 3000 doesn't concern me since I'm not going to be around. But thinking about my future sounds like a lot of fun for me. So here are some plans to ensure my having a profitable and interesting future.

I will finish college by getting my degree in business administration. Then I picture myself finding a job in retail business, probably managing a store. After five years of experience, my dream is running my own small business, maybe a ski shop with a tie-in to nearby resorts. I have skied since I was a child, so skiing is something I know about.

I'll stock my store with the best and latest equipment—skis, poles, boots, clothing, goggles—and have lots of information about resorts, weather, slope conditions, and snow depths. I can imagine advising skiers on resorts, equipment, and technique; maybe I'll even ski with some of them. I'll take managing a ski shop to whole new dimensions by making the shop a ski center and community resource.

I will be active in local boys' and girls' clubs, the Chamber of Commerce, and other organizations. I will probably be helping them with activities and benefits, so I will be promoting my ski shop as well as encouraging people to try the slopes. I won't make it look too obvious, however. Skiing the slopes will be my whole life.

Of course, I'll get married and have children. Then my whole family can ski with me. I think my future looks really bright.

Exercise 10.3   Identifying Uses of Noun Verbal Phrases

*A. Underline the **one noun verbal phrase** in each sentence and label its function in the sentence as follows:*

S *subject*	**SC** *subjective complement*
IO *indirect object*	**A** *appositive*
DO *direct object*	**OP** *object of a preposition*

                        S

Example   <u>Visiting Italy</u> is my dream.

1. Playing tennis is definitely good exercise.

2. An average player can manage with using second-hand equipment.

3. The one big expense is buying new tennis balls.

4. Most towns and cities have inexpensive public tennis courts, playing surfaces with a net and little else.

5. We don't like waiting our turn at popular courts, however.

6. Spending an afternoon with a friend on the court can be fun.

7. We get lots of exercise too by running back and forth.

8. When I serve, I always try acing the ball but rarely succeed.

9. The hardest part is rushing the net for a low ball.

10. Everyone should give playing tennis a serious try.

B. *Underline the* **one noun verbal phrase** *in each sentence and label its function in the sentence as follows:*

   S *subject*   **SC** *subjective complement*
   IO *indirect object*   **A** *appositive*
   DO *direct object*   **OP** *object of a preposition*

1. In tennis, having just one person to play with is easy.

2. Team sports require signing up with a whole group of people.

3. Then you have problems of scheduling practice sessions.

4. I play two times a week just by calling up one of my friends.

5. For me, tennis means playing with friends whom I like.

6. I like playing outdoors, but we go to an indoor court in bad weather.

7. I don't like the indoor court, but I'm thankful for having it around.

8. Competing against a better player than I certainly improves my game.

9. But lobbing the ball back and forth with a child can also make me run around.

10. I don't often have to do the hardest part, jumping over the net at the end.

Exercise 10.4   Identifying Parts of Noun Verbal Phrases

In these sentences, underline the **noun verbal phrase** *and label the* **gerund** *and any of these other parts as follows:*

   G *gerund*   **DO** *direct object*
   IO *indirect object*   **SC** *subjective complement*

                   G   *SC*
Example   Being too rich can cause problems.

1. Springtime allergies may be alleviated by taking various steps.

2. The first step is avoiding the allergens.

3. Sufferer can lessen pollen by limiting yard work.

4. Working outdoors should be restricted.

5. Cleaning our hair and shoes will reduce indoor pollen.

6. We can help by keeping the doors and windows closed.

7. Washing clothes used outdoors will also help.

8. Giving pets a bath keeps them pollen free also.

9. Using antihistamines can help reduce sneezes and coughs.

10. Turning on the air conditioner will keep the air cleaner.

Exercise 10.5   Writing with Noun Verbal Phrases

The following phrases can be used in many ways, but try to make them **noun verbal phrases** *in sentences.*

Example   (taking the train) __I like taking the train to Chicago.__

1. (walking the dog) _____

   _____

2. (considering the weather) _____

   _____

3. (announcing the event) _____

   _____

4. (raising the curtain) _____

   _____

5. (enjoying the flowers) _____

   _____

6. (keeping fit) _____

   _____

7. (looking for trouble) _____

   _____

8. (furnishing an apartment) _____

   _____

9. (cheating on the exam) _____

_____

10. (eating the cake) _____

_____

11. (breaking up the fight) _____

_____

12. (selling all my assets) _____

_____

13. (pleasing my parents) _____

_____

14. (being from California) _____

_____

15. (being an athlete) _____

_____

16. (having thrown the ball) _____

_____

17. (having stopped smoking) _____

_____

18. (having devoted my life) _____

_____

19. (having sought refuge) _____

_____

20. (having collected the rent) _____

_____

Exercise 10.6   Writing with Noun Verbal Phrases

*Use each of the following phrases as a **noun verbal phrase**, and make each one a **subject, direct object, subjective complement, object of a preposition**, or **appositive**, as indicated.*

Example   writing a term paper (as direct object)

I don't like writing a term paper.

1. using a cell phone (as subject) _____

    _____

2. using a cell phone (as direct object) _____

    _____

3. sending a fax (as indirect object) _____

    _____

4. sending a fax (as appositive) _____

    _____

5. e-mailing a friend (as subjective complement) _____

    _____

6. e-mailing a friend (as object of a preposition) _____

    _____

7. buying DVDs (as subject) _____

    _____

8. buying DVDs (as direct object) _____

    _____

9. carrying my laptop (as appositive) _____

    _____

10. carrying my laptop (as object of a preposition) _____

    _____

11. shucking peas (as indirect object) _____

    _____

12. shucking peas (as appositive) _____

    _____

13. picking blueberries (as subject) _____

    _____

14. picking blueberries (as direct object) _____

    _____

15. sitting in a rocking chair (as object of a preposition) _____

    _____

16. climbing trees (as subjective complement) _____

_____

17. climbing trees (as subject) _____

_____

18. growing watermelons (as direct object) _____

_____

19. growing watermelons (as an appositive) _____

_____

20. having a great life (as object of a preposition) _____

_____

Exercise 10.7   Proofreading

*In the following paragraph, underline the **ten noun verbal phrases** and correct the **three** that have errors. Don't confuse adjective phrases with noun verbal phrases.*

Anarchism was a political movement advocating the elimination of all government. By having no government, it would mean relying completely on each individual's ability to behave well. Anarchists believed that people were capable of behaving properly without laws or authorities. By being rational and clear-thinking, it would suffice for keeping people in order. William Godwin, an English political theorist, wrote about anarchism in the nineteenth century. Emma Goldman popularized the movement by lecturing throughout the United States in the early twentieth century. Finally deporting her to Russia ended her lectures. By idealizing faith in humankind, it made an attractive movement. It opposed class divisions and capitalism, both allowing for rich and poor people. For that reason, many people connected the anarchist movement with communism and socialism. Anarchy, however, was against structuring society in any way. But many people opposed anarchy, which is now practically synonymous with chaos and disorder. Trusting people's honesty cannot be advocated. What a shame.

Summary

I. Noun Verbal Phrases (also called Gerund Phrases)
   A. Definition: A **noun verbal phrase** (gerund phrase) is a group of words that go together using the *-ing* form of the verb (gerund).
   B. As nouns
      1. Noun verbal phrases are used as subjects.
         Example: ***Singing in the shower*** *is fun.*
      2. Noun verbal phrases are used as indirect objects.
         Example: *I'll give* ***singing on stage*** *a chance.*
      3. Noun verbal phrases are used as direct objects.
         Example: *I prefer* ***walking in the park.***
      4. Noun verbal phrases are used as subjective complements (but not as objective complements).
         Example: *My preference is* ***jogging outdoors.***
      5. Noun verbal phrases are used as objects of the preposition.
         Example: *He finds peace by* ***meditating every day.***
      6. Noun verbal phrases are used as appositives.
         Example: *Our job,* ***sending faxes,*** *is boring.*
   C. Parts of noun verbal phrases
      1. A **gerund** must be part of a noun verbal phrase.
         Examples: ***seeing*** *the sky,* ***finding*** *happiness*
      2. A gerund may take an indirect object.
         Examples: *taking* ***them*** *for a ride, wiring* ***Tom*** *money*
      3. A gerund may take a direct object.
         Examples: *throwing a* ***tantrum,*** *kissing* ***her***
      4. A gerund can take a subjective complement.
         Examples: *feeling* ***exhausted,*** *appearing* ***happy***
   D. Problems and special uses of noun verbal phrases
      1. Use pronouns appropriate for modifying nouns: ***my, our, your, his, her, its, their.***
         Examples: *Sue likes* ***my*** *going with her. I like* ***their*** *giving me a gift.*
      2. Use adverbs rather than adjectives to modify gerunds.
         Examples: *singing* ***quietly*** *on stage, being* ***often*** *at home, having been finished* ***quickly***
      3. Avoid using *by* with a noun verbal phrase to form a prepositional phrase if the phrase has nothing to modify.
         Example: NOT: *By going now, it would cause trouble.*
         CORRECT: *Going now would cause trouble.*

Clauses

Chapter 11

Independent Clauses: Simple and Compound Sentences

Underline the **simple sentences** and double underline the **compound sentences** in the following paragraph. Don't worry if you are not sure.

Two challenges face American education today. We must raise overall achievement levels, and we must make opportunities for achievement more equitable. The importance of both derives from the same basic condition—our changing economy. Never before has the pool of developed skill and capability mattered more in our prospects for general economic health. And never before have skill and knowledge mattered as much in the economic prospects for individuals. (Lauren B. Resnick, "From Aptitude to Effort," *American Educator*)

A *clause* is a group of words that go together and have a subject and verb. That is, clauses have *predication*, a subject that goes with a verb. *Independent clauses* (also called sentences) are complete clauses that can stand alone as sentences. *Dependent clauses* cannot stand alone and must be a part of an independent clause.

Simple Sentences

A *simple sentence* is one kind of *independent clause.* It is called simple, not because of length, but because of its structure. A simple sentence has just one clause with one or more subjects and one or more verbs but cannot be divided by a period to form two or more sentences:

Jo runs. (*Jo* = subject; *runs* = verb)
Jo and Jack run. (*Jo, Jack* = subjects; *run* = verb)
Jo and Jack run and jump. (*Jo, Jack* = subjects; *run, jump* = verbs)

A simple sentence does not include any other clauses but may contain adjectives and adverbs, prepositional phrases, verbal phrases, appositives, objects, and complements:

Jo, my best friend, likes to run on the beach often.
Running on the beach makes Jo very happy to be alive.

A simple sentence may have conjunctions (*and, but, nor, or*) joining its parts, but the verb(s) have the same subject(s), and the parts are *not* separated by a comma:

> My father **and** my mother both like the beach **and** the park.
> Jo often runs on the beach **but** never exercises indoors.
> Jo walks to the beach **or** takes the bus.

A simple sentence may have parts joined by **correlatives** (*either . . . or, neither . . . nor, not only . . . but also*), and the parts are *not* separated by commas:

> Jo **either** walks to the beach **or** takes the bus.
> Jo likes **neither** indoor exercise **nor** indoor swimming pools.
> Jo will **not only** run **but also** jump and skip on the beach.

Remember that a simple sentence *cannot* be divided into two or more sentences and does not have a dependent clause in it.

Compound Sentences

A **compound sentence** has two or more independent clauses, each of which could stand alone:

> Jo walks to the beach, but Jack takes the bus. (compound)
> Jo walks to the beach. But Jack takes the bus. (2 simple)

Compound sentences may be connected by a comma and the coordinating conjunctions *for, and, nor, but, or, yet, so* (which you can remember by the acronym FANBOYS):

> Jo walks to the beach, **for** he likes the fresh air.
> Jo does not like indoor exercises, **nor** does he like pools.
> Jo runs on the beach, **yet** he prefers swimming in the ocean.

If the two parts are closely related and the relation between them is clear without a conjunction, connect the independent clauses by a semicolon:

> Jo runs on the beach; he likes outdoor exercise.

Use a semicolon even if adverbs and adverb phrases precede the second independent clause:

> First Jo runs on the beach; then he swims in the ocean.
> Jo runs on the beach; however, he prefers swimming.
> Jo runs on the beach; in addition, he swims.
> Jo runs on the beach; therefore, he is very fit.

Make sure that *both* (or more) parts of the compound sentence are complete sentences before using a semicolon between the parts.

Notice that coordinating conjunctions differ from adverbial modifiers in that the coordinating conjunctions connect the two parts while the modifiers may show some connection but may be placed elsewhere in the sentence, unlike the coordinating conjunctions. So the comma with the coordinating conjunction and the semicolon with the modifier are important differences.

Exercise 11.1   Identifying Simple and Compound Sentences

Label each sentence with **S** *for simple or* **CD** *for compound.*

Example   The pipes are old and rusty. __S__

1. My apartment is so small and cramped and crowded. _____

2. The kitchen is really in the front hallway along one wall right after the front door. _____

3. The tiny refrigerator has a wooden board on top for the only work space in the kitchen. _____

4. The two-burner stove has a little microwave oven over it and a tiny oven under it. _____

5. The main room serves as living room, dining room, bedroom, and study. _____

6. I pull out the futon every evening and then fold it back up in the morning. _____

7. I can't leave it open, for it takes up almost the entire room. _____

8. I can either sleep in the bed or eat at the table, not both. _____

9. The one closet is small and narrow, and the bathroom is not big enough for a bathtub. _____

10. My bath mat covers practically the entire bathroom floor. _____

11. I feel cramped, and I want to move. _____

12. I have found another apartment with a separate, yet small, bedroom and two closets. _____

13. The kitchen is also small, but it is separate and has a little window at one end. _____

14. The bathroom is about the same size as my present one, so I still won't be taking any baths soon. _____

15. The rent is only $50 more a month for a lot more space. _____

16. This new apartment has no view at all, for just brick walls and a tall fence are outside. _____

17. The neighborhood is all right but doesn't have convenient public transportation. _____

18. I will have to walk a little farther to catch the bus, and the bus will take longer to get me to work, but I won't mind. _____

19. I will be much closer to school, so I can walk there. _____

20. Sometimes I want to move back with my parents. _____

Exercise 11.2   Identifying Simple and Compound Sentences

*In each of the following paragraphs underline the **two simple sentences** and double underline the **one** or **two compound sentences**.*

Example   I like pizza, but she likes pasta. We agree on scungilli.

1. The importance of being well hydrated cannot be too emphasized. Most people should drink about eight cups of liquid a day. Liquids may include sodas, juice, and soup, but they do not include coffee, tea, or alcoholic drinks. Herbal tea may count as a liquid; it has no caffeine in it.

2. Small people may not need quite as much as eight cups of liquid a day, but average and large people do. A large orange juice in the morning and then two cups of liquid with each meal should be enough. This liquid will not only hydrate the body but also ease digestion.

3. Everyone should drink plenty of liquid before, during, and after exercising. Most people simply drink water, but many people drink a sports drink instead. Some people favor one, and some prefer the other. People should have a thorough knowledge about the pros and cons of sports drinks versus water.

4. Sports drinks provide sodium (salt) and carbohydrates to the body. The sodium stimulates the body to crave even more liquid, so people drink even more. The sodium also speeds up absorption and causes people to drink more. Sports drinks really help people stay hydrated, so they can continue exercising.

5. The carbohydrates in a sports drink also provide energy for the body. While exercising, the body uses up the available carbohydrates already stored there. The sports drink provides more energy, so the person can continue exercising without feeling depleted.

6. Endurance sports such as marathons and bicycle racing need nutrients added while the racer is exercising. Of course, the racer could eat some food as well, but drinking something nutritious might be easier. In any case, participating in endurance sports requires planning.

7. However, sports drinks have about 250 calories per quart, but water has no calories. A person wanting to lose weight may actually gain weight from a sports drink. He or she would have to exercise very vigorously for a long time to burn off the sports drink calories.

8. A person may lose three or four pounds of sweat with strenuous exercise lasting over ninety minutes. But most people do not do that much exercising at a time. Thus they do not need anything beyond water to hydrate the body, and they do not need the added carbohydrates.

9. In general, a person taking an aerobics class or using a cardio machine, such as a stepper or treadmill, does not exceed an hour at a time. Drinking plain water during this time is hydrating enough to meet the average person's needs. The water need not be mineral water, so safe tap water is fine.

10. Usually a person urinates every two to four hours. The urine should have little or no color. Frequent urination should not be an embarrassment, for it demonstrates a healthy, well-hydrated body. However, coffee, tea, and beer make the body overactivated, so they should be limited.

Exercise 11.3 Identifying Simple and Compound Sentences

In the following sentences, label each sentence as **S** *(**simple**) or* **CD** *(**compound**) and punctuate with nothing, a comma, or a semicolon.*

Example He enjoys all Italian food, but he hates scungilli. _CD_

1. Honoré de Balzac is the author of *La Comédie Humaine,* an overall title comprising around ninety novels and novellas. _____

2. He was born in 1799 and died in 1850. _____

3. Raised in Tours, France, he moved to Paris at age sixteen to study law and write stories. _____

4. He changed his name from Balssa to Balzac and added *de* to sound aristocratic. _____

5. He wrote many plays and novels but they all failed so he became a businessman. _____

6. Balzac also failed at business and went into serious debt for the rest of his life. ____

7. He became involved in get-rich-quick schemes to make money but these schemes always went bankrupt. ____

8. At age thirty he wrote two successful novels and did not stop until his death twenty years later. ____

9. He changed from a preference for equal opportunity to a desire for royal and noble privilege. ____

10. Balzac stopped portraying upstarts from the provinces (like himself) as successful he considered them disruptive and greedy. ____

11. He showed characters motivated by a desire for money. ____

12. One of Balzac's most famous novels, *Le Père Goriot*, showed an exploited father. ____

13. Everyone wants this father's money they will do anything for it. ____

14. *Cousine Bette* portrays a poor relative staying with rich ones yet she schemes and connives against them. ____

15. Balzac's family believed in middle-class values of individual achievement and enterprise. ____

16. With his first successful novels, however, Balzac changed his values and politics he no longer praised initiative. ____

17. He preferred the status quo of the rich staying rich and the poor staying poor. ____

18. He was in favor of a stable society for he did not like the upheavals of social change. ____

19. Balzac was a monarchist he supported royalty despite the French Revolution. ____

20. However, Marxists still support Balzac's work they see him as a champion of democratic ideals. ____

Exercise 11.4 Punctuating Compound Sentences

Each of these **compound sentences** *needs punctuation. Punctuate the sentence correctly by adding a comma + for, and, nor, but, or, yet, so OR adding a semicolon. Choose which method suits the sentence better. Sometimes either way will work well.*

1. Kinetics is the study of body language it involves our movements and gestures.

2. Our movements are important in cross-cultural misunderstandings we can sometimes be misinterpreted.

3. Sometimes looking people straight in the eye is a sign of honesty for some people it is a sign of disrespect.
4. Asian children are taught to look down they are not supposed to stare people, especially adults, in the eye.
5. Americans often slouch or slump down in chairs to show ease many people think slouching is a sign of disrespect.
6. Pointing the sole of one's foot or shoe at another person is rude in Asia Americans think nothing of doing that.
7. The hitchhiking sign with the thumb can be a sign of approval, a number, or an obscenity it depends on the country.
8. Arabs and South Americans face people more closely than Americans their conversations seem overly intimate or threatening to us.
9. Nodding and shaking the head may mean yes and may mean no people know their intent you may not.
10. Sneezing or blowing one's nose in front of people is very rude in most parts of the world a person should go to a private place instead.

Exercise 11.5   Using Simple and Compound Sentences

A. Combine the simple sentences into a **compound sentence** *using a comma and coordinating conjunction (*for, and, nor, but, or, yet, so*) OR a semicolon.*

Example   Pizza is my favorite. I like pasta, too.

    Pizza is my favorite, but I like pasta, too.

1. Other people had invented electric cars. Thomas Davenport built the first practical one in 1834.

   Compound _____

2. This British electric car began to catch on. The United States had fifty companies making them in the 1800s.

   Compound _____

3. These cars used Thomas Edison's DC battery. He predicted widespread use of electric cars.

   Compound _____

4. Men found the cars hardly ever broke down. Women no longer needed to crank them.

   Compound _____

5. Gasoline-powered cars would often stop. Then they had to be restarted by cranking.

   Compound _____

6. By 1912, there were 34,000 electric cars in the United States. Use of electric cars diminished for many reasons.

   Compound _____

7. Charles Kettering invented the electric starter in 1912. Cranking the engine was no longer needed.

   Compound _____

8. The internal combustion engine was revolutionized. Gasoline cars could go 50 mph instead of 20 mph.

   Compound _____

9. Gasoline cars could go much faster than electric cars. They could go for a longer time without having to stop.

   Compound _____

10. The highway system expanded. People wanted to drive for longer distances.

    Compound _____

B. In each paragraph, combine the simple sentences to form one or two compound sentences along with one or two simple sentences. Change or add some words if you need to and use commas, coordinating conjunctions, and semicolons.

Example   Everyone likes calamari. Everyone likes clams. No one likes scungilli.

   Everyone likes calamari and clams, but no one likes scungilli. _____

1. The electric car was abandoned. The electric car was not practical. The electric car could not go far enough. The electric car could not go fast enough. The electric car could not compete.

   _____

   _____

   _____

   _____

2. We want to have less pollution. Recent emissions regulations have toughened. Gas-burning cars pollute the air. Electric cars do not pollute. Electric cars seem more appealing again.

   _____

   _____

   _____

   _____

3. California has the toughest clean-air regulations for cars. New York also has the toughest clean-air regulations for cars. California and New York have the most electric cars on the road. Consumers have demanded electric cars. Major manufacturers have made electric cars.

_____

_____

_____

_____

4. The average electric car costs about $25,000. The electric car costs at least 90 percent less to run. The electric car hardly ever needs repairs. The electric car rarely needs any maintenance. Recharging the electric car's battery is easy.

_____

_____

_____

_____

5. The electric car can go about one hundred miles at a stretch. The electric car needs recharging for another one hundred miles. It can also be recharged before running out of electricity. Ordinary household outlets may be used. Southern California has many recharging stations.

_____

_____

_____

_____

Exercise 11.6   Writing Simple and Compound Sentences

Write a simple and then a compound sentence for each set of words. Add any words necessary to form complete sentences.

Example   tiger, lion, zoo, wild

Simple ___We capture tigers and lions in the wild for the zoo.___

Compound ___Tigers and lions live in the wild, but we see them in the zoo.___

1. sit, eat, chair, table

   Simple _____

   Compound _____

2. eat, sit down, 7:00 A.M., 1:00 P.M., 7:00 P.M.

   Simple _____

   Compound _____

3. skip, miss, breakfast, lunch, dinner

   Simple _____

   Compound _____

4. want, eat, corn flakes, muffins, eggs

   Simple _____

   Compound _____

5. serve, drink, coffee, tea

   Simple _____

   Compound _____

6. grab, eat, yogurt, doughnuts

   Simple _____

   Compound _____

7. snack, buy, chips, popcorn

   Simple _____

   Compound _____

8. sip, guzzle, soda, water

   Simple _____

   Compound _____

9. cook, prepare, potatoes, vegetables

   Simple _____

   Compound _____

10. wake up, smell, coffee, tea

    Simple _____

    Compound _____

11. drink, want, cranberry juice, orange juice

    Simple _____

    Compound _____

12. gulp, sip, wine, beer

    Simple _____

    Compound _____

13. make, consume, pancakes, waffles

Simple ————————————————————————————

Compound ——————————————————————————

14. enjoy, pour, milk, cream

Simple ————————————————————————————

Compound ——————————————————————————

15. imbibe, drink, grape juice, fruit punch

Simple ————————————————————————————

Compound ——————————————————————————

16. eat, taste, brains, sweetbreads

Simple ————————————————————————————

Compound ——————————————————————————

17. splurge, indulge, Mississippi mud pie, chocolate cake

Simple ————————————————————————————

Compound ——————————————————————————

18. order, try, carrot juice, wheat grass juice

Simple ————————————————————————————

Compound ——————————————————————————

19. buy, treat, ice cream, chocolates

Simple ————————————————————————————

Compound ——————————————————————————

20. sneak, hide, candy bars, cookies

Simple ————————————————————————————

Compound ——————————————————————————

Exercise 11.7   Proofreading

*Correct the **five errors** in punctuating the simple and compound sentences in this paragraph.*

Many colleges and universities are debating the need for a physical education requirement. Some schools have already done away with one and others are thinking about it. Formerly, all students tended to be full time, able bodied, and young.

Now students may be part time, physically disabled, pregnant, and older so they are exempt already from physical education. Students should be adult enough to regulate their own exercise, or choose not to exercise. Or perhaps schools could compromise with a time requirement. Students would log in perhaps two hours a week of exercise. They could sign up for a sport or they could sign in for a workout in the gym. They would be creating habits and they would find activities to enjoy for a lifetime.

Summary

   I. Simple Sentences
      A. Definition: A **simple sentence** has one independent clause and cannot be divided into more than one sentence.
      B. Parts of simple sentences
         1. Simple sentences have a single subject or multiple subjects.
            Examples: *The **lake** is far away.* (single)
                      *The **lake** and **village** are near.* (multiple)
         2. Simple sentences have a single verb or multiple verbs.
            Examples: *The forest **grew** larger.* (single)
                      *The forest **grew** for a long time and then **died** after a blight.* (multiple)
         3. Simple sentences can have adjectives and adverbs, phrases, objects, and complements.
            Example: *The green field along the road looked inviting.*
  II. Compound Sentences
      A. Definition: A **compound sentence** has two or more joined independent clauses.
      B. Parts of compound sentences
         1. Compound sentences have two or more subjects.
            Example: *The **lake** is far, but the **forest** is near.*
         2. Compound sentences have two or more verbs, each going with a separate subject.
            Example: *The **field looks** green, and the **flowers have** nice petals.*
         3. Compound sentences can have adjectives and adverbs, phrases, objects, and complements.
            Example: *The tall maples grew rapidly in the sunlight, yet they fell in the big storm.*

C. How compound sentences are connected
  1. Compound sentences can be connected by a comma and a coordinating conjunction: *for, and, nor, but, or, yet, so* (remembered by the acronym FANBOYS).
    Examples: *He is strong,* **for** *he exercises.*
              Mary is bright, **and** *she has good habits.*
              My chair is not soft, **nor** *is it comfortable.*
  2. Compound sentences can be connected by a semicolon.
    Examples: *Your plan is good; it is also simple.*
              I like reading; however, my eyes get tired.

Chapter 12

Dependent Clauses

Underline the **dependent clauses** in the following paragraph. Don't worry if you are not sure.

The invention of the wheel is often held up as the proudest accomplishment of civilization. Many textbooks point out that no animal has evolved wheels and cite the fact as an example of how evolution is often incapable of finding the optimal solution to an engineering problem. But it is not a good example at all. Even if nature *could* have evolved a moose on wheels, it surely would have opted not to. Wheels are good only in a world with roads and rails. They bog down in any terrain that is soft, slippery, steep, or uneven. Legs are better. Wheels have to roll along an unbroken supporting ridge, but legs can be placed on a series of separate footholds, an extreme example being a ladder. Legs can also be placed to minimize lurching and to step over obstacles. (Steven Pinker, *How the Mind Works*)

A clause is a group of words that has at least one subject that goes with one verb (called predication). Independent clauses, as the name implies, are complete clauses that can stand alone as sentences. **Dependent clauses** cannot stand alone as a sentence and must be part of independent clauses.

An independent clause that contains a dependent clause (whether at the beginning, middle, or end) is called a **complex sentence.** Unlike the compound sentence, in which the two or more parts are equal in importance, the complex sentence has a more important part (the independent clause) and a subordinate part (the dependent clause). Subordinating one part of a sentence permits further meaning to be conveyed and emphasizes the relationship of the parts:

My dog is hungry. She had a walk. (Are the ideas connected? Maybe, but we are not sure.)

My dog is hungry because she had a walk. (clear connection)

Types of Dependent Clauses

A dependent clause may have a **conjunction** at the beginning, such as *although, because, if, when, while,* that prevents it from being able to stand alone, and the dependent clause may come at the beginning, middle, or end of a sentence:

After she takes a walk, she eats dinner.

My dog, **because she takes a walk,** gets hungry.

She gets hungry **if she takes a walk.**

A dependent clause may have a **relative pronoun** (that, what, whom, who) or a **relative adjective** or **adverb** (when, where, which, whose):

A dog **that likes to walk** will get exercise.

The dog likes to walk, **which takes a lot of time.**

My dog walks **where he wants.**

My dog is happy **when he walks.**

We use *who, whom, whoever, whomever* for persons (and sometimes dogs), and *which* and *what,* for animals, concepts, and things. *That* and *whose* may be used for people, animals, and things although some people do not accept *that* for people. *When* is used for time and *where* for places.

Sometimes the dependent clause looks independent but often *that* has been omitted; it could be inserted and have the same meaning:

Many people (that) **I know** walk their dogs.

They feel sure (that) **many people walk their dogs.**

Some dependent clauses serve as part of the whole sentence, such as a subject or direct object. For example, in *Whoever walks dogs gets exercise,* the subject of the whole sentence is *whoever walks dogs,* a dependent clause. The subject of the sentence is not *whoever* alone since the sentence would mean *whoever gets exercise.* Also in *The dog ate what was available, what was available* is the dependent clause and serves as the direct object.

Nonrestrictive Dependent Clauses

Normally if the dependent clause adds information that is not essential to the sentence, it is surrounded by commas (omitting the first comma if it comes at the beginning of the sentence, and omitting the last comma if it is at the end of the sentence):

Although Mina doesn't own a dog, she walks dogs for a living. (The basic sentence is not changed.)

Mina, **who doesn't own a dog,** walks dogs for a living. (The basic sentence is not changed)

The dogs like Mina, **who doesn't own a dog.** (The basic sentence is not changed.)

These dependent clauses are called **nonrestrictive** since they do *not* restrict, or limit, the noun or pronoun but simply add further information.

Restrictive Dependent Clauses

If the dependent clause restricts (defines, limits, or identifies the word it modifies to the extent that it is essential to the meaning), it does not have commas around it:

People **who walk dogs** get exercise. (The dependent clause restricts *people* to only those who walk dogs.)

Dogs **that like walking** get exercise. (The dependent clause restricts *dogs* to those that like walking.)

If the dependent clause serves as the subject, direct object, or object of the preposition in a sentence, it does not have commas:

Whoever likes dogs will be enriched. (The dependent clause is the subject.)

My dog likes **anyone who feeds it.** (The dependent clause is the direct object.)

I'll give my dog to **someone who will love it.** (The dependent clause is the object of the preposition.)

These dependent clauses are called *restrictive* since they restrict the noun or pronoun and are essential to the basic meaning of the sentence.

Distinguishing Nonrestrictive and Restrictive Dependent Clauses

Dependent clauses that have a conjunction (*because, if, when, while,* etc.) do not normally need a comma if they come at the end of the sentence: *Mina likes dogs because they are loyal.* However, dependent clauses beginning with *although, even though, though,* and *whereas* usually present a contrast to the main idea and are often preceded by a comma:

Jane hates dogs, **although she's thinking of getting one.**

Jane hates dogs, **whereas her family loves them.**

You will have to decide whether you are presenting a contrast or not.

In some cases, the dependent clause will be nonrestrictive or restrictive depending on the intended meaning:

We need dogs, **who add joy to our lives.** (All dogs add joy.)

We need dogs **who add joy to our lives.** (We need only those dogs that add joy, not others.)

My dog, **who is not bright,** runs in the street. (My dog runs in the street, maybe because it isn't bright.)

My dog **who is not bright** runs in the street. (My unbright dog runs in the street; the other dog or dogs don't.)

We should abolish leash laws, **which limit our rights.** (All leash laws limit our rights and should be abolished.)

We should abolish leash laws **that limit our rights.** (We should abolish only those leash laws that limit our rights, not all leash laws.)

Many misunderstandings can occur because of imprecision about nonrestrictive and restrictive dependent clauses, so deciding which to use is crucial.

Exercise 12.1   Finding Dependent Clauses

A. Underline the dependent clause in each of these sentences.

Example   <u>Since my dog ran away,</u> I have been so lonely.

1. ENIAC, which stands for Electronic Numerical Integrator and Computer, was the first computer.
2. The U.S. War Department wanted a method that would accurately hit enemy targets.
3. However, ENIAC was not developed until 1946, after World War II had ended.
4. Although it could not hit enemy targets, it could do extremely fast calculations.
5. ENIAC could multiple a five-digit number by itself five thousand times in a split second, which was faster than any other machine.
6. It was just an electronic calculator that was very fast.
7. The two scientists who invented ENIAC wanted to increase its ability.
8. They worked for two more years before they finally added the idea of stored programs or memory.
9. Because ENIAC could do more, it became more useful for the government and large companies.
10. It still did not have widespread applicability, which would come later.

B. Underline the dependent clause in each of these sentences:

1. The scientists knew they had to make ENIAC more practical.
2. The machine they invented was one hundred feet long and weighed around thirty tons.
3. Whoever used it would have to have a very large room.
4. ENIAC worked on 17,468 vacuum tubes that often broke down.
5. A company would have to hire someone who had the patience and knowledge to find the broken vacuum tube.

6. ENIAC was a big help when it worked, but it was often down.
7. The electricity it used was extremely costly.
8. What made the early computer practical was reducing the size and weight.
9. Word processing added another function, although the computer remained very large.
10. Now small, easy-to-use computers are available to whoever wants them.

C. *Underline the dependent clause in each of these sentences:*

1. The 18th Amendment to the Constitution, which was passed on January 17, 1920, was called the Volstead Act.
2. This act prohibited the sale, manufacture, and distribution of alcoholic beverages, although it did not seem to prohibit drinking.
3. A strong educational campaign was aimed mostly at young people, who were considered most vulnerable.
4. Children took a pledge not to deal with alcohol as long as they lived.
5. They promised to avoid alcohol if they wanted to play sports.
6. The Anti-Saloon League, which engineered much of Prohibition, proclaimed an era of clear minds and bodies.
7. Parents, particularly fathers, could read literally tons of pamphlets that detailed the evils of drink.
8. Outwardly, enforcement of the new law did not seem a problem that would cause much trouble.
9. Since bars and liquor stores were closed, adults could not find alcoholic beverages.
10. Children who were not exposed to alcohol should lose any desire for such drink.

D. *Underline the dependent clause in each of these sentences:*

1. Education on the evils of liquor, which would affect many more people, would take much longer.
2. While enforcement of laws against drinking was not seen as a problem, it became the biggest one.
3. What was dubbed "bootleg" liquor could be had everywhere.
4. People could buy drinks at a "speakeasy," a secret place that everyone knew.
5. People who wanted to drink held private parties all the time.
6. Organized crime, the "mob," distributed liquor to anyone who wanted it.
7. Drinking became desirable as it took on the aura of glamour and intrigue.
8. Far from repelling them, liquor became a rite of passage that children wanted.

9. Whatever glamorous adults did seemed attractive to children.
10. Although the 18th Amendment was not overturned until almost fourteen years later, enforcement had already proven impossible.

Exercise 12.2   Combining Sentences for Subordination

Combine the two simple sentences into a complex sentence by making one part into a dependent clause. You may have to change some words, but try to keep the general meaning intact.

Example   Akitas are fine dogs. Not many people own them.

Although akitas are fine dogs, not many people own them.

Not many people own akitas, though they are fine dogs.

Akitas, which are fine dogs, are not owned by many people.

1. The first movie was invented in 1895. It must have been wonderful.

2. The first movies had no sound. They had separate shots with captions.

3. They were in grainy black and white. They seemed realistic.

4. The movements were jerky and fast. They showed real people.

5. The Lumière brothers of France made an early movie. It was called *The Arrival of a Train at La Ciotat Station*.

6. People saw the movie. They gasped at the realism.

7. Some people thought the train would run them over. Some leaped away and screamed.

8. Nowadays it would not seem realistic. It was silent, jerky, dim, and colorless.

9. Movies also became "talkies." They did not need the dialogue frames anymore.

_____

10. Color was another big innovation. It really made movies more realistic.

_____

Exercise 12.3   Combining Sentences for Subordination

Combine the three simple sentences into a complex sentence by making one or two parts into dependent clauses. You may have to change some words, but try to keep the general meaning intact.

1. Georges Bizet was a composer of operas. His name was originally Alexander. His godfather always called him Georges.

_____

_____

2. He was born in Paris in 1838. He died near Paris in 1875. He was only thirty-seven years old.

_____

_____

3. Bizet started studying music at the Paris conservatory. He was only nine years old. He showed extraordinary talent.

_____

_____

4. He studied the piano. He could sight-read music very well. He could compose music.

_____

_____

5. He won a prize for an operetta in 1857. He was nineteen years old. This operetta was entitled *Doctor Miracle.*

_____

_____

6. He won the Prix de Rome. He won this prize in 1857. This prize allowed him to study in Italy.

_____

_____

7. Bizet was in Naples, Italy, for three months in 1859. He composed a comic opera. He developed a serious throat ailment.

   _____

   _____

8. In Italy, he studied many composers of comic opera. He studied Rossini, Mozart, and others. He studied serious German composers.

   _____

   _____

9. Bizet had great early promise. He won many prizes. He was highly sought after by opera producers and theater directors.

   _____

   _____

10. The lyric theater in Paris commissioned an opera. Bizet wrote *The Pearl Fishers*. Many people looked forward to it.

    _____

    _____

11. *The Pearl Fishers* ran for only eighteen performances. Two other operas ran for very few performances. People were disappointed.

    _____

    _____

12. Bizet was not doing very well. He had shown such extraordinary early talent. He continued to work very hard.

    _____

    _____

13. He wrote some musical numbers. He wrote them to accompany a drama. The drama by Alphonse Daudet was called *L'Arlesienne*.

    _____

    _____

14. The drama was a failure. The drama ran for only fifteen performances. Bizet's musical numbers were a success.

    _____

    _____

15. Bizet wrote the opera *Carmen*. Many people criticized the opera severely. It was fairly successful.

    _____

    _____

16. *Carmen* ran for fifty performances. People seemed to like the music and the story. The story was originally by Prosper Mérimée.

    _____

    _____

17. Bizet died before the complete run of *Carmen.* He was thirty-seven years old. He had always had throat troubles.

    _____

    _____

18. Legend says that Bizet died because of *Carmen's* reception. He died just three months into its run. He was shocked by the criticism.

    _____

    _____

19. *Carmen* was first seen in 1875. It was produced thousands of times soon after. Now it is the most famous opera in the world.

    _____

    _____

20. Bizet did not live long enough to see the success of *Carmen.* The music is well known. The music will live forever.

    _____

    _____

Exercise 12.4   Correcting Punctuation in Dependent Clauses

In each of the following paragraphs, **one dependent clause** *is incorrectly punctuated. Underline it, and either add or delete the comma(s).*

Example   The dogs I really like are dachshunds. <u>Since they are long and low,</u> they have a cute walk.

1. Insects have the ability to adapt to life almost anywhere. Although they have short lives they have the ability to reproduce in great numbers. They greatly outnumber humans.

2. Cockroaches live well in hot and cold climates. They can eat only once every six or seven days if they must. Since they need water every three days they are found in damp places.

3. It is not possible to prevent cockroaches from entering a home. They can live wherever water is present. The kitchen and bathroom which both have damp pipes make good cockroach hotels.

4. Kitchens that have crumbs and garbage containers are more attractive than bathrooms to cockroaches. But even if no food is around the cockroaches like the dampness.

5. Cockroaches will migrate to another part, if one part of a building is fumigated. They will even migrate to another building if they want to. So fumigation does little to prevent them.

6. Spiders can be helpful insects. They weave their webs, where other insects might crawl or fly. Usually webs can be found in corners or near windows that are not open.

7. Flies often get tangled in the web. If they are large they might actually escape. But usually they cannot fly away, so the spider injects them with a poison and then wraps them up.

8. An active web that is still guarded by a spider should be left where it is. The web is doing the work, that it was meant to do. But abandoned webs can be cleaned away since they look messy.

9. Crickets rarely come inside; if one of them does come in it is harmless. They do not bite or cause unsanitary conditions. Although they might sing, they rarely do indoors.

10. Many people think that crickets bring good luck, if they are found in the hearth. They certainly would not kill one, if they could catch it. They probably would cage it.

11. Crickets probably do not care to be in a cage. They would rather be outdoors where they can move around and sing. But we don't know, if they sing out of happiness.

12. Crickets do not "sing" in the conventional sense, which is by voice. They sing by rubbing their wings together to produce that special sound, that tells us crickets are near.

13. Mosquitoes are insects, that definitely need to be exterminated. They bite humans and can carry diseases that could be fatal. At the least, they leave annoying bites that itch.

14. Mosquitoes do not really bite but "drill" into our skins. Then they extract a bit of blood which is their food. In the process they leave behind a bit of irritant that causes itching.

15. Mosquitoes like dampness and warmth, so they live in the summertime in humid climates. Although they can bite anytime they prefer the evenings and nights for doing their work.

16. Many areas of the world have mosquito-abatement programs, that try to control the infestation. They get rid of still water where mosquitoes reproduce. They also spray insecticide.

17. Flies are also very annoying pests that are sometimes dangerous. They may carry disease, since they frequently feed off dead and rotting matter and then land on our food.

18. Flies can be controlled but probably not totally exterminated. If their breeding grounds can be eliminated fewer flies will come into existence. Then we have to swat as many as possible.

19. Most of our common houseflies do not bite, but various ones, such as the horsefly, do bite. They have a very unpleasant sting, that may need treatment or at least some ointment.

20. Although most people do not care for insects bugs obviously have their place on earth. Even if we got rid of most of them, others would replace them. And they will outlive us anyway.

Exercise 12.5   Writing with Dependent Clauses

*Use the following **dependent clauses** in complete sentences. Be sure to add punctuation where it is needed.*

Example   (whose collar this is)

     My dog, whose collar this is, has run away.

1. (since I went away) _____

2. (because I'm busy) _____

3. (although I think of those back home) _____

4. (that I don't write) _____

5. (which is not that easy) _____

_____

6. (if I go out) _____

_____

7. (when I look for a new address) _____

_____

8. (while I adjust to a new schedule) _____

_____

9. (if I need different clothes) _____

_____

10. (whom I haven't met yet) _____

_____

11. (where I should go shopping) _____

_____

12. (whoever invites me over) _____

_____

13. (whose house is hard to find) _____

_____

14. (who shares my interests) _____

_____

15. (how I get to know them) _____

_____

16. (who don't like bars) _____

_____

17. (that everyone can enjoy) _____

_____

18. (that will help me) _____

_____

19. (who at least has a lot of work) _____

_____

20. (who really misses everyone) _____

_____

Exercise 12.6   Writing with Dependent Clauses

*Use **two dependent clauses** in one complete sentence. Use any order of dependent clauses you wish. Change any words that need changing. Be sure to add punctuation where it is needed.*

Example   (if I get a dog, because it will need care)

   Because a dog will need care, my life will change if I get one.

1. (because America is a country of immigrants, since America was a land of opportunity)

_____

_____

2. (since the east coast was closer to Europe, that was called Ellis Island)

_____

_____

3. (since the west coast was closer to Asia, where the boats landed)

_____

_____

4. (because most of New Mexico and Texas were part of Mexico, as Mexicans were not really immigrants)

_____

_____

5. (where they felt comfortable, when they had the chance)

_____

_____

6. (why the Scandinavians preferred the north, that reminded them of home)

_____

_____

7. (until they learn English, given that they did not know the language)

_____

_____

8. (before so many Asians arrived in California, since Latinos were closer)

_____

_____

9. (as they move around the country, what can bring a decent job)

_____

_____

10. (that seems like a good opportunity, before they move to another area)

_____

_____

11. (unless social conditions are too difficult, in order that they can work)

_____

_____

12. (even though many are exploited, because some of them have entered illegally)

_____

_____

13. (although they love their country, where they now live)

_____

_____

14. (wherever you go in Los Angeles, if you walk around the city)

_____

_____

15. (as soon as you are in southern Texas, if you go down any busy street)

_____

_____

Exercise 12.7   Proofreading

*Correct the **five comma errors in the dependent clauses** in the following paragraph.*

Classical ballet is a very special art form, that takes years of study and training. Girls usually start training at around five years old but do not wear toe shoes until a few years later. Boys can wait, until their muscles develop. They do not wear toe shoes as high leaps are more important for them. Serious dancers usually go to class six days a week. Even when they become professional dancers they start the day with class and then rehearse for the rest of the day. Dancers even when properly trained, have many injuries, especially to their legs. And later in life, they may suffer from chronic pain from old injuries. Although it is a difficult, all-consuming life most dancers would not choose any other.

Summary

I. Dependent Clauses
    A. Definition: A **dependent clause** has at least one subject and one verb but cannot stand alone as a sentence.
    B. Types of dependent clauses
        1. Some dependent clauses start with a conjunction such as ***although, because, if, while.***
            Examples: *because I care, when he arrives*
        2. Some dependent clauses start with a relative word such as *that, when, which, where, who, whose.*
            Examples: *that was my idea, where we are going*
        3. **Nonrestrictive dependent clauses** add information that is not essential for the meaning of the sentence.
            Example: *The schedule,* ***which isn't very good anyway,*** *is out of date.*
        4. **Restrictive dependent clauses** provide essential meaning by restricting, limiting, or defining the words they modify.
            Example: *The schedule* ***that I got*** *is out of date.*
        5. Some dependent clauses may be either nonrestrictive or restrictive depending on the intended meaning.
            Examples: *We like tourists, who are fun.* (All tourists are fun, and we like them all.)
            We like tourists who are fun. (Not all tourists are fun, but we like the ones who are.)
    C. Uses
        1. Dependent clauses can serve as subjects in a sentence.
            Example: ***Whoever arrives late*** *can't eat.*
        2. Dependent clauses can serve as direct objects in a sentence.
            Example: *My dog eats* ***whatever is there.***
        3. Dependent clauses can serve as objects of prepositions in sentences.
            Example: *She will take it to* ***whichever house is nearest.***
    D. Punctuation
        1. Nonrestrictive dependent clauses are set off with commas, omitting the first comma if they start a sentence or the last comma if they end a sentence.
            Example: *Dr. Parker,* ***who teaches yoga,*** *lives here.*
        2. Restrictive dependent clauses are not set off with commas.
            Example: *The woman* ***who teaches yoga*** *lives here.*

Chapter 13

Adjective Dependent Clauses

Underline the one **adjective dependent clause** in each of the following sentences. Don't worry if you can't find them all.

1. Jai alai, which originated in the Basque region, is played in many countries in the world.
2. The Basque region is an area that includes parts of southern France and northern Spain.
3. The jai alai court, called a *fronton*, resembles a racquetball or squash court that has been enlarged.
4. Two players who stand side by side toss a ball against a wall.
5. Each player wears a *cesta*, which is a curved basket tied to the wrist.
6. Catching a ball that has bounced off a wall is very tricky.
7. Jai alai is popular in those parts of Asia where there was Spanish influence.
8. Spain, where some of the best Basque players live, loves jai alai.
9. In the United States, several states that had Spanish influence also have jai alai *frontons.*
10. Sports fans who like gambling have been attracted to jai alai.

Like independent clauses, dependent clauses are a group of words that go together and have at least one subject and one verb that goes with the subject. Unlike independent clauses, dependent clauses cannot stand alone as sentences but must be attached to independent clauses. One kind of dependent clause is the adjective dependent clause.

An *adjective dependent clause* (also called an *adjective clause* or a *relative clause*) acts the same as an adjective: It modifies nouns and pronouns. An adjective dependent clause is embedded, that is, placed inside the independent clause of which it is a part, sometimes in the middle and sometimes at the end:

My favorite shoes, **which I got in Maine,** fit well.

I prefer shoes **that are comfortable.**

Usually the adjective dependent clause comes immediately after the noun or pronoun it modifies:

Shoes **that fit well** are important. (modifies *shoes*)

Sneakers, **which come in many styles,** can be costly. (modifies *sneakers*)

He **who hesitates** is lost and shoeless. (modifies *he*)

Relative Pronouns, Adjectives, and Adverbs in Clauses

Most adjective dependent clauses start with one of these words:

relative pronouns: **that, which, who, whom**
relative adjectives: **which(ever), whose**
relative adverbs: **when, where**

These words are called ***relative*** because each connects, or relates, the information in the adjective dependent clause to the word they modify. These relative words serve as pronouns, adjectives, and adverbs within the adjective dependent clause itself:

A man **who looks pained** wears tight shoes. (*who* = relative pronoun, subject of dependent clause)

The woman **whose shoes are tight** is uncomfortable. (*whose* = relative adjective, modifies *shoes*)

The store **where he bought those shoes** has closed. (*where* = relative adverb, modifies *bought*)

Who (for subjects) and *whom* (for objects) refer to people (and sometimes dogs and other pets), while *that* and *which(ever)*, refer to ideas, concepts, and things. Some people allow *that* for people; others do not. *When* refers to time, and *where* refers to place:

The dancer **who bought the shoes** needs them today.

The athlete **whom you spoke of** wears those shoes.

Shoes **that fit well** are rare.

The season **when we go barefoot** is coming soon.

In matching a preposition with the relative word, such as *to which* and *for whom*, use the preposition that would sound right if placed at the end of the adjective dependent clause:

The man **to** whom you gave the shoes needed them.   OR

The man whom you gave the shoes **to** needed them.

The shoes **about** which you raved cost $200.   OR

The shoes which you raved **about** cost $200.

The shoes **in** which she arrived looked sturdy.   OR

The shoes which she arrived **in** looked sturdy   OR

[better] The shoes **that** she arrived in looked sturdy.

The preposition before the relative word usually sounds more formal, but the other less formal way is perfectly acceptable. However, make sure not to mix the two ways or to use another pronoun or noun meaning the same in addition to the relative pronoun. Do not say, for example, "The shoes in which I told you about . . ." or "The shoes which I told you about them . . . ."

Restrictive and Nonrestrictive Adjective Dependent Clauses

Those adjective dependent clauses that give a sentence its basic meaning are called *restrictive* because they restrict, limit, identify, or define the noun or pronoun they modify. They are not surrounded by commas:

Shoes **that look good** may not fit well. (*Shoes* are restricted to those that look good, not all shoes.)

Give those shoes to a man **who needs them.** (*A man* is restricted to one who needs shoes, not any man.)

Shoes **whose time is up** should be discarded. (*Shoes* are restricted to those that are worn out, not all shoes.)

Return those shoes to the store **where you got them.** (*Store* is restricted to the one where you bought the shoes, not any store.)

The relative word is sometimes omitted in restrictive clauses, but the sentence has the same meaning:

The shoes (that) **he likes** have tassels.

The place (where) **they bought** their shoes is nearby.

A woman (whom) **I know** has 100 pairs of shoes.

The summer (when) **I went shoeless** was great.

Normally *that* is restrictive and *which* is nonrestrictive (but *which* is often used in a restrictive sense, especially with a preposition, such as *to which*).

Those adjective dependent clauses that add information but are not essential are called *nonrestrictive.* The adjective dependent clause is surrounded by commas, unless it comes at the end of a sentence, when a period will supersede the second comma. Usually the word being modified is sufficiently precise on its own so as not to need further restriction:

Jim, **who lives in Alaska,** wears hiking boots.

Her boots, **which she wears everywhere,** are worn out.

I like Shoe City, **where shoes are cheap.**

I bought shoes for my mother, **whose feet are very small.**

Whether an adjective dependent clause is restrictive or unrestrictive is usually clear, but sometimes the punctuation will change the meaning:

My sister who goes barefoot lives at the beach.   OR

My sister, who goes barefoot, lives at the beach.

The first means that the writer's particular sister who goes barefoot lives at the beach; another sister or sisters do not. The second means that the writer's one sister lives at the beach and goes barefoot probably because of living at the beach.
Or consider this:

I like wearing sneakers **which are comfortable.** (I like wearing only sneakers that are comfortable, not all sneakers.)

I like wearing sneakers, **which are comfortable.** (All sneakers are comfortable.)

This problem could be solved partly by using *that* for restrictive and reserving commas + *which* for nonrestrictive, a generally preferred usage that is not always followed. Most of the time, this issue will not be important or relevant in a piece of writing, but you should be careful not to cause these misunderstandings.
All adjective dependent clauses, of course, are adjectives and usually modify the nearest noun or pronoun. But sometimes a phrase will come between the adjective dependent clause and the word it modifies:

The teacher in my school **who won the award** is Ms. Parker. (modifies teacher)

My trip last year **that was a disaster** had its good side. (modifies trip)

Make sure that the meaning of the sentence is clear and cannot cause misunderstanding. Also have a clear modifier for the relative word; do not let it modify something indefinite or too much in the sentence. For example, in *I worked in Miami for three years as a shoe salesperson, which was wonderful,* what was wonderful? Perhaps the writer meant either Miami or working as a shoe salesperson, or perhaps the writer meant the whole experience was wonderful, but the reference is unclear. However, a broad reference is acceptable if the meaning of the sentence is clear.

Parts of the Adjective Dependent Clause

Just as independent clauses have subjects, verbs, phrases, and modifiers, so do dependent clauses. Notice that each of these dependent clauses has its own subject, verb, modifiers, and complements:

	subject	*verb*	*adverb*	
Shoes	**that**	**fit**	**well**	are important.

	direct object	subject	verb	prepositional phrase	
These shoes,	**which**	**I**	**bought**	**in Maine,**	are good.

Which changes order since it must come directly after the noun or pronoun the adjective dependent clause modifies (in this case, *shoes*).

	adverb	subject	verb	
The street	**where**	**she**	**lives**	is nice.

Where changes order since it must come directly after the noun or pronoun the adjective dependent clause modifies, in this case, *street*.

Exercise 13.1   Identifying Adjective Dependent Clauses

*A. Underline the **one adjective dependent clause** in each of the following sentences.*

Example   The shoes you gave me are beautiful.

1. Humans are among the few animals that stand upright and walk on two legs.
2. Chickens and other birds that also stand and walk on two legs still have horizontal bodies.
3. Penguins, which are birds, stand upright but have squat bodies and very short legs.
4. Primates, which include gorillas, monkeys, chimpanzees, and apes, can also stand upright but do not most of the time.
5. Lots of small animals that can stand on hind legs only do so occasionally and do not walk upright.
6. We can teach a dog, which is basically four legged, to stand and even walk on hind legs.
7. But walking on two legs, which cannot be sustained, is unnatural to dogs.
8. Humans, who start out by crawling on all fours, always become upright.
9. Babies that are normal will pull themselves upright and learn to walk without any help.
10. Parents who encourage baby's first steps don't really help.

*B. Underline the **one** or **two adjective dependent clauses** in each of the following sentences.*

1. Walking upright, which all humans do, has some advantages and some disadvantages.
2. Any position that makes the animal taller is helpful for seeing the lay of the land.

3. Being taller than predators that might be nearby gives advance warning.
4. Admittedly predators were more of a problem outdoors in places where wild animals roamed.
5. Using two legs to walk also freed our arms and hands, which could be used for carrying food.
6. We could also defend ourselves or attack with weapons that we carried in our hands.
7. However, running on only two legs, which made us slower and which made us less balanced, was a disadvantage.
8. Also, with greater height, the spine, which supports the whole upper body, has too much work.
9. Humans are susceptible to back trouble, which is caused by our relatively weak spines that must support so much.
10. Animals that have horizontal bodies do not generally have back trouble.

C. *Underline the* **one adjective dependent clause** *in any sentences that have one. Not all sentences have adjective dependent clauses.*

1. Another aspect of being upright has both advantages and disadvantages for humans.
2. Our esophagus, which we use for many things, is relatively long and narrow.
3. Its narrowness causes us to choke more frequently on our food.
4. Animals gulp down food, sometimes without chewing, but they rarely choke.
5. We can choke fairly easily on food lodged in the esophagus and blocking the passage of air.
6. Our narrow esophagus has its advantages that might outweigh the disadvantages.
7. The sensitivity of our larynx, a part of the esophagus, allows us to make very precise sounds.
8. These sounds, along with our mouth armature, have made us the only animals with language.
9. Our highly developed brains also have helped.
10. We have brains, weapons, and precise larynxes; we don't need our upright positions anymore.

D. *Underline the* **one** *or* **two adjective dependent clauses** *in any sentences that have them. Not all sentences have adjective dependent clauses.*

1. Other animals can make sounds which we cannot make, but humans have precision that they do not have.

2. Humans can make about 250 sounds, not counting shouts, screams, cries, and coughs.
3. These sounds, which closely resemble those made by many animals, are universal among humans.
4. People of all races and languages have close to the same emotional or physical sounds.
5. The area of the larynx and the mouth are not the sole areas that we need for speech.
6. As important and maybe more important is the brain, which gives us abilities that we have not seen in any other animal.
7. The quantity of sounds that humans can make is not very important.
8. None of the languages in the world uses anywhere near the 250 sounds we are capable of making.
9. But all languages can express anything that needs to be expressed.
10. All languages can recount the past and future, not only of real occurrences but also of feelings, hopes, and wishes.

Exercise 13.2   Identifying Adjective Dependent Clauses

*Underline the **ten adjective dependent clauses** in this essay.*

The Aging of the World

Life expectancy, which has continually risen in industrial countries, has taken great leaps not only in the United States but also all over the world. Many more people now live longer.

In America, where life expectancy is now age seventy-four for males and seventy-nine for females, longer life means that many people who reach those ages can expect actually to reach one hundred and even more. Many children born at the beginning of the millennium can expect to see the next century.

In other parts of the world, people have really lived a long time. The longest documented life was that of the Frenchwoman Jeanne Calment, who lived to age 120. Possibly other countries of eastern Europe, which is well known for the longevity of its population, have people who have lived even longer.

But the issue of more people living to over seventy-five years of age is even more important. In India, China, and many African countries, the number of people who are over seventy-five has increased tremendously, and this number will continue to grow.

Every country will have to rethink its attitude toward the elderly. No longer should they be considered a burden on society, which considers them useless, obsolete, and expensive. The elderly will need not only services—social, medical, and financial—but also opportunities for work and play. Retirement age, which is usually sixty-five, may well be changed. Or retired people may start a different career that will take into account both their talents and limitations.

Exercise 13.3   Identifying Nonrestrictive and Restrictive Adjective Dependent Clauses

*In each paragraph underline the **adjective dependent clause.** Then add commas if it is nonrestrictive, or do not add commas if it is restrictive.*

Example   My slippers, <u>which were made in China</u>, have embroidery.

1. Echolocation is a method of emitting sounds that reflect back information to the animal.
2. These sounds which are reflected back in the form of waves tell the location of prey or obstacles.
3. Not only can the animals tell the direction where the prey or obstacle is located but also the distance and the size of the object.
4. Bats, dolphins, whales, and one bird are the only creatures that have this remarkable ability.
5. The microbat and just one genus of megabats use echolocation for location of prey and navigation which they can do in total darkness.
6. These bats emit high-frequency sounds that reflect back to their ears from surrounding areas.
7. These sounds which begin in the larynx are transmitted through the mouth or nostrils depending on the species.
8. Most megabats, which have rather large eyes, use vision for orientation, but microbats also can see.
9. The echolocation system that is used by dolphins consists of clicks and whistles.
10. These sounds that the dolphin emits almost constantly send back waves.
11. The dolphin's system which is similar to the bat's enables the dolphin to swim among other dolphins and to detect food.
12. Dolphins which are considered highly intelligent can learn and perform rather complex tasks.

13. Whales use both echolocation and vocalization which are both produced by air moving in and out of nasal sacs.
14. Whales can send sounds that are produced in the head toward objects and receive sound waves back.
15. This echolocation system has great advantages in water that is dark or murky.
16. Whales can make roughly the same differentiations that humans can make by eyesight.
17. Whales which have very large brains seem very intelligent but very hard for humans to study.
18. The oilbird which is also called the *guacharo* navigates by echolocation.
19. It lives in caves where it remains all day and comes out at night to search for fruit.
20. Echolocation certainly has its uses in darkness and water where eyes would be at a disadvantage.

Exercise 13.4   Filling in Adjective Dependent Clauses

In each paragraph fill in the blanks with your own **adjective dependent clauses.** *You may choose from these relative words:* that, when, where, which, whichever, who, whom, whose. *Be sure to add commas where they are needed.*

Example   I bought some shoes ___, which were on sale._____

1. This summer I am going to visit New York City _____.
   I will only visit Manhattan _____. I wish I had time
   for Brooklyn, the Bronx, and Queens _____.

2. My parent _____ had visited Manhattan many years
   ago. They said that the parts of the city _____ did not
   seem very nice. Times Square _____ was very dirty
   and run down.

3. Many bums _____ asked for money. The subway stations and cars had graffiti _____. The streets were in
   bad shape and needed repairs _____.

4. More recently, I read that New York City has cleaned up the
   mess _____.   The   transportation   system

_____ is safe and clean. Crime _____ is way down and well below most other cities.

5. I am planning on staying in midtown _____. Then I can take the bus and subway to various sights _____. Taxis _____ probably will also be available.

6. I will be able to walk to any Broadway shows _____. Times Square has really been cleaned up and has lots of bright lights _____. I will try to get tickets _____ at the half-price booth.

7. The World Trade Center _____ is near the tip of Manhattan and farther away. Another tall building is the famous Empire State Building _____. In both of them, I want to go to the top _____.

8. Greenwich Village _____ should be very quaint and picturesque. Cafés and jazz clubs _____ will be fun to visit. However, I'll bet that Greenwich Village has not kept the charm _____.

9. I also want to hear gospel music in a church in Harlem _____. My uncle _____ really enjoyed that on his visit. After the service he went to lunch at a famous soul food restaurant _____.

10. I don't want to miss the great museums _____. And I'm hoping to walk around Columbia University and New York University _____. All these places _____ will really occupy my ten days in Manhattan.

Exercise 13.5   Writing with Adjective Dependent Clauses

Write complete sentences using the following as ***adjective dependent clauses.***

1. (that I rented yesterday) _____

_____

2. (which cost a lot of money) _____

   _____

3. (who told me about it) _____

   _____

4. (which is a good part of town) _____

   _____

5. (who will collect the rent) _____

   _____

6. (when the ventilator is on) _____

   _____

7. (where the wall meets the ceiling) _____

   _____

8. (which has missing tiles) _____

   _____

9. (whose place this was) _____

   _____

10. (who didn't leave a forwarding address) _____

   _____

Exercise 13.6   Adding Adjective Dependent Clauses

*To each of these sentences add an **adjective dependent clause** in an appropriate place. You may choose from these relative words:* that, when, where, which, whichever, who, whom, whose.

Example   The child has real talent.
                    who drew that picture

1. Old houses had fireplaces in every room.
2. The fireplace in the kitchen was probably used often.
3. Meals could be cooked in the fireplace.
4. The kitchen was probably quite hot in the summer.
5. But the kitchen was very cozy and warm in the winter.
6. The bedrooms also had fireplaces.

7. Sitting rooms were small and probably not used often.

8. People usually sat in the kitchen.

9. Sometimes two fireplaces might be in a room.

10. Getting and chopping wood was always a chore.

Exercise 13.7   Proofreading

Correct the **three errors** *of prepositions and relative words and* **three errors** *of punctuation*

Bees have developed a remarkable society, that works very efficiently for them. The queen bee has the sole function of reproduction. Male bees, which also have just one function, mate with her and then quickly die. Worker bees take care of the hive where the bees live. Some bees search for food in the surrounding fields in which they will find flowers in it. They ingest the nectar from flowers but also transport pollen. Back at the hive they do a sort of dance in which it resembles the Charleston to indicate the location of the nectar. Other bees follow the dancing carefully and then go out searching for the flowers. Some bees tend to the young by forming the honeycomb cubicles to which they live at and by feeding them. Each bee has a time, when it works and a place, where it belongs.

Summary

  I. Adjective Dependent Clauses
   A. Definition: An **adjective dependent clause** is a dependent clause that acts as an adjective.
    1. An adjective dependent clause modifies a noun or pronoun.
       Examples: *The desk* **that I bought** *is beautiful.*
       Someone **who is dishonest** *took the book.*
    2. An adjective dependent clause usually comes immediately after the word it modifies.
       Example: *The sun* **that shines on me** *shines on you.*
   B. Recognizing adjective dependent clauses by relative words
    1. Some adjective dependent clauses begin with relative pronouns: *that, which, who, whom.*
       Examples: *My sister,* **who** *lives in Seattle, is here.*
       The actor about **whom** *you spoke is performing in our town.*

2. Some adjective dependent clauses begin with relative adjectives: *which(ever), whose.*

    Example: *The tree* **whose** *leaves are red is a maple.*

3. Some adjective dependent clauses begin with relative adverbs: *when, where*

    Example: *The time* **when** *we were young was long ago.*

C. Using a preposition with the relative word

1. Make sure of the correct preposition by trying the preposition at the end.

    Example: *the actor* **about whom** *you spoke* OR *the actor* **whom** *you spoke* **about**

2. Do not use the wrong relative pronoun.

    Example: NOT *the actor which you spoke about*

D. Types of adjective dependent clauses

1. Restrictive adjective dependent clauses restrict the words they modify and are crucial to the meaning.

    Examples: *Here is the book* **that I love.**

                Citizens **who obey the law** *help the country.*

2. Nonrestrictive adjective dependent clauses do not restrict the word they modify and give added but not crucial information.

    Examples: *This book,* **which I bought Monday,** *is good.*

                 We should have strict drunk driving laws, **which will make our streets safer.**

E. Punctuation

1. Restrictive adjective dependent clauses are not set off with commas.

    Example: *The students* **who study hard** *will pass.*

2. Nonrestrictive adjective dependent clauses are set off with commas unless a period supersedes the final comma at the end of a sentence.

    Examples: *The students,* **who study hard,** *took a break.*

                 The students took a break, **which helped them.**

Chapter 14

Noun Dependent Clauses

Underline the **noun dependent clauses** in the following sentences. Don't worry if you are not sure of any of them.

1. Whoever has been to an ice skating rink has seen the Zamboni.
2. Ice skaters know that this machine comes out periodically.
3. Whatever needs doing on the ice surface is done by this machine.
4. The fact that the Zamboni does many chores is obvious.
5. How this Zamboni works needs explaining.
6. One cannot tell by how it moves around the ice.
7. Water hoses, a pump, conveyors, a blade, and a towel are what the machine uses on the ice.
8. What the blade and water do is smooth out and fill in the cracks.
9. What the pump and conveyors do is collect excess water and snow.
10. That is why ice skaters should be grateful for the Zamboni.

A dependent clause contains a subject and its verb and often modifiers, objects, and complements. It cannot stand alone as a sentence, so the dependent clause must be joined with an independent clause. Such a sentence is called a ***complex sentence.*** One kind of dependent clause is the noun dependent clause.

Unlike some dependent clauses that are added to the independent clause, ***noun dependent clauses*** make up a part of the independent clause. A noun dependent clause functions the way a noun would function in a sentence: as subject (or delayed subject), as direct object, as subjective complement, as object of the preposition, or as appositive (but rarely as indirect object and *not* as objective complement):

Whoever rides bicycles stays in good shape. (subject)

It's good **that you ride a bicycle.** (delayed subject)

He likes **that I ride a bicycle.** (direct object)

This bicycle is **what I want.** (subjective complement)

Ride the bicycle to **wherever you wish.** (object of preposition)

The fact **that I own a bicycle** bodes well. (appositive)

As Subject and Delayed Subject

Noun dependent clauses may be used as subjects of sentences. Since the whole dependent clause together makes the subject, another verb, the verb for the independent clause, must also exist. For example, in *Whoever rides bicycles stays in good shape*, the noun dependent clause is *Whoever rides bicycles* and serves as subject of the independent clause. The verb *rides* goes with the noun dependent clause; *stays* serves as the verb both for the independent clause and for the noun dependent clause.

The delayed subject, as the word implies, comes later in the sentence and is signaled by *it* at or near the beginning of the sentence. This pronoun *it* stands for nothing else but the noun dependent clause that follows. For example, in *It is good that you ride a bicycle*, the actual subject, *that you ride a bicycle*, could replace *it*: *That you ride a bicycle is good*. Delayed subjects add variety to sentences and also give emphasis to the subject.

As Direct Object

As with a single word after a transitive verb, a noun dependent clause can also be a direct object. For example, in *He likes that I ride a bicycle*, the transitive verb *likes* takes the direct object *that I ride a bicycle*. Any single word in the noun dependent clause could not serve as the whole direct object; the whole noun dependent clause must be the direct object. Sometimes the subordinating word *that* may be omitted, but the sentence has the same construction: I think (**that**) **you'll like this bicycle.**

As Subjective Complement

A linking verb that takes a subjective complement may have a noun dependent clause as that subjective complement. In *That bicycle is what I want*, the subjective complement *what I want* renames *bicycle*, the subject of the independent clause.

As Object of a Preposition

Any preposition that can be used in a prepositional phrase can also have a noun dependent clause as the object of the preposition. In *Ride the bicycle to wherever you wish*, the preposition *to* has as its object *wherever you wish*. Any single word of the noun dependent clause could not serve as the object of the preposition; the whole noun dependent clause must.

As Appositive

An appositive is a renamer. With such words as *argument, belief, contention, fact, hope, opinion, statement, news,* and *vow,* among others, sometimes a noun dependent clause starting with *that* renames that word:

The fact **that I own a bicycle** bodes well. (renames *fact*)
The belief **that bicycles are good** is common. (renames *belief*)
Her vow **that she will ride the bicycle** was broken. (renames *vow*)

Notice that the appositive resembles the adjective dependent clause, but the appositive renames; that is, the noun dependent clause means the same as the word it follows. The adjective dependent clause modifies the word it follows. Notice the difference here:

The statement **that I love bicycles** is a lie. (appositive)
The statement **that she made** is a lie. (adjective dependent clause)

In the first sentence, *statement* is renamed by *that I love bicycles;* they mean the same. In the second sentence, *statement* is not renamed; *that she made* modifies *statement.*

Subordinating Words for Noun Dependent Clauses

These words introduce noun dependent clauses:

Conjunctions: **if, that, whether**
Pronouns: **what(ever), which(ever), who(ever), whom(ever)**
Adjectives: **what, which, whose**
Adverbs: **how, when, where, why**

Of course, these words are also used to introduce other phrases and clauses in addition to noun dependent clauses.

Punctuation of Noun Dependent Clauses

No commas separate a noun dependent clause from the rest of the sentence since normally the subject, direct object, subjective complement, and object of the preposition are not separated by commas from the rest of the sentence.

Most appositives that are noun dependent clauses do not need punctuation, but one construction will need a colon:

He has one problem: **how he will pay for the bicycle.**
There remains a dilemma: **who will take the bicycles.**

Parts of Noun Dependent Clauses

As with any clause, independent or dependent, a noun dependent clause in itself has a subject and its verb, and possibly modifiers and complements:

Conjunction	*subject*	*verb*	*adjective modifier*	*direct object*
That	**you**	**like**	**yellow**	**bicycles** is odd.

	pronoun subject	*verb*	*adjective* *subjective complement*
I like	**whichever**	**is**	**yellow.**

Exercise 14.1   Identifying Noun Dependent Clauses and Appositives

A. Underline the **one noun dependent clause** in each of the following sentences:

Example   How to ride a bicycle is not a problem.

1. What we know as our modern English alphabet is based on the Latin alphabet.
2. The task of writing down an oral language was given to whoever was literate around 800 A.D.
3. Christian monks in England decided that the Latin alphabet would serve well.
4. They wrote down what they could for each word in Old English.
5. They added what seemed necessary for new sounds.
6. The Norman Conquest in 1066 changed what we now know as Old English.
7. That Norman French would become the dominant language was a real possibility.
8. What we now call Middle English is a mixture of Old English (Anglo-Saxon) and Norman French.
9. When Shakespeare's English flourished at the end of the sixteenth century is known as the period of Early Modern English.
10. No dictionaries of English existed, so people spelled the way they pronounced a word.

B. Underline the **one** or **two noun dependent clauses** in each of the following sentences:

1. Whoever has studied English spelling knows it has problems.
2. Why spelling reforms were needed was very obvious.
3. People often judge others by whether they spell correctly.
4. The question was not if we need to reform spelling but when we will reform it.

5. Many predicted that we would eliminate the letters *C*, *Q*, and *X*.
6. People said we would use *K* or *S* for *C*, *Q*, and *X*.
7. In 1900, we thought this would happen by 2000.
8. How we would change spelling was not a difficult problem.
9. But whatever was proposed met with fierce opposition.
10. Our literature would be lost to whoever wanted to read it.

C. *Underline the **one appositive** in each sentence and draw an arrow to the noun that it renames.*

Example   The plan that I go bike riding became impossible.

1. The idea that a uniform system of spelling would be beneficial is widespread.
2. The Spanish system carries the assumption that phonetically spelled words are helpful for spellers.
3. But Spanish has the problem that some sounds have more than one spelling and some sounds are silent.
4. Spanish spelling is complicated by the fact that *ll* and *y* are pronounced the same.
5. Spanish also has the difficulty that *h* is silent, so whether to spell words with or without that letter is unclear.
6. The quandary that the language's literature will be lost has some solutions.
7. The answer that all the literature could be respelled is possible.
8. The faith that computers could handle the job is not totally unfounded.
9. Passing judgment on the spelling of various words would give rise to the argument that words are pronounced differently by people in different regions.
10. However, the contention that spelling tests would be eliminated and that spelling bees would be obsolete does not seem adequate reason for spelling reform.

Exercise 14.2   Finding Noun Dependent Clauses

*Underline the **one** or **two noun dependent clauses** in each of the following paragraphs.*

1. In 1755, Samuel Johnson wrote what we call the first dictionary of English. Before that time lists of hard words were compiled by teachers of writing. They considered that everyone already knew the easy words.
2. Johnson's dictionary listed thousands of words. Whatever spelling Johnson gave them became the standard spelling, and other spellings then became "wrong." Definitions also became standardized.

3. Johnson listed only "proper" English words, not substandard or improper ones, according to him. Thus, whichever spelling was given a word had to be known by any literate person. Unlike previously, people could now be poor spellers.

4. At the end of the eighteenth century in America, John Adams already recognized that we needed spelling reform. He wanted a language academy to establish standards for the American language and to keep it pure. Many supported this idea.

5. Benjamin Franklin also was interested in English spelling. He offered what he thought would improve spelling. He wanted to drop the letters *C, J, W,* and *Y.* But he proposed that we add six newly created letters.

6. Franklin suggested that we have a new alphabet. Most of the letters would be the same, but he wanted new letters such as an upside down *h* and curlicues on letters to designate different sounds. Nobody liked his ideas.

7. Noah Webster was at work on a dictionary even before Adams and Franklin. Webster eliminated what he considered unnecessary. He wrote *color* for *colour, center* for *centre, shop* for *shoppe,* and many others.

8. Webster also proposed that we eliminate the letter *C.* That even Noah Webster could not rid the language of this letter means that we must have wanted it. He managed to change *frolick* to *frolic* but could not replace that *C* with *K.*

9. Webster's *American Dictionary of the English Language,* published in 1828, has set the standard for dictionaries ever since. In addition to standard words, this dictionary also included what were then considered slang words.

10. Webster may have changed and standardized American English, but we still like to use former spellings. For example, we still see *programme, theatre,* and *ye olde shoppe.* These spellings tell us that we miss the old ways.

Exercise 14.3   Finding Noun Dependent Clauses

In the following essay, underline the **ten noun dependent clauses.**

Give Me Heat

How we heat houses is different from country to country and certainly has changed over the centuries. Basically, however, we heat with fire. But differences are created by how we use the fire, which may involve water, wood, oil, coal, gas, and electricity. Or we may even use the sun's fire for solar heating.

In very ancient times, a fire in the middle of a room was what most people had. It was smoky, and rain came in from the hole in the ceiling. The idea that the fire could go up a chimney was innovative. Thus a fire in a fireplace soon became what was commonly used for heat. Sometimes the heat from the fire could be sent where people sat on a platform, as in the *kang* of old China, or in a pit with people sitting around a *hibachi,* as in old Japan. In many countries, potbelly stoves in the middle of a room radiated heat all around.

Whatever material was abundant in an area was burned. Wood appeared to be the most used. Coal used in the fireplace or in a basement furnace was longer lasting than wood. Great coal mines all over the world attest to the utility of coal. Heating water and sending it up to radiators worked particularly well, but pipes and radiators had to be installed.

Although coal is still used, modern houses normally use oil or gas to heat water. Some people use electricity, but it can be more expensive. Solar power can be used effectively in some regions. Why some houses are heated one way and some another depends on the availability of materials and the costs.

Now we think burning wood in a fireplace is very romantic and charming. Whether ancient people would feel the same is doubtful. They would have found a nice radiator romantic and charming.

Exercise 14.4   Filling in Noun Dependent Clauses and Appositives

*A. In the following sentences, fill in the blank space with a suitable **noun dependent clause.***

Example _____ Whoever needs a ride _____ should ask for one.

1. At the town meeting, the mayor proposed _____.

2. She thought _____, but everyone disagreed.

3. The police chief suggested _____.

4. A store owner agreed _____.

5. _____ could not be agreed upon.

6. Some students envisioned _____.

7. Older people recalled _____.

8. A town elder remembered _____.

9. _____ really did seem possible.

10. Everyone agreed to do it by _____.

*B. In the following sentences, fill in the blank space with a suitable **noun clause appositive.** Remember that they begin with* that.

Example   The idea _____ *that I can't ride a bicycle* _____ bothers me.

1. The news _____ was exciting.

2. I hope the problem _____ won't matter.

3. My opinion _____ is valid.

4. After all, the argument _____ is true.

5. The contention _____ is always possible.

6. Take into account the vow _____.

7. The conviction _____ stays with me.

8. No one will change my belief _____.

9. The feeling _____ won't go away.

10. It won't change the fact _____.

Exercise 14.5   Writing with Noun Dependent Clauses

*Use the following **noun dependent clauses** to make up sentences.*

Example   (whoever wants it)
            I'll give the bicycle to whoever wants it. _____

1. (why he did that) _____

   _____

2. (when he could have done it) _____

   _____

3. (how dangerous it is) _____

   _____

4. (whether he would be caught) _____

   _____

5. (that anyone would tell) _____

   _____

6. (what the consequences were) _____

_____

7. (whichever way we look at it) _____

_____

8. (whatever he was thinking) _____

_____

9. (who would know) _____

_____

10. (how he would get away with it) _____

_____

11. (why she put it off) _____

_____

12. (that the assignment was due) _____

_____

13. (how anyone could forget) _____

_____

14. (who could she blame) _____

_____

15. (where she was) _____

_____

16. (that require some research) _____

_____

17. (whatever she was thinking) _____

_____

18. (whose notes she borrowed) _____

_____

19. (what information she already had) _____

_____

20. (that she will never do it again) _____

_____

Exercise 14.6 Writing with Noun Dependent Clauses and Appositives

Use each **noun dependent clause** *as a subject, delayed subject, direct object, subjective complement, object of the preposition, or appositive, as indicated.*

Example   that people should vote *(direct object)*

I think that people should vote.

1. that my neighbor borrows things *(subject)* _____

   _____

2. whatever he needs *(object of a preposition)* _____

   _____

3. that he borrows my tools *(direct object)* _____

   _____

4. that he forgets to return things *(delayed subject)* _____

   _____

5. what he needs *(direct object)* _____

   _____

6. when he needs sugar in a hurry *(subjective complement)* _____

   _____

7. that he can borrow anything *(appositive)* _____

   _____

8. whoever is around *(object of a preposition)* _____

   _____

9. why he doesn't buy his own ladder *(subject)* _____

   _____

10. whether he returns it *(appositive)* _____

    _____

11. how he can use a dozen eggs *(direct object)* _____

    _____

12. that I might need the punchbowl *(subjective complement)* _____

    _____

13. what he will ask for next (*appositive*) _____

_____

14. whether he is aware of his borrowing (*direct object*) _____

_____

15. whatever I say to him (*subject*) _____

_____

16. where he hides my tools (*direct object*) _____

_____

17. when he returns anything (*appositive*) _____

_____

18. how he will escape my notice (*object of a preposition*) _____

_____

19. whether I should charge him (*direct object*) _____

_____

20. why he is this way (*subject*) _____

_____

Exercise 14.7   Proofreading

*Correct the **five comma errors** in the noun dependent clauses in the following paragraph.*

"It's in the dictionary," once meant a word was correct. Samuel Johnson certainly believed, that the dictionary would help people write properly. Noah Webster agreed, that dictionaries should be sources of correct usage, although he added some slang words. But everything changed with *Webster's Third International Dictionary* in 1961. Whether a word was used by a native speaker of English, comprised the sole criterion for that word. Thus formerly unprintable, ungrammatical, and regional words found their way into that dictionary. Many people objected to these inclusions. But the dictionary had become descriptive; that is, it described the existing language. Formerly, all dictionaries had been prescriptive; that is, they told, which words could be used and how to use them.

Summary

I. Noun Dependent Clauses
   A. Definition: A **noun dependent clause** is a dependent clause that acts as a noun within a sentence.
   B. Uses
      1. Noun dependent clauses may be used as subjects and delayed subjects.
         Examples: ***Whenever we go*** *is fine with me.*
         It is fine ***that we go on Tuesday.***
      2. Noun dependent clauses can be used as direct objects.
         Example: *We prefer* ***what you like.***
      3. Noun dependent clauses can be used as subjective complements.
         Example: *My goal is* ***whatever makes me happy.***
      4. Noun dependent clauses can be used as objects of the preposition.
         Example: *I will go to* ***wherever you want.***
      5. Noun dependent clauses can be used as appositives.
         Example: *The news* ***that you won the game*** *is great.*
   C. Subordinating words used in noun dependent clauses
      1. Noun dependent clauses use conjunctions: *if, that, whether*
         Example: ***Whether*** *you win or not is fine with me.*
      2. Noun dependent clauses use pronouns: *what(ever), which(ever), who(ever), whom(ever)*
         Example: ***Whichever*** *tastes best has my vote.*
      3. Noun dependent clauses use adjectives: *what, which, whose*
         Example: ***Whose*** *boat we use doesn't matter.*
      4. Noun dependent clauses use adverbs: *how, when, where, why*
         Example: *We'll go* ***when*** *you feel like it.*
   D. Punctuation
      1. Do not use a comma between the noun dependent clause and the preceding word.
         Example: *I like* ***whatever you like.***
      2. Do not use a comma between the noun dependent clause and the following word.
         Example: ***Whoever is hungry*** *should sit down here.*

Chapter 15

Adverb Dependent Clauses

Underline the **adverb dependent clauses** in the following sentences. Don't worry if you are not sure.

1. Although they were once considered part of the raccoon family, giant pandas are actually bears.
2. Since they have black patches around their eyes and ears, they have a resemblance to raccoons.
3. Pandas mostly live where they can find their staple food, bamboo.
4. Unfortunately, bamboo is not very nutritious even if pandas eat vast quantities of it.
5. When bamboo blooms and produces seeds every sixty years or so, it becomes inedible.
6. Many pandas die at this time since they cannot find enough food.
7. Female pandas give birth to one cub a year if they manage to mate during the few days a year of fertility.
8. Because giant pandas live in a small mountainous area of western China and cannot survive elsewhere, they will soon be extinct.
9. Only about a thousand giant pandas still exist, although many efforts have been made to preserve them.
10. Even though pandas have been protected in zoos, they have rarely reproduced successfully.

A *complex sentence* is made up of an independent clause, which can stand alone as a sentence, and one or more dependent clauses, which are part of the independent clause.

One kind of dependent clause is the *adverb dependent clause.* As its name implies, the adverb dependent clause acts as an adverb by modifying a verb, adjective, or adverb in the independent clause to which it is attached. It may come at the beginning, middle, or end of a sentence. As is true of adverbs in general, the adverb dependent clause can concede and compare and can give information about the time or place; the manner, condition, or purpose; the reason (cause) or result:

The snow is lovely, **although it is dangerous.** (concession)

After the snow has fallen, we must shovel it. (time)

The snow, **if it is moist,** will look nice. (condition)

The snow looked **as if it would melt.** (manner)

I like snow **because it covers ugliness.** (reason)

The snow fell **where we like it.** (place)

I shoveled **so that the walk is clear.** (purpose)

The snow melted **so fast that I missed it.** (result)

This snow is drier **than last week's snow** [was]. (comparison)

Notice that with comparisons, the verb in the adverb dependent clause may or may not be expressed.

Subordinating Conjunctions

Many *subordinating conjunctions* may introduce an adverb dependent clause:

after	provided that
although	since
as	so that
as if	than
as though	that
as soon as	though
because	unless
before	until
even though	when(ever)
given that	where
if	wherever
in order that	while
on condition that	

These words also serve in other capacities besides subordinating conjunctions, so do not assume they always form adverb dependent clauses. Subordinating conjunctions help make up complex sentences, unlike the coordinating conjunctions (*for, and, nor, but, or, yet, so*) that connect compound sentences (two or more independent clauses).

Some other subordinating words are the two-part adverb dependent clauses that describe the extent of something:

so (adjective) that

The snow was **so** deep **that** I couldn't walk in it.

such (noun) that

The snow caused **such** a mess **that** we missed the train.

Note that *being as, being as how,* and *being that* are not on the list of subordinating conjunctions. They are not considered standard; replace them with *because* and *since.*

Elliptical Clauses

Sometimes part of the adverb dependent clause is not expressed:

When [she was] delayed by snow, she called a cab.
The snow, **although [it is] beautiful,** causes problems.
The snow will cause problems **unless [it is] shoveled.**
This snow is deeper **than last year's [snow was].**
This snow is worse **than that in Minneapolis [is].**

Filling in the **ellipsis** (omitted word or words) will help you see that *He is taller than I (am)* is correct while *He is taller than me (am)* is incorrect. However, *She loves you more than I* and *She loves you more than me* are both correct, but they have very different meanings, as completing the ellipsis will reveal: *She loves you more than I [love you]* and *She loves you more than [she loves] me.* Fill in the ellipsis to find out if you are saying what you want.

Identifying What the Adverb Dependent Clause Modifies

Most adverb dependent clauses modify the verb of the independent clause:

Since the snow melted, he shoveled the walk. (modifies *shoveled*)
I bought a new shovel **in order that you may clear the snow.** (modifies *bought*)

Some adverb dependent clauses modify an adjective in the independent clause:

She was sad **that the snow had melted.** (modifies *sad*)
I'm happier to see snow **than you (are).** (modifies *happier*)

Sometimes the adverb dependent clause may modify an adverb in the independent clause:

My snow melts faster **than yours [does].** (modifies *faster*)
My shovel works better **than it did before.** (modifies *better*)

Punctuating Adverb Dependent Clauses

An adverb dependent clause that comes at the beginning of a sentence usually takes a comma before the independent clause that follows:

While the snow is falling, we shouldn't be shoveling.

In order for the snow to clear, we must wait an hour.

The adverb dependent clause in the middle of an independent clause will always be surrounded by commas:

The snow, **unless it is shoveled,** will be dangerous.

My shovel, **although (it is) brand new,** isn't working well.

An adverb dependent clause at the end of an independent clause normally does *not* take a comma since it is considered the natural flow of a sentence:

Minnesota is a great place **even if it has a lot of snow.**

I'll shovel the driveway **since the snow stopped.**

However, to indicate contrast or hesitation, a comma is almost always used:

I cleared the walk, **although he could have done it.** (contrast)

Can you shovel the walk, **if it isn't too much trouble?** (hesitation)

However, sometimes you must use your own judgment to decide if you need the comma for contrast or hesitation.

Identifying Parts of Adverb Dependent Clauses

As with all clauses, the various words in the clause serve as subjects, verbs, adjectives and adverbs, objects, and complements:

subordinating conjunction	subject	verb	direct object	
Even though	**I**	**like**	**snow,**	I can't wait for spring.

	subordinating conjunction	subject	verb	adverb	adjective subjective complement
I like snow	**because**	**it**	**is**	**so**	**beautiful.**

Exercise 15.1   Finding Adverb Dependent Clauses

*Underline the **one adverb dependent clause** in each of the following sentences.*

Example   Snow tires are required <u>because they help a lot.</u>

1. Since the Himalayas were revered by local people, no one climbed them in former times.

2. Because Mount Everest, the tallest peak, straddled the border between Tibet in the north and Nepal in the south, it was difficult to approach.

3. Anyone wanting to climb in the Himalayas could not do so because Nepal had closed its borders.

4. Some people went to Tibet so that they could climb the less difficult northern route.

5. In the early 1900s, British climbers also went into Tibet so that they could survey the land.

6. When China occupied Tibet in the 1950s, Tibet was also closed to foreigners.

7. As Nepal became influenced by Western ways and money, the people succumbed to demands.

8. Nepal finally opened the border on condition that climbers apply for a permit before climbing.

9. The local Sherpas became guides since they were experts at climbing in the area.

10. In 1924, the Britishers George Mallory and Andrew Irvine climbed almost to the top before they disappeared.

11. Mallory's body was found seventy-five years later on a ledge, although Irvine's was not found.

12. Because his body had fallen at a particular spot, Mallory apparently was ascending and did not reach the top.

13. After the British had made ten attempts, in 1953 the Britisher John Hunt, along with New Zealander Edmund Hillary and Sherpa Tenzing Norgay, succeeded in reaching the top.

14. Although the northern route through Tibet was easier, they had climbed the southern route.

15. This route became so popular that many climbers have attempted it since then.

16. Junko Tabei of Japan became the first woman to reach the top when she did so in 1975.

17. Although the Sherpas had guided many foreigners on expeditions, they did not climb Everest themselves until 1991.

18. By the turn of the century, over four thousand people had tried to climb Mount Everest though under seven hundred of them reached the summit.

19. About one hundred fifty people died before they reached the top.

20. Although modern methods and equipment have changed mountain climbing, Mount Everest still remains the ultimate challenge.

Exercise 15.2   Finding Adverb Dependent Clauses

Underline the **one** *or* **two adverb dependent clauses** *in each of the following paragraphs.*

1. Mount Everest has such a reputation that many people have wanted this ultimate challenge. George Mallory said he wanted to climb it because "it is there." Others preceded him and many have followed him, but the danger is always there.

2. The first challenge is being granted permission. Since Mount Everest lies in Tibet to the north and Nepal to the south, one of those two countries must grant permission for a climb. Although they charge hefty fees, they have been issuing permits.

3. The high cost of equipment and guides adds to the expense. Tents, clothing, and climbing gear must be the best so that they can withstand the harsh weather. Good guides must be expert climbers and very experienced.

4. Avalanches of either snow or ice pose one of the biggest threats even though climbers choose the safest routes. An avalanche can bury valleys, passages, and routes instantly. Of course, they also may bury the climber.

5. Sudden blinding snowstorms also add to the danger. The strong wind blowing the snow has such force that tents, equipment, and clothing may be torn to shreds or tossed down the mountainside. This loss will probably lead to death.

6. Climbers must be very careful of hypothermia, a rapid decrease in body temperature. If his or her body is exposed to the elements without adequate protection, such as tents, heaters, and insulated clothing, a person will die.

7. Although in 1978 some climbers refused to use additional oxygen, most climbers need it. If they do not acclimate to the thin air of such a high altitude, they lose energy, become debilitated, and lose the ability to think clearly.

8. A rapid shift of a glacier over abrupt rocks, called an icefall, causes vertical cliffs. Deep crevices between the cliffs, if not filled with snow, change the route and sometimes make the climb impossible to continue.

9. Usually the chasm between these cliffs fills quickly with blowing snow so that a smooth surface forms. One step on this seemingly firm snow, however, will plunge the climber down the chasm to be buried in deep snow.

10. So that they may meet the expense of climbing Mount Everest, experienced climbers have recruited wealthy people to join them. However, the severe weather and some inexperienced climbers have led to difficulties.

Exercise 15.3   Finding Adverb Dependent Clauses

*Underline the **ten adverb dependent clauses** in the following essay.*

Care for the Elderly

More and more people are living much longer than they used to. Although the upper limit of longevity has not changed that much, more people have become centenarians. And even more people have become octogenerians and nonagenarians. It is not unusual for a twenty-year-old to have parents, grandparents, and great-grandparents. When people are in reasonably good health, they don't need any special care. When they can no longer live independently, many problems ensue.

The first step for an elderly person at home is to have a regular daily visit of a few hours from a home care aide. In addition, a charitable organization or care center may send daily meals. This person is still able bodied and mentally acute. The next step for an elderly person at home is full-time care because he or she needs help doing everyday tasks such as preparing food, bathing, or shopping. This type of care is sometimes called "assisted living."

The final step consists of moving out of the home and into a nursing home where twenty-four-hour care is available. These elderly people often are no longer ambulatory and have several medical problems. Unless they are assisted every day, they cannot really function independently. Most of them still function well in many aspects of their lives.

Before they go into a full-scale nursing home, however, older people have several options. Retirement villages exist in order that elderly people may have some measure of independence. They have private apartments and may cook for themselves but may also eat in a communal dining room. Doctors and nurses live on the premises in order to help at any time. However, these retirement villages may be distant, unavailable, too expensive, or inadequate.

If everyone plans ahead, elderly parents can receive the right care for them. But making such plans is fraught with heartache, guilt, distress, and sadness for everyone.

Exercise 15.4   Making Adverb Dependent Clauses

*A. Combine the two simple sentences into a complex sentence by making one of the two sentences into an **adverb dependent clause.** Add a subordinating conjunction and change some words if you need to.*

Example   I like snow. I go skiing often.

_____Because I like snow, I go skiing often._____

1. I want to go camping. Camping is so much fun.

   _____

2. One or two friends can go. They can help with preparations.

   _____

3. We can each bring food. We will each have our preferences.

   _____

4. I hope someone can cook. I don't want to eat beans.

   _____

5. I have four sleeping bags. I will lend them to friends.

   _____

6. My parents have a large tent. They used to go camping.

   _____

7. I'll borrow their tent. They don't go camping anymore.

   _____

8. I have chosen a favorite campground. It is next to a lake.

   _____

9. We will bring bathing suits. We can swim during the day.

   _____

10. The hiking trails may be rugged. We need good boots.

    _____

B. *Combine the three simple sentences into a complex sentence by making* **one or two** *of the three sentences into an* **adverb dependent clause.** *Add a subordinating conjunction and change some words if you need to.*

1. I am taking a cruise. I have booked tickets. I have two weeks of vacation.

   _____

   _____

2. I planned almost six months ahead. I made a down payment. I didn't get any information.

   _____

   _____

3. I made many phone calls. I talked to several people. I was patient.

   _____

   _____

4. I had many questions. I tried writing a letter. My phone calls didn't work.

   _____

   _____

5. I have never been on a cruise. My clothes are a problem. What and who should I tip?

   _____

   _____

6. I want to know about mail. My parents are elderly. I need to contact people.

   _____

   _____

7. I want to visit the sights. I want to sign up for shore excursions. I want to know the prices of the excursions.

   _____

   _____

8. I have special dietary requirements. I need certain foods. I can eat most foods.

   _____

   _____

9. I am looking forward to the cruise. We will visit the Yucatan Peninsula. I have been to Mexico before.

   _____

   _____

10. I usually enjoy boats. I like the water. I want to have a good time.

   _____

   _____

Exercise 15.5   Writing with Adverb Dependent Clauses

Use the following **adverb dependent clauses** *in sentences of your own.*

Example   (because I said so)

   You may not have the car tonight because I said so.

1. (although I don't want to) _____

_____

2. (as soon as you called) _____

_____

3. (as if you didn't know) _____

_____

4. (even though I had told you) _____

_____

5. (given that you knew my plans) _____

_____

6. (in order that I have enough time) _____

_____

7. (on condition that you try) _____

_____

8. (so that it doesn't happen again) _____

_____

9. (unless you help me) _____

_____

10. (until I have time) _____

_____

11. (wherever I want to go) _____

_____

12. (provided that you come, too) _____

_____

13. (since you couldn't care less) _____

_____

14. (as I don't really care) _____

_____

15. (after I made plans) _____

_____

16. (as I am very busy) _____

_____

17. (before you make a decision) _____

_____

18. (if I were you) _____

_____

19. (whenever I make an attempt) _____

_____

20. (while I still have time) _____

_____

Exercise 15.6   Writing with Adverb Dependent Clauses

Use some or all of the following conjunctions in **adverb dependent clauses** *to write a paragraph.*

1. after   although   before   until

2. because   if   since   unless

3. as soon as   even though   in order that   provided that

4. even if   on condition that   so [adjective] that

5. even though   so that   such [noun] that   than

Exercise 15.7   Proofreading

*Find and correct the **five comma errors** in adverb dependent clauses in the following paragraph.*

Many people have visited Egypt, because it has so many fascinating sights. Flying into Cairo is easy, since the airport is very modern and convenient. Although Cairo itself has interesting mosques, marketplaces, monuments, and old neighborhoods people flock to Giza, just outside Cairo. In Giza, they will see the famous pyramids. Going down, but really up, the Nile to Luxor and Aswan is also popular. They will see Karnak and, across from Luxor, the Valley of the Kings and the tombs of the pharaohs. The building of the Aswan Dam caused such a controversy, that it has become a popular resort area. If time permits people should continue to Abu

Simbel. But unfortunately many people lack the time to see Alexandria, a very European city. They also probably will miss the pyramids at Memphis and Sakara unless they plan a longer stay.

Summary

I. Adverb Dependent Clauses
   A. Definition: An **adverb dependent clause** is a dependent clause that acts as an adverb.
   B. Purposes
      1. Adverb dependent clauses concede and compare.
         Example: *I like the sun,* **although it is hot.**
      2. Adverb dependent clauses give information about time and place.
         Example: **Before you go,** *we must talk.*
      3. Adverb dependent clauses tell the manner, condition, or purpose.
         Example: *We'll talk now* **if you want to.**
      4. Adverb dependent clauses give the reason, cause, or result.
         Example: *I spoke* **because I needed to.**
   C. Uses
      1. Adverb dependent clauses modify verbs (most often).
         Example: **When I got up,** *I opened the window.*
      2. Adverb dependent clauses modify adjectives.
         Example: *I was glad* **that the sun was shining.**
      3. Adverb dependent clauses modify adverbs.
         Example: *I see the sky more clearly* **than you do.**
   D. Recognizing adverb dependent clauses
      1. Most adverb dependent clauses start with a subordinating conjunction: *although, because, if, since,* etc.
         Examples: **Although I went,** *I didn't like it.*
         I didn't like it **because it rained.**
      2. Some adverb dependent clauses have two words: *so that, such that.*
         Example: *I slept* **so that I would look better.**
      3. Some adverb dependent clauses are elliptical clauses with some words omitted.
         Example: *The sky is bluer* **than Monday's** [*sky was*].
   E. Punctuation
      1. An adverb dependent clause at the beginning of a sentence takes a comma at the end.
         Example: **Since the storm passed,** *the sky is bright.*
      2. An adverb dependent clause in the middle of a sentence is set off with commas.
         Example: *The sky,* **even if you don't think so,** *is bluer now than before.*

3. An adverb dependent clause at the end of a sentence normally takes no preceding comma unless it shows contrast or hesitation.

Examples: *I won't be there **before you get there.***

*I won't go, **although I want to.*** (contrast)

*I won't go, **unless you take me.*** (hesitation)

Sentence Structure

Chapter 16

Inverted Sentences and Passive Voice

Underline the **inverted sentence parts** in the following paragraphs.

1. Why do so many people study Spanish? Do they think that Spanish is easy? Spanish is not easy to learn, nor does it come easily to most of us. So I will not think it is easy, nor will I assume I'll be speaking Spanish in a few days.

2. Had I gotten a good Spanish teacher, I would have learned much faster. The teacher would drill me on verb forms and give me lots of tests to make sure that I did my work. Why else would anyone want a teacher? Certainly it's not for the fun of it.

3. I won't tell anyone I'm studying Spanish, nor will I try to practice on anyone. Why would I want this kind of embarrassment? I'll just study quietly. Then one day, were someone to say something in Spanish, I would surprise everyone by responding.

The normal English sentence puts the subject before the verb, but this order may be changed. ***Inverted sentences*** serve various purposes.

WH Questions

Questions often begin with these ***question words,*** also called ***WH words:***

how	when	which	whom	why
what	where	who	whose	

The question word is usually followed by the verb and then the subject, inverting their usual order:

How is your cold? (*is* = verb; *cold* = subject)

Why is your cold worse? (*is* = verb; *cold* = subject; *worse* = subjective complement)

Who are your doctors? (*are* = verb; *doctors* = subject)

Notice that a plural subject (*doctors*) takes a plural verb form (*are*).

When action verbs, past, present, or future, are used in a question, the subject is inverted with the helping verb only (only the first helping verb if there is more than one), not the complete verb:

> Why **might I** be sick? (*might be* = complete verb)
>
> When **am I** going to get well? (*am going* = complete verb)
>
> Where **will I** see the doctor? (*will see* = complete verb)
>
> How **had you** been feeling? (*had been feeling* = complete verb)

Even when the past or present tense verb is a single word, a helping verb, *do*, is added in the questions form:

> I catch cold often. = Why **do** I catch cold often?
>
> I caught cold. = When **did** I catch cold?

English does not have single-word future tense verbs, so that problem does not exist.

Notice, however, that when the question word is the subject or part of the subject of the sentence, the order is not inverted:

> Who wants some aspirin? (*Who* = subject)
>
> How many pills are in the bottle? (*How many pills* = subject)
>
> Which pills should be here? (*Which pills* = subject)
>
> Whose pills are new? (*Whose pills* = subject)

Yes-No Questions

Yes-no questions do not need a question word, but the subject and verb are still inverted:

> Is your doctor here?
>
> Will you be all right?
>
> Do you want some aspirin?
>
> Did the doctor arrive?

They are called yes-no questions because they can be answered in this way, unlike other questions that ask for information. Yes-no questions, however, can take other answers, such as *maybe, I'll see,* and the like.

A variation of the yes-no question is the *tag question.* At the end of statements, a tag question is sometimes added to make the whole sentence a question:

> Maria isn't sick, is she?
>
> She will recover, won't she?
>
> She could be sick, couldn't she?
>
> She should see a doctor, shouldn't she?

Follow these steps: (1) If the statement is positive, the tag is negative, and vice versa. (2) If the main sentence uses a *be* form of the verb (*am, is, are, was, were, will*) or *can, could, would,* and *should,* the tag question uses the same. Other verbs change to *do* forms for tags:

> He ran a fever, **didn't** he?
> He eats well, **doesn't** he?

(3) Use the same tense in the main sentence and the tag. (4) Use a pronoun in the tag whether the subject in the main sentence is a noun or pronoun:

> **You** have a cold, don't **you**?
> **Maria** has a cold, doesn't **she**?

(5) Add a verb if the tag reference is not to the main sentence:

> **Maria** looks sick, don't **you think**?

Tag questions are preceded by a comma and followed by a question mark.

Direct and Indirect Questions

Direct questions are those that take question marks at the end and include WH-questions, yes-no questions, and tag questions.

A sentence that tells about asking a question is called an ***indirect question,*** does *not* take a question mark, and does *not* involve a subject-verb inversion:

> He asked if I wanted medicine.
> She questioned why I caught cold.
> They inquired whether my cold was better.
> We wondered who gave me the cold.

Notice that commonly *if* and *whether,* along with regular questions words—*what, when, where, who, why*—are used. Do not invert or change to question form for indirect questions:

> He asked if I caught cold.   NOT   He asked did I catch cold.
> He inquired whether I was well.   NOT   He inquired was I well.
> She asked who my doctor was.   NOT   She asked who was my doctor.

Informally we also ask questions without inverting the subject and verb by simply adding a rising intonation in speech or a question mark in writing:

> The doctor is here?
> You're feeling better?

Nor *and* as *Constructions*

When part of a sentence, usually a compound sentence, has a *nor* part, the subject and verb are inverted in that part:

I do not have a cold, nor **do I** feel sick.

He neither has a cold, nor **does he** feel sick.

Occasionally the sentence starts with *neither* and is followed by *nor*. In this case, both parts have inverted subject and verb:

Neither do I feel sick, nor do I want medicine.

Neither will she take medicine, nor will she lie down.

Notice that the sentence parts following *neither* and *nor* have the same structure. This form is rarely used.

When the sentence is positive, *as* serves the same purpose as *nor:*

She caught cold last week, as did I.

She takes aspirin, as do many people for their colds.

Dependent Clauses without if

Although adverb dependent clauses usually start with a subordinating conjunction such as *although, because, if,* or *since,* one construction omits the subordinating conjunction and inverts the subject and verb of the adverb dependent clause:

Were you sick, you'd feel bad. (If you were sick,)

Had you taken it, you'd feel well. (If you had taken it,)

This construction seems rather formal but is still used in speech as well as in writing.

Passive Voice

Active voice means that the subject of a sentence is the doer of the action of the verb:

She called the doctor.

Passive voice means that the direct object becomes the subject but is not the doer of the action:

The doctor was called by her.

The verb always has the auxiliary verb *be* and the past participle of the verb. The forms of *be* used for passive voice include *is, are, was, were, will be, has been, have been, had been, will have been, can be, could be, should be, would be, is being, are being, was being, were being,* all used along with a past participle verb:

> The doctor **was called.**
>
> The doctor **had been called.**
>
> The doctor **should be called.**
>
> The doctors **are being called.**

Since the passive voice is formed by making the direct object the subject of the sentence, only transitive verbs (those having a direct object) can be used for passive voice.
The actual doer of the action can be added as the object of the preposition *by:*

> The doctor was called **by her.** (*She called the doctor* = active voice.)
>
> The doctors are being called **by the nurse.** (*The nurse calls the doctors* = active voice.)

You can often test for passive voice by adding *by someone* (or *by anyone* for negative sentences) to the sentence and seeing if it makes sense:

> The patient was being examined [*by someone*].
>
> Tests were performed [*by someone*].
>
> The results are made available to the patient [*by someone*].
>
> No problems were detected [*by anyone*].

Questions using passive voice may be formed in the same way as active voice questions. Invert the auxiliary verb and the subject:

> Has the doctor been called?
>
> Are the doctors being called by the nurse?

Although people are criticized for using the passive voice to avoid taking responsibility for their actions (*Mistakes were made*), passive voice has its uses. When you want to emphasize that an event has taken place, not who caused it, use the passive voice. For example, in *The furniture was moved*, that the move was done by movers or by someone may not be the point. Instead of *Somebody finished the job*, use *The job was finished* if the completion of the job is more important than who did it.

Inverted Construction Exercises

Exercise 16.1   Finding Inverted Constructions

*Find the **inverted subjects** and **verbs** in the following sentences and label them as follows:*

Q *question*

T *tag question*

N nor *construction*
A as *construction*
DC *dependent clause with inversion*

Example   She's getting well, isn't she? __T__

1. Were people to eat more fish, they would be healthier. _____
2. But why should people eat fish? _____
3. Fish is not free of fat, nor is it always safe. _____
4. Fish has fat, as does chicken and red meat. _____
5. Does all fish contain omega-3 fatty acids? _____
6. Do only herring, mackerel, and sardines have fatty acids? _____
7. Some fish is fairly lean, isn't it? _____
8. Do chicken and red meat have omega-3 fatty acids, as do many fish? _____
9. Most people think eating fish once or twice a week is a good idea, don't they? _____
10. Had we known about the benefits of fish earlier, we would have eaten more of it. _____

Exercise 16.2   Finding Inverted Sentence Parts

*A. In the following short essay, underline the **inverted parts** in questions, tag questions, and* nor *sentences.*

Example   A dog is following me, <u>isn't it</u>? What <u>does it</u> want?

Forever Cod?

Cod is one of the most versatile of fish. It has been eaten for centuries and probably will go on being a food source forever. Or will it?

Beginning in the early Middle Ages, the Basque people in the mountainous areas of southern France and northern Spain perfected the technique for salting cod. Why did the Basques salt cod? This method preserved the fish for long periods of time to accommodate transporting it from the sea inland and for use later in the season. It was definitely the most practical thing to do, wasn't it?

Cod cannot be ruined by any cooking method, nor can it be bad tasting. And most of all, cod is cheap. But all good things change, don't they? The waters off Russia and Newfoundland and the North Sea no longer have abundant schools of cod, nor do the New England waters have the vast supplies they once did.

The supply of cod is running out. Why has this happened? The species has been seriously diminished in all waters by overfishing. Only some Scandinavian countries still have adequate stocks because of strict controls on fishing. Soon cod may become a delicacy eaten only in expensive restaurants. This would be a shame, wouldn't it?

Exercise 16.3   Writing with Questions

*Change each of the following statements into (1) a **yes-no question** and (2) an information question.*

Example   A dog is following Mary.

Is a dog following Mary?

What is following Mary?

1. People eat cod fish all over the world.

2. Salmon and trout possess high percentages of omega-3 fatty acids.

3. Scientists think that shellfish is low in fat.

4. Many people like some shellfish, such as lobster, shrimp, and crab.

5. Eating fish oils helps prevent heart attacks.

6. Vegetarians can eat flax and purslane, both with fatty acids.

7. People know olive oil is healthful for us.

_____

_____

8. Avocados, heavy in oil, also contain good oils.

_____

_____

9. Some nuts also have beneficial oils.

_____

_____

10. Oily food does not necessarily cause clogged arteries.

_____

_____

Exercise 16.4   Writing Direct and Indirect Questions

A. *Change the following* **direct questions** *into* **indirect questions.**

Example   When did she catch cold?

I asked her when she caught cold.

1. Why is butter salted?

_____

2. Is it for the taste?

_____

3. Do Americans prefer salted butter?

_____

4. Why is most butter in other countries unsalted?

_____

5. Do we salt butter to make it last longer?

_____

6. What does "shelf life" mean?

_____

7. Does it mean that a product will last longer?

_____

8. Does a long shelf life save money for the producer?

   _____

9. Don't producers care about the taste of the butter?

   _____

10. Have other products changed because of shelf life?

   _____

B. *Change the following* **indirect questions** *into* **direct questions.**

Example   I asked her how she caught cold.
   <u>   How did you catch cold?   </u>

   1. I asked if many foods have been changed to increase shelf life.

   _____

   2. I wondered if milk was homogenized for that reason.

   _____

   3. I asked whether pasteurizing had to do with shelf life or not.

   _____

   4. I wondered whether stamping dates on milk is right or not.

   _____

   5. I asked if the date was just another trick.

   _____

   6. I inquired about how eggs have been changed.

   _____

   7. I wondered how vegetables are treated for shelf life.

   _____

   8. I asked if all foods are processed to last longer.

   _____

   9. I pondered why we really need such fresh food.

   _____

10. I wonder if refrigeration helps prolong food also.

   _____

Exercise 16.5   Proofreading

*Find and correct **three errors** of **faulty inversion** and **three errors** of **end punctuation**.*

Why do most countries in the world have cafés. Ask Europeans do they sit in cafés? They will definitely answer that they meet friends, take a rest, read the papers, have something to eat or drink, or all of the above. Many Europeans must have their daily dose of espresso. In the Middle East, some Egyptian men smoke elaborate water pipes at cafés while Turkish men meet for tea in cafés. Do women go to these cafés. Inquire would they let women in, and all of them will. But ask women do they go often to cafés, and they will say no. Customarily women stay at home and visit with other women at home.

Passive Voice Exercises

Exercise 16.6   Understanding Passive Voice

*In each of these **passive voice sentences**, underline the **subject** and the **complete verb** and copy the doer of the action in the blank. If the doer is not stated, write in an appropriate doer with by.*

Example   Cough syrup is often used. ____by people____

1. Formerly, oysters and clams were eaten frequently. _____
2. Oyster and clam chowders were served in many homes. _____
3. They were consumed as ordinary fare by New Englanders. _____
4. Clam bakes on weekends were featured often. _____
5. They were sponsored by church and community socials. _____
6. Batter-fried oysters were put into sandwiches. _____
7. Lobster was also eaten often by many people. _____
8. Shellfish was found abundantly in the local waters. _____
9. Vast quantities of shellfish were wasted. _____
10. Sometimes the price for them was considered too cheap to bother with. _____
11. Supplies were depleted by disease and waste. _____

12. Various diseases and pollution can be contracted rather easily by clams and oysters. _____

13. Whole populations of shellfish were depleted by diseases and water pollution. _____

14. Some shellfish is still not considered safe to eat. _____

15. Careful controls and licensing were instituted to bring back our shellfish. _____

Exercise 16.7   Understanding Passive Voice

*In each of these **passive voice** sentences, underline the **subject** and the **complete verb**. Copy the doer of the action in the blank. If the doer is not stated, write in an appropriate doer with the word* by.

Example   The <u>money was stolen</u> by somebody. ___*somebody*___

1. Oprah Winfrey is celebrated by her fans as one of television's premier women. _____

2. At Tennessee State University, the subjects of speech and drama were studied by Oprah Winfrey. _____

3. At age nineteen, Winfrey was hired as a news anchor for the local CBS television station. _____

4. Following her graduation in 1976, she was made reporter and co-anchor for the ABC news affiliate in Baltimore, Maryland. _____

5. In 1977 she was chosen to be the cohost of the Baltimore morning show *People Are Talking.* _____

6. Later, in Chicago, she was hired to turn the faltering *A.M. Chicago* into a success, outperforming the leading talk show host, Phil Donahue, in his own market. _____

7. In 1985, *A.M. Chicago* was renamed *The Oprah Winfrey Show*, which entered national syndication in 1986. _____

8. *The Oprah Winfrey Show* was recognized as the best of the genre. _____

9. A wide audience of viewers was attracted by Winfrey's intelligence, honesty, and engaging personality. _____

10. Because of the show's success, Winfrey was established as one of the wealthiest women in entertainment. _____

Exercise 16.8   Identifying Passive Voice and Active Voice

Label each of these sentences as
  AV *active voice*
  PV *passive voice*

1. American people in general eat very little fish. _____
2. Fresh fish is eaten by Americans only occasionally. _____
3. Of all fish, canned tuna is consumed the most often in the United States. _____
4. Canned sardines were used sometimes as snacks. _____
5. Formerly, breaded fried shrimp were featured by restaurants as the only seafood on the menu. _____
6. Some specialty restaurants carried lobster or clams as well. _____
7. But the general demand for fish was very small. _____
8. Only frozen and canned fish were on the market. _____
9. A fish market was hardly ever found in ordinary communities even near the ocean. _____
10. Various ethnic groups should be credited with helping to popularize fish for general consumption. _____
11. Greek, Italian, and Chinese restaurants were known for their fish preparations. _____
12. Now, fresh fish can be found in most supermarkets and restaurants. _____
13. A larger variety of fish is also being offered in fish stores, supermarkets, and restaurants. _____
14. Some restaurants feature fish almost exclusively. _____
15. Many Americans have discovered the wonders of fish. _____

Exercise 16.9   Identifying Passive Voice and Active Voice

Label each of these sentences as
  AV *active voice*
  PV *passive voice*

1. The tornado is known by meterologists and lay people alike as one of nature's most violent storms. ⎯⎯⎯

2. In an average year, 800 tornadoes are reported by citizens across the United States. ⎯⎯⎯

3. Each year, tornadoes result in 80 deaths and over 1,500 injuries. ⎯⎯⎯

4. A tornado is a violently rotating column of air extending from a thunderstorm to the ground. ⎯⎯⎯

5. Tremendous destruction is created by the most violent tornadoes. ⎯⎯⎯

6. Wind speeds of 250 mph or even more have been measured by scientists who study strong tornadoes. ⎯⎯⎯

7. The damage path of a tornado can be in excess of one mile wide and fifty miles long. ⎯⎯⎯

8. Tornadoes come in all shapes and sizes and can occur anywhere in the United States at any time of the year. ⎯⎯⎯

9. In the southern states, peak tornado season is March through May. ⎯⎯⎯

10. For residents of the northern states, peak tornado months are during the summer. ⎯⎯⎯

Exercise 16.10   Changing Passive Voice to Active Voice and Vice Versa

*A. Change the following **active voice** sentences to **passive voice**.*

1. Bob preferred meat and potatoes.

   _____

2. He ate a big steak or hamburger almost every day.

   _____

3. He almost never ate green vegetables.

   _____

4. He liked potatoes in any form.

   _____

5. Apple pie contains the only fruit in his diet.

   _____

6. Bob usually skipped breakfast.

   _____

7. He consumed a hamburger and french fries at noon.

   _____

8. He had a steak or beef stew with a baked potato for dinner.

   _____

9. He ate cookies, doughnuts, and candy between meals.

   _____

10. Bob didn't really want other food on a regular basis.

   _____

B. *Change the following passive voice sentences to **active voice**. You may have to supply a subject.*

1. One day, fried calamari was eaten by Bob.

   _____

2. That it was not a potato puff was known immediately by Bob.

   _____

3. But the taste was not considered so bad.

   _____

4. Fried clams and oysters were tried a week later.

   _____

5. Steamed lobster might be eaten the next time in a restaurant.

   _____

6. Tempura vegetables were served to him at a party.

   _____

7. At first, the vegetables weren't going to be eaten by Bob.

   _____

8. Then they were found to be pretty good.

   _____

9. Cajun shrimp also was presented to him.

   _____

10. Seafood and vegetables are being made part of his diet.

   _____

Exercise 16.11   Writing with Passive Voice

*Write sentences using **passive voice** with the following subjects and verbs.*

1. (sandwich, eat) _____

2. (orange juice, drink) _____

3. (apple pie, devour) _____

4. (piece of cake, finish) _____

5. (box of cookies, share) _____

6. (dessert, take) _____

7. (coffee and tea, pour) _____

8. (banana, consume) _____

9. (junk food, buy) _____

10. (diet, start) _____

Summary

I. Inverted Sentences
   A. Definition: **Inverted sentences** are sentences with the subject and verb inverted.
   B. Types of inverted sentences
      1. **Information Questions** (called **WH Questions**)
         a. Invert the first helping verb and the subject.
            Example: *What must you be thinking now?*

    b. Use *do* forms for present and past tense, *will* for future tense.
       Examples: *Why **do** we want that bus?*
                *Where **will** she find us?*
    c. No inversion if a question word is the subject.
       Example: *Who is here?*
  2. **Yes-No Questions** (no question word)
       Example: *Should we leave tomorrow?*
  3. **Tag Questions**
    a. Use negative tag if statement is positive and vice versa.
       Examples: *You like it, **don't you?***
              *It's not right, **is it?***
    b. Use *be* forms, *can, could, would,* and *should* if the main sentence uses one of them.
       Examples: *He wasn't here, **was he?***
              *You can go, **can't you?***
              *We should tell him, **shouldn't we?***
    c. Use *do* forms for other verbs.
       Examples: *She swims, **doesn't she?***
              *They don't run, **do** they?*
C. Punctuation
  1. Use a question mark at the end of direct questions.
       Example: *Who are you?*
  2. Use a period at the end of indirect questions.
       Example: *I asked who he was.*
D. *Nor* and *as* constructions
  1. Invert the subject and verb in the *nor* part of the sentence.
       Example: *He's not here, nor is she.*
  2. Invert the subject and verb in the *as* part of the sentence.
       Example: *You like sunshine, as do I.*
F. Dependent clauses without *if*
       Example: *Had you left, you'd be sad. (If you had left)*

II. Passive Voice
A. Definition: **Passive voice** is a variation of the standard sentence and tells that something is being acted upon rather than performing the action.
B. Forming the passive voice
  1. The direct object in an active-voice sentence becomes the subject in a passive-voice sentence.
       Examples: *The child threw the **ball.** (active)*
              *The **ball** was thrown by the child. (passive)*
  2. An auxiliary verb form of *be* must be part of the complete verb.
       Example: *The party **was** given in my honor.*
  3. The doer of the action is expressed with *by* or left unexpressed.
       Examples: *The dog was walked **by** his **owner.***
              The dog was walked.
  4. Only transitive verbs (taking a direct object) can be used.
       Example: *Steve was **hit** by a baseball.*

Chapter 17

Parallel Structure

Underline examples of **parallel structure** in the following paragraph. Don't worry if you miss some.

In my next life, when I am an architect, I always will design houses with kitchens that open to the outdoors. I love stepping out to head and tail my beans while sitting on the stone wall. I set dirty pots out to soak, dry my dishcloths on the wall, empty excess clean water on the arugula, thyme, and rosemary right outside the door. Since the double door is open day and night in summer, the kitchen fills with light and air. A wasp—is it the same one?—flies in every day and drinks from the faucet, then flies right out. . . . The leisure of a summer place, the ease of prime ingredients, and the perfectly casual way of entertaining convince me that this is the kitchen as it's meant to be. (Frances Mayes, *Under the Tuscan Sun*)

A sentence does not have to be formed with ***parallel structure*** (also called ***parallelism***), but if a series of parts has similar functions, the parts should have similar forms. These parts may be words, phrases, or clauses.

Parallel Words

Most parallel structure in words concerns nouns and pronouns, verbs, adjectives, and adverbs. When you are setting up a sentence that has a series of items, make sure the items are the same part of speech:

The **sun,** the **heat,** and the **humidity** caused discomfort. (nouns)
Ahmed, Pei, Maria, and **I** like the sun. (nouns and pronoun)
Whether it **rains** or **shines,** we'll go. (verbs)
The weather is **hot, humid,** and **muggy.** (adjectives)
The sun shone **strongly** and **relentlessly.** (adverbs)

Notice that nouns and pronouns may be mixed, but other parts of speech should not be mixed.

Parallel Phrases

Phrases, such as prepositional phrases and all verbal phrases (adjective, infinitive, noun), as well as groups of words that go together should also have parallel structure:

> **On the beach** and **in the sun** are two deck chairs. (prepositional phrases)   NOT
> On the beach and sitting in the sun . . .

> I want **to get a tan** and **to look good.** (infinitive phrases)   NOT   *I want a tan and to look good.*

> Abby, **tanning well** and **liking the sun,** goes to the beach. (adjective verbal phrases)   NOT   *Abby, who tans well and liking the sun . . . ;*   NOT   *Abby, tanning well and who likes the sun . . .*

However, a combination of words and phrases may still be parallel if they have the same structure:

> The sun **tans, causes sunburn, quickens the onset of wrinkles, dries,** and **supplies Vitamin D.** (verbs—some intransitive, some transitive)

The number of words may vary in each part and still be parallel. See if each part of the parallel structure can be said separately with the main sentence. For example, in the example, *The sun tans, the sun causes sunburn . . .* , the issue is that the phrases function similarly in the sentence; in this case, they are all verbs or verb phrases.

Parallel Clauses

A compound sentence (two or more independent clauses) in itself has parallel structure already. Dependent clauses (adjective, noun, and adverb) in a series of two or more should also be parallel.

> She's a person **who loves the sun** and **who doesn't get sunburned.**   NOT
> *She loves the sun and who doesn't get sunburned.*

> I hate the rain **that made me wet** and **(that) ruined my plans.**   NOT   *I hate the rain that made me wet and my plans were ruined.*

> **When it's a nice day or if we feel like it,** we'll go.   NOT   *When it's a nice day or if feeling like it.*

> **Whatever food we have** and **wherever we go** is fine with me.   NOT   *Whatever food we have and anywhere is fine.*

The absence of parallel structure usually does not damage the sense of the sentence. However, parallel structure makes for clearer and smoother writing.

Exercise 17.1   Finding Parallel Structure

*Underline the **one set of parallel words, phrases, or clauses** in the following sentences.*

Example   The tropics have <u>relentless heat</u> and <u>extreme humidity</u>.

1. Mexico because of its geographical location is a North American country but because of its heritage is a Central and South American country.
2. Mexico may be divided roughly into three parts: the north along the border, the center dominated by Mexico City, and the south with its indigenous population.
3. The North Atlantic Free Trade Agreement (NAFTA) has caused the increase of heavy industry but the decrease of small industry.
4. With a two thousand mile border and with many small towns dotting that border, northern Mexico has some immigration problems.
5. Many large factories have established themselves permanently and successfully in this northern region.
6. Because of Mexico City, the center of Mexico has been enriched by people who flock to the city and impoverished by people who leave the rural areas.
7. Large heavy industry created many urban jobs, improved the economic level, but ruined many small factories (*maquiladoros*).
8. The southern part of Mexico is dominated by indigenous groups that clash with the central government and that rebel against inequities.
9. Differences among racial groups are religious, social, economic, regional, and linguistic.
10. The government is changing also, supporting various political parties, holding clean elections, ridding itself of corruption, and becoming more self-sufficient.

Exercise 17.2   Finding Parallel Structure

*Underline the **one** or **two sets of parallel words, phrases, or clauses** in each of the following paragraphs.*

1. Mexico City is both the largest and the highest city in Mexico. With a population of over eight million and at an altitude of 7,710 feet, Mexico City is a sprawling metropolis. Located in the middle of the country, it rests in the Valley of Mexico.

2. Originally the center of the Aztec empire, Mexico City was founded by a group of people coming from further north. Around 1325, they established themselves in the Valley of Mexico and grew to a population of a quarter million people.

3. Hernan Cortes arrived from Spain and conquered the city in 1521. He destroyed the Aztec city and built his own on top. Although the Spanish architecture used by Cortes was attractive, many Aztec artifacts were lost forever.

4. This valley is a highland basin, surrounded by three mountains. The city itself covers a vast and sprawling urban area, the largest in the world. The population expands to over fifteen million if it includes the metropolitan area around Mexico City.

5. Mexico City has a mixed population of people who have immigrated from all over the world. It is truly a city with a cosmopolitan feel and with many international attractions.

6. The city has an attractive mixture of narrow streets, wide boulevards, open plazas, and forested parks. Aztec architecture has been preserved in the central plaza as well as in the numerous parks. Tall, modern buildings dominate the skyline.

7. The climate in Mexico City is usually dry and temperate because of the high altitude and the mountain barriers. Unfortunately, the mountains also prevent the urban smog from dispersing, causing Mexico City to become dangerously polluted at certain seasons.

8. The rapid growth of the population and the soft earth underneath the city have contributed to other problems. The center of the city has been sinking so that costly major construction is needed. New and existing buildings must be strengthened.

9. The city's sinking causes water pipes and sewage lines to break. So water service is disrupted. Bringing in water from outside the Valley of Mexico has proven expensive and difficult. This problem continues to plague the city.

10. Mexico City has worked hard to overcome its problems. Sordid slums have been cleared, and proper housing has replaced them. Pollution from industries has been strictly regulated; emissions from cars have been controlled.

Exercise 17.3   Correcting Faults of Parallel Structure

*Arrange the words in parentheses so that the sentence is **parallel**. In some cases you should remove the parenthetical phrase altogether.*

Example   They are healthy and (with a lot of energy) __*energetic*__.

1. As a poet, Carl Sandburg is one of America's most famous and (he has popularity)

    _____.

2. He got his first job at the age of eleven and held a variety of jobs: barber-
   shop porter, (he drove a milk truck) _____, (to work
   in a brickyard) _____, (and he harvested wheat)

    _____.

3. He decided it was better to fight for his country than (sitting at home)
   _____ and so enlisted in the army during the Spanish-
   American War in 1898.

4. He moved to Chicago in 1913 and (was joining) _____
   the "Chicago Renaissance" movement, publishing his most famous poem,
   "Chicago," in 1914.

5. Sandburg's   collections   include   "Chicago   Poems,"   (he   wrote)
   _____ "Cornhuskers," "Smoke and Steel," and (writ-
   ing) _____ "Slabs of the Sunburnt West."

6. Sandburg's poems address America's industrialization and (how America was becoming urbanized) _____; they also celebrate the work-
   ing population as having drive and (with energy) _____.

7. He was a poet who championed the causes of the lower classes and (he tried to
   find poetry) _____ in the sometimes brutal arena of
   everyday life.

8. Sandburg wrote simply, (he was honest) _____, and
   (his poems are vivid) _____.

9. His   experiences   working   as   a   child   and   (his   army   enlistment)
   _____ can account for his recurring themes of war,
   immigrant life, death, love, loneliness and the beauty of nature.

10. He won the Pulitzer Prize in Poetry in 1951 for *Complete Poems* and (dying)
    _____ in 1967 in Flat Rock, North Carolina.

Exercise 17.4   Correcting Faults of Parallel Structure

*Rewrite each sentence to give it **parallel structure**.*

Example   They are healthy and with a lot of energy.

   They are healthy and energetic.

1. In Greek mythology, Persephone was the daughter of Demeter and who was extraordinarily beautiful.

2. Wherever she stepped and sleeping anywhere, flowers grew and birds sang.

3. Hades, the god of the underworld, fell in love with her utterly and complete, and decided to carry her off.

4. Demeter was distraught; she wanted her daughter back and to get revenge.

5. As she grieved, the earth grew barren, wilted flowers and trees losing their leaves.

6. In the underworld and being in the dark, Persephone was tempted by the fruit of the dead, which would tie her to Hades forever.

7. Zeus, seeing that the earth was suffering from Demeter's loss, ordered Hades to say goodbye and returning Persephone to her mother.

8. Demeter, overjoyed at her daughter's return, and who was content to have her back, let the earth blossom again.

9. Hades knew that Persephone had eaten a pomegranate and emitted a loud laugh which was hooting.

10. Persephone admitted to her mother that she had eaten the fruit and forcing her to return to the Underworld.

11. Zeus, powerful and who was mighty, declared that Persephone would spend one month underground for every seed consumed.

   _____

12. That's why in winter trees are losing their leaves, grass withers, and flowers will become dead.

   _____

   _____

Exercise 17.5   Correcting Faults of Parallel Structure

*Each sentence has **one error of parallel structure.** Rewrite each so it has parallel structure. Write another version if you want.*

Example   This computer is cheap and which does a lot.

   This computer is cheap and versatile.

   This is the computer that is cheap and that does a lot.

1. My best friend Maria lives next door and going to college.

   _____

   _____

2. She works hard and with determination, and very lucky.

   _____

   _____

3. She participated in the science fair, art club, and orphans.

   _____

   _____

4. She works part time in a fast food restaurant, running to club meetings, and her little brother needs babysitting.

   _____

   _____

5. She is an artist with great talent and who should go far.

   _____

   _____

6. Studying, working, babysitting, and my best friend takes up all her time.

   _____

   _____

7. One day, a customer who was in the restaurant and needing help walking home, asked Maria to go with him.

_____

_____

8. Maria had to take time off work and which would make her lose money, but she walked him home.

_____

_____

9. When she applied to college, he helped by writing a letter of recommendation and which got her in.

_____

_____

10. Of course, good grades, talented, a kind person, and working hard also helped her get in.

_____

_____

Exercise 17.6   Writing with Parallel Structure

*A. Use a variety of words, phrases, or clauses to complete sentences with **parallel structure**. Change* and *to* but *or* or, *if you want.*

Example   He is tall, ____dark_____, and ____handsome_____.

1. High school students usually feel _____, _____, and _____.

2. Before entering college, they should _____ and

_____.

3. They need time to _____ and _____.

4. _____ and _____ they should do something else.

5. They could _____, _____, and

_____.

6. If they work _____ and _____, they will want to

go to college.

7. If they travel, they _____ and _____.

8. If they loaf _____ and _____, they will really

   welcome something to do.

9. College demands _____, _____, and

   _____.

10. A breather from school will _____ and _____.

*B. Use a variety of words, phrases, or clauses to complete sentences with **parallel
structure**. Change* and *to* but *or* or, *if you want.*

1. Playing soccer _____ and _____.

2. It requires _____, _____, and

   _____.

3. _____, _____, and _____ have

   soccer teams.

4. Many countries _____ and _____ worship their

   soccer teams.

5. The United States has a soccer team that _____ and

   _____.

6. Soccer is probably the _____ and _____.

7. Many children have started playing soccer for _____ and

   _____.

8. "Soccer moms" typically _____ and _____.

9. Soccer camps teach children _____ and _____.

10. _____ and _____ requires hours of practice.

Exercise 17.7   Proofreading

*Find and correct the **five errors of parallel structure** in the following paragraph.*

   Edgar Degas, the French Impressionist painter and wanting to visit a different

place, stayed in New Orleans for five months from October 1872 to March 1873. He

decided to stay with his eighteen relatives and who had a large house on Esplanade

Avenue, east of the French Quarter. He could not stand the bright light, so he did no paintings outdoors. Degas painted many relatives who seemed somewhat impatient and with sad expressions. Degas himself must not have been easy to live with. He never married, had no immediate family, and liking solitude. Nevertheless, he was the only famous French Impressionist to visit the United States. And he used his time profitably and with diligence.

Summary

I. Parallel Structure
   A. Definition: **Parallel structure** means that parts of a sentence that have similar functions must have similar grammatical structure.
   B. Types of parallel structures
      1. Parallel words
         a. Nouns and pronouns in a series should be parallel.
            Example: ***Bill, Alice,** and **you** are going.*
         b. Verbs in a series should be parallel.
            Example: *She **slept** and **ate.***
         c. Adjectives in a series should be parallel.
            Example: *The day was **sunny, bright,** and **hot.***
         d. Adverbs in a series should be parallel.
            Example: *He ate **fast, noisily,** and **sloppily.***
      2. Parallel phrases
         a. Prepositional phrases in a series should be parallel.
            Example: *Go **into the house** and **through the room.***
         b. Verbal phrases (adjective, infinitive, noun) should be parallel.
            Examples: ***Feeling good** and **wanting sunshine,** she stayed on the beach.* (adjective)
            *They want **to have fun** and **to win money.** (infinitive)*
            ***Whomever you want** and **whenever you can** is all right with me.* (noun)
      3. Parallel clauses
         a. Compound sentences are naturally parallel.
            Example: ***We camped,** but **they went home.***
         b. Dependent clauses (adjective, noun, adverb) should be parallel.
            Examples: *A cat **that catches mice** and **that eats flies** is helpful.* (adjective)
            ***Whoever arrives** and **whatever we do** is up to you.* (noun)
            ***Since you returned** and **because I have time,** let's go out.* (adverb)

Chapter 18

Faulty Predication

Underline the one sentence that is an example of **faulty predication** in each of the following short paragraphs. Don't worry if you miss some of them.

1. I have great plans for the future. I will be married with children and a pharmacist. We'll live in a nice house in the suburbs, and both my husband and I will work in the city.

2. Happiness is when I am at home playing with my children while my husband barbecues in the back yard. We'll take a swim in our in-ground pool and then sit down for a picnic.

3. My ambitions reveal my personality. I feel a high achievement as well as a dreamer. I want what a lot of people want perhaps, but I won't have to work very hard for it.

4. The reason why I am ambitious is because my parents raised me to aim high. They said I could have anything I really wanted. So I want this life, and I will get it.

The predicate of any sentence is the part that completes the subject. **Faulty predication** means that the subject and the rest of the sentence do not fit together either logically or grammatically.

Matching Subject and Verb

Sometimes the subject of the sentence cannot have the verb it is given:

My **brain angered** at the idea of poverty. (*Brain* cannot anger)

The **reason** for his failure **showed** his incompetence. (*Reason* cannot "show" something. *Failure* is a better subject here.)

Rewriting these sentences with a subject and verb that match should solve the problem:

I **am angered by** (or "get angry at") the idea of poverty.

His failure **showed** [or *demonstrated*] his incompetence.

Sometimes the verb is suitable for part of the predicate but not the rest of it:

> I will buy a big car and two children. (You cannot buy children. Change to: *I will buy a big car and have two children.*)

Faulty predication particularly affects **linking verbs** (*appear, be, continue, feel, get, grow, look, mean, seem, smell, taste, turn*) since the subjective complement renames or describes the subject. For example, the famous saying *Happiness is a warm puppy*, although expressing a nice sentiment, tries to equate *happiness* with a *warm puppy*. But that is not a logical equation. A warm puppy might *bring* happiness, happiness might *be caused* in part by having a warm puppy, but *happiness* cannot *be* a warm puppy. One does not rename or describe the other. The following sentences also have a subject and linking verb that cannot be followed logically by the given subjective complement:

> My **definition** of happiness **is ambition.** (*Definition* cannot be *ambition.*)
>
> **Success** looks **tall, dark,** and **handsome.** (*Success* cannot look like something.)
>
> My **meaning** of happiness **feels wonderful.** (*Meaning* cannot *feel. Happiness* is the intended subject.)

Using is how, is what, is when, is where, is who, is why

Using these expressions creates faulty predication because they equate one idea with something that it cannot be equated with:

> Hard work is when you feel satisfied. (*Hard work makes me feel satisfied.*)
>
> Ambition is how I succeeded. (*I succeeded through ambition.*)
>
> Achievement is what he put into the job. (*He made great achievements in his job.*)
>
> Happiness is where I want to be. (*I want to be happy.*)

There are some correct uses for these words:

> Three o'clock **is when** you will arrive.
>
> Seattle **is where** you will be.
>
> A suit **is what** you will wear.

These sentences actually tell when (time), where (location), and what (thing). But such uses tend to be wordy and awkward. You can usually say the same thing in a more direct way:

> You **will arrive** at three o'clock.
>
> You **will be** in Seattle.
>
> You **will wear** a suit.

Using the reason why . . . is because . . .

A very common form of faulty predication is seen in the sentence *The reason (why) . . . is because. . . .* Here *reason*, the subject, cannot be equated with *because. . . .* Sentences constructed in this way are also wordy and awkward. Such sentences can easily be improved:

WORDY AND AWKWARD: The reason why he was fired is because he was late.

IMPROVED: He was fired because he was late.

WORDY AND AWKWARD: The reason I am ambitious is because my parents were.

IMPROVED: I am ambitious because my parents were.

Making Faulty Comparisons

Another type of faulty predication occurs with comparisons in which one thing cannot be compared with something else because of illogic or incongruity:

My idea of wealth is greater than Bill Gates. (Can an idea be greater than a person? Change to: *My idea of wealth is greater than Bill Gates's [idea of wealth]*. But probably the writer meant, *My idea of wealth is having more money than Bill Gates does.*)

Success is better than a warm puppy. (An abstract concept cannot be compared to an object. Does the writer mean success is better than love?)

Exercise 18.1   Recognizing Faulty Predication

*Decide which kind of **faulty predication** is contained in each of the following sentences and label it as follows:*

1   *subject and nonlinking verb*
2   *linking verb*
3   is how, is what, is when, is where, is who, is why
4   the reason (why) . . . is because . . .
5   *comparison*

Example   Success is a Rolls-Royce. __2__

1. The reason why many people want to exercise is because they want to be in good shape. _____

2. Summertime is where they start going outdoors. _____

3. Exercising in the sun means higher temperatures. _____

4. The heat might drain a person's energy more than feeling like a workout. _____

5. Making some adjustments to a workout schedule is better than never mind. _____

6. Air conditioning is why you can exercise at home or in a gym. _____

7. Drinking a lot of water or other liquid stays hydrated. _____

8. The reason is because the sun makes you perspire more. _____

9. Loose clothing means perspiration dries more quickly. _____

10. Wearing a hat is where you will protect your head. _____

Exercise 18.2   Recognizing and Labeling Faulty Predication

*Decide which kind of **faulty predication** is contained in each of the following sentences and label it as follows:*

  1 *subject and nonlinking verb*
  2 *linking verb*
  3 *is how, is what, is when, is where, is who, is why*
  4 *the reason (why) . . . is because . . .*
  5 *comparison*

Example   Love is never saying I'm sorry. __2__

1. When it was first invented, rock and roll said the feelings of teenagers. _____

2. This kind of music is when entertainers married rhythm and blues, country, and popular tunes. _____

3. The reason why rock and roll is so popular is because it's easily accessible and fun to dance to. _____

4. Music is when people want to express themselves and search for appropriate outlets. _____

5. My opinion of music likes it better than the other arts. _____

6. My feet get happy just thinking about it. _____

7. Listening to music is where I want to be. _____

8. The reason I love rock and roll is because everyone can enjoy it. _____

9. Talent is playing musical instruments well. _____

10. Rock and roll is how music is. _____

Exercise 18.3   Finding Faulty Predication

Underline the **one sentence that has faulty predication** *in the following paragraphs:*

1. James Baldwin is who many think of as a great writer. He lived from 1924 to 1987 and wrote many novels, essays, and plays. He was very successful despite many hardships and difficulties.

2. He was born in Harlem, a section of New York City. His mother was poor and unmarried, so Baldwin's first stigma was being illegitimate. Racial discrimination also felt bad.

3. He took the name of his stepfather, although he and his stepfather did not get along with each other. His stepfather's feelings of bitterness and frustration were greater than Baldwin.

4. Although young James aspired to the influence of Countee Cullen, a black poet, he became a minister. Since his stepfather was a minister, James must have had positive feelings about him.

5. The ministry was where Baldwin acquired some ability with language. But after only three years of preaching at a church, he moved to a more artistic life in Greenwich Village.

6. Baldwin and a friend began a literary magazine called *This Generation*. His concept for a novel was first written as a short story. Baldwin received a fellowship to complete it.

7. At this time Baldwin moved to France. The reason why he moved was because he wanted the freedom of living in Paris and also of acknowledging his homosexuality.

8. His novel *Go Tell It on the Mountain* was published in 1953. His next novel *Giovanni's Room* pursued the first one. Both novels were quite successful and made Baldwin's name.

9. Although he returned for visits to the United States, Europe was what he preferred. He felt that Europeans accepted him as black and gay without difficulties.

10. Baldwin is perhaps best known for his collections of essays: *Notes of a Native Son, Nobody Knows My Name,* and *The Fire Next Time.* These works are why he is still remembered.

Exercise 18.4   Correcting Faulty Predication

*Each of these sentences has **faulty predication.** Rewrite it correctly. If more than one possibility exists, write another one. Consider what the writer probably wanted to say.*

Example   Success is a big house.

> One sign of success is having a big house.

> Owning a big house is a sign of success.

1. On a daily basis, the average American eats less than half of his or her vegetables.

2. Buying more vegetables to keep at home is how you can help.

3. Clean and cut them up, so they seem prepared to eat.

4. Broccoli florets, carrot sticks, and sliced peppers could be where to start.

5. Hummus and eggplant relish are better than dipping in butter and mayonnaise.

6. In the morning, drinking vegetable juice is where you will get a good start.

7. For lunch, lots of greens in a sandwich means health.

8. Adding a salad to lunch continues your health.

9. Vegetable juice for lunch is better than choosing soda or coffee.

   _____

   _____

10. If you don't want vegetable juice, lunchtime is where you might drink green or black tea.

    _____

    _____

11. The reason why tea is good for you is because it is made from tea leaves, a vegetable.

    _____

    _____

12. A few cups of tea a day mean antioxidants that reduce heart disease and some cancers.

    _____

    _____

13. Unfortunately, herbal teas are not when you get these same antioxidants.

    _____

    _____

14. Chinese food can be more healthful and vegetables.

    _____

    _____

15. Order meat mixed with vegetables seems like a good idea.

    _____

    _____

16. The reason why this is a good idea is because you'll get a smaller quantity of meat and more vegetables.

    _____

    _____

17. The dish will taste full of good minerals and vitamins.

    _____

    _____

18. Bake bread containing vegetables rather than store bought.

    _____

    _____

19. Carrot, pumpkin, or zucchini cake or bread is why you can combine health and good food.

    _____

    _____

20. More vegetables in the American diet is better than living in poor health.

    _____

    _____

Exercise 18.5   Finding and Correcting Faulty Predication

*Underline the **one sentence that has faulty predication** and then rewrite it correctly.*

1. The Long Island Rail Road travels the length of Long Island and Pennsylvania Station in Manhattan. It connects Nassau and Suffolk counties with Manhattan, Brooklyn, and Queens. It is vital to commuters both going to or from Manhattan.

    _____

2. This commuter railroad is the largest in the country. The reason it is so big is because it has about 80 million customers a year. Every day the LIRR operates more than 700 trains.

    _____

3. The railroad has over 700 miles of track. These are divided among eleven lines that branch out of Pennsylvania Station in Manhattan. The lines roughly parallel each other and go to the eastern end of Long Island.

    _____

4. The eleven lines have 124 stations with almost as many parking lots. The whole system also includes hundreds of rail bridges and pedestrian crossings. The complex system is why it must operate smoothly.

    _____

5. The large number of commuters is the purpose of the Long Island Rail Road. The vast majority of them live somewhere on Long Island in Nassau or Suffolk counties and commute to jobs in Manhattan. Some also go to Brooklyn or Queens.

    _____

6. In the morning until about 10:00, the trains from Long Island to Manhattan are called "peak trains." Passengers going that way must pay more for a ticket and crowded into the trains. Going the other way is not considered "peak."

_____

7. In the afternoon from about 4:00 to 7:00, the trains from Manhattan to Long Island are also called "peak." Once again, the passengers, most of them the same as in the morning, pay extra. The best customers is why they should get a discount.

_____

8. If passengers commute five days a week and peak trains both ways, they can buy a monthly pass. This pass is much cheaper than single tickets for a month. For less frequent travelers, a "ten-trip" lasts a year and costs less.

_____

9. These commuters also pay to park in the parking lot connected to the station. Some of them get rides to the station or car pooling to save money. These parking lots are almost always full, so they are rarely useful for the noncommuter.

_____

10. The Long Island Rail Road has added new trains, built more overpasses, and renovated stations. They have installed automated ticket machines now for off hours and still human ticket sellers. The trains are cleaner also.

_____

Exercise 18.6   Finding and Correcting Faulty Predication

*Underline the **one sentence in each paragraph that has faulty predication**. Then rewrite it correctly.*

1. Most people know that the definition of the word *boycott* is to abstain from using, buying, or dealing with something or someone, as a means of protest. But few know the word's origin. Though the word comes from Captain Charles Cunningham Boycott, his importance in history is less than the great Irish nationalist Charles Parnell. Captain Boycott would have died in obscurity had he not been the first victim of Parnell's political tactics in the battle for Irish independence.

_____

_____

2. Captain Boycott returned from years at sea in the late 1870s to an Ireland that was depressed and poverty stricken. Unfair and absentee landlords governed hungry and oppressed peasants. Though the Land Act of 1870 guaranteed the rights of tenants to purchase the land they farmed, most were too poor to do so. A feeling of unfairness is why the people started a nationalistic movement.

   _____

   _____

3. There did appear to be hope. At that time Charles Parnell was a member of Parliament and president of the Irish National Land League. In 1880, he made a successful voyage to America traveling down the east coast from Boston to Baltimore. He returned carrying 70,000 pounds in Irish-American donations for the cause. Winning Americans over with his persuasive speeches is how Parnell became the darling of the Irish-American population.

   _____

   _____

4. Parnell had decided on a new tactic: ostracism. Under this new policy, a tenant could be ostracized for buying land from which another tenant had been evicted. The reason why a landlord could be ostracized was because he failed to accept a reduced rent which the tenants fixed themselves. The implementation appeared severe and unyielding.

   _____

   _____

5. In his new job as the executor of Lord Erne's estate, Captain Boycott refused the drastically reduced rent the tenants suggested. This refusal was a nightmare. A band of hostile peasants approached the captain's house and forced his servants to leave. There were no laborers to gather the harvest and no stablemen. There was no cook to prepare the evening meal, and no one to serve it.

   _____

   _____

6. Boycott was not allowed to enter stores or purchases. The blacksmith refused to shoe his horse. The laundress refused to wash his clothes; even the postman refused to deliver his letters. This trouble was the extent of the organized tenants' power.

   _____

   _____

7. In the end, it took fifty imported workers guarded by British soldiers to harvest Lord Erne's crops. The government's intervention was how the tenants' campaign was successful. The tenants protested on the shores of Lough Mask. They put increasing pressure on the landlords. Captain Boycott and his wife were sheltered by friends, then forced to hide in a barn. They eventually escaped Ireland.

_____

_____

8. Parnell's "boycott" worked; his goals achieved a larger scale. In 1881, an act was passed guaranteeing tenants fair rent, fixity of tenure, and freedom of sale. This Irish farmer's "Magna Carta" is what the results were. This was another step closer to the freedom of Home Rule.

_____

_____

9. It is to the Irish people's credit that they bore no ill will against Captain Boycott. Nor was his animosity of longer duration than the people. On a visit to Ireland years later, he was recognized at a public gathering in Dublin. The people's cheers greeted him thunderously, illuminating their forgiveness. They chalked up his behavior to his army-trained sense of duty and bore him no grudge.

_____

_____

10. What lessons can we take from this story? Togetherness can achieve change, and one individual makes a difference. And don't forget that language is continuously evolving. We add words from unlikely sources.

_____

_____

Exercise 18.7   Proofreading

*Underline the **three errors of faulty predication** in the following paragraph.*

Basically there are three kinds of curving staircases. One kind has a few steps up and then a small landing with steps continuing either to the right or left. This is called a *boxed* staircase. These take up space but safest. Next is the *circular* staircase. This is when the steps are of equal width and length and attached to the wall. Circular staircases are safe but expensive and take up room. The last is the *spiral* staircase, which has steps attached to a center pole. The steps vary in width from narrow to normal. This kind is not very safe. The reason why they are popular is because they are the cheapest and take up very little space. The best curved staircases would combine the best features of each kind.

Summary

I. Faulty Predication
  A. Definition: **Faulty predication** occurs when the subject of the sentence does not go with the predicate (the rest of the sentence).
  B. Types of faulty predication
    1. Subject and verb incompatibility
      a. A verb is incorrectly used with the subject.
        Example: *The idea for the trip was canceled.*
        CORRECT: *The trip was canceled.*
      b. A verb that goes with one part is incorrectly used with another part of the sentence.
        Example: *I will marry a rich man and children.*
        CORRECT: *I will marry a rich man and have children.*
      c. A linking verb is incorrectly used with a subjective complement that does not rename or describe the subject.
        Example: *California is a great life.*
        CORRECT: *You can have a great life in California.*   OR   *Living in California is great.*   OR   *California is a great place to live.*
  C. *is how, is what, is when, is where, is who, is why*
    1. The subject cannot be equated with this kind of phrase or clause.
        Example: *Love is how you feel.*
        CORRECT: *Love is a particular feeling.*   OR   *I feel I'm in love.*
    2. These phrases can be used when the subject deals with the word itself (time for **when,** person for **who,** etc.), but the resulting sentence is wordy and awkward and should be avoided.
        Example: *A student is who you are.* (BETTER: *You are a student.*)
  D. *The* reason (why) . . . is because . . . construction
    1. **Reason** cannot be equated with a **because** phrase or clause.
        Example: *The reason why I left is because I was busy.*
        CORRECT: *I left because I was busy.*
    2. The sentence becomes awkward and wordy.
  E. Faulty comparisons
    1. Ideas and concepts cannot be compared with unlike things or people.
        Example: *Failure is better than no money.*
        CORRECT: *Being a failure is better than having no money.*
    2. The sentence becomes illogical.

Chapter 19

Subject-Verb Agreement

Indicate **subject-verb agreement** by drawing an arrow from the subjects to the verbs that go with them in the following paragraphs. Underline any two-word verbs.

In most sports, such as baseball, football, and basketball, play is stopped when substitutions are made. But ice hockey allows unlimited substitution while the game is in progress, one of the features that make hockey such a fast-paced game.

It is the goalie's job to be a dispatcher, announcing to his teammates when traffic patterns are changing on the ice. For example, a minor penalty involves the offender serving two minutes in the penalty box. Some goalies bang the ice to signal to teammates that they are now at even strength. (David Feldman, *How Does Aspirin Find a Headache?*)

Subject-verb agreement is the grammatical concept that the subject of a sentence must have a verb that matches it in number (singular or plural); that is, a singular subject takes a singular verb form, and a plural subject takes a plural verb form:

singular	*singular*	
I	**like**	seeing movies.

plural	*plural*	
People	**enjoy**	going to the movies.

singular	*singular*	
Everyone	**enjoys**	the movies.

For almost all verbs in English, the singular form occurs only in the present tense; -*s* or -*es* is added to a present-tense verb when its subject is a singular noun or a third person singular pronoun (*he, she, it, one, something, everybody,* etc.):

singular noun	*singular verb*	
Juan	**goes**	to the movies.

singular pronoun	*singular verb*	
He	**wants**	me to go, too.

singular pronoun		*singular verb*	
Nothing	good	**plays**	there.

Two verbs—*be* and *have*—are exceptions to this rule. *Have* changes to *has,* and *be* changes to *is:*

singular noun	*singular verb*	
Juan	**is**	a movie buff.
singular pronoun	*singular verb*	
He	**has**	a collection of videos.
singular pronoun	*singular verb*	
Everything	**has**	a place.

Be is the only verb that has a singular form in the past tense. We use *was* with *I,* with singular nouns, and with third person singular pronouns:

singular pronoun		*singular verb*	
I		**was**	interested in the movie.
singular pronoun		*singular verb*	
Juan		**was**	also interested.
singular pronoun		*singular verb*	
Who	else	**was**	interested?

Otherwise, we use *were:*

The movies were all good.

The idea of subject-verb agreement is simple, but many problems make it more complicated in practice.

Multiple Subjects

When more than one subject (also called a **compound subject**) occurs in a sentence, agreement depends on whether the subjects are joined by *and* or by *or-nor.* If they are joined by *and,* usually a plural verb is necessary:

Juan and I go to the movies often.

The seats and the aisle are wide.

Dick, Paula, and Brian love the movies.

However, if the compound subject forms a single unit that would not have the right meaning if its parts were separated, use a singular verb form:

Popcorn and butter is my favorite snack at the movies. (You would not have butter by itself.)

Peanut butter and jelly is messy at the movies. (You would eat these together as one unit.)

If the subjects are considered separate units, often modified by *each* or *every*, they take a singular verb form.

Each aisle and every seat is covered with popcorn.

Every man, woman, and child goes to the movies.

When the multiple subject is linked by *or* and *nor*, each subject is considered separate from the others. So the verb agrees in number with the nearest subject:

singular
Dick, Paula, or **Brian** wants to go to the movies.

plural
Dick, Paula, or the **boys** want to go to the movies.

singular
Neither Dick nor **Paula** is going to the movies.

plural
Neither Dick nor the **boys** are going.

singular
Neither the boys nor **Dick** is going.

Collective Nouns

Collective nouns refer to a number of people or things taken as a unit. Some common ones are *audience, band, club, committee, couple, family, group, union*. American English speakers usually treat these words as singular and use a singular verb form:

The movie committee is voting on a film.

The club wants to find a good movie.

When each member of the group is acting separately or individually, the words are plural and take a plural verb form:

The committee are casting their votes.

The band take home their instruments.

But usually American English speakers prefer to change the sentence to, for example, *committee members*, to indicate plural rather than use the plural verb form.

Singular and Plural Pronoun Subjects

Because pronouns replace nouns, many of them can take either a singular or a plural verb depending on the pronoun reference (what the pronoun is referring to). These pronouns include *all, most, number, rest,* and *some.*

plural
All of the foreign films **are** French.

singular
All of the movie **is** dubbed.

singular
The number of films **has** doubled.

plural
A number of films **are** dubbed.

plural
Most of the films **are** interesting.

singular
Most of the film **is** interesting.

Plural-Looking Nouns

Some nouns have a plural form and are treated as plural even though they refer to single items: *clippers, eyeglasses, jeans, pants, scissors, shears, shorts, thanks, tweezers.* Use plural verbs with them:

My glasses are too dark for the movie.

Your thanks are enough reward for me.

Another group is nouns that look plural (because of the *s* at the end) but are treated as singular: *aesthetics, economics, mathematics, measles, mumps, news, physics:*

The news about the movie is good.

Mathematics is not often a movie subject.

Plural nouns indicating a unit of measure (distance, money, time, etc.) are considered a singular unit and need a singular verb form:

Three hours is too long for a movie.

Ten dollars is too much to pay for a movie.

Fifty miles is too far to go for a movie.

Titles and names of companies, even when they look plural, are treated as singular:

Sense and Sensibility is a good movie.

Trident Films makes many of the movies I've seen.

Allyn & Bacon is a publisher, not a movie company.

Intervening Phrases and Clauses

Phrases and clauses that come between the subject and its verb must not be considered part of the subject:

Dick, along with the boys, is going to the movies.

The price of tickets for adults and children was the same.

All of the tickets for the entire committee were free.

Paula, who already saw the film, is not going.

The film that won two Oscars is really good.

Reverse Order of Subject and Verb

For any kind of reverse order sentence, question, and *there is* sentence, subject-verb agreement is still necessary. Locating the subject and verb is the only problem:

               verb subject   verb

At the movies are people eating popcorn.

              verb subject verb

Which movie are you going to see?

    verb   *subject*

There are two movie theaters to choose from.

               verb   *subject*

The street on which are two theaters is not far.

Singular and Plural Relative Pronouns

Relative pronouns used as subjects of adjective clauses take verbs that agree with pronouns' antecedents:

  singular   *singular*

A movie that plays there can't be good.

plural   plural
The   movies that play   there are good.

singular   singular
This   seat, which is   nice, is the last one.

plural   plural
These   seats, which are   in front, are bad.

singular   singular
Brian,   who rarely sees   movies, is going.

plural   plural
The   boys, who rarely see   movies, are going.

singular singular
   I, who am   rarely free, went to a movie. (Notice that *am* goes with *I.*)

plural   plural
Paula is one of those   people who enjoy   movies.

plural   plural
The Ritz is one of those   theaters that charge   ten dollars.

Some people use a singular verb form in the *one of those . . . who (that, which)* construction, but saying just the last part of the sentence, *of those theaters that charge ten dollars,* by itself sounds right. However, some will argue that *one* is the subject that *that* replaces and thus is singular. This becomes true when *the only one* is used:

singular   singular
The Ritz is **the only one** of those theaters **that charges** ten dollars.

Exercise 19.1   Recognizing Subject-Verb Agreement

*A. In the following sentences, indicate **subject-verb agreement** by drawing an arrow from the subject to its verb. Some sentences have more than one set of subjects and verbs.*

Example   My book on entomology is interesting.

1. People in hot places have always wanted to cool down.
2. To sit in the shade with a fan is one old method.
3. Water, especially running water, also helps to bring down the temperature.
4. Bathing in a cool stream brings down the body's temperature.

5. In ancient Rome, wealthy property owners built a room especially for the hot season.
6. It has marble walls with water running steadily down them.
7. With a servant waving a large fan, a person was ten degrees cooler in this room.
8. Blocks of ice were also transported from nearby mountains.
9. Ice transport, however, requires many servants, horses, and vehicles.
10. Economics was a factor; only the leisure classes could keep cool.

*B. In the following sentences, indicate **subject-verb agreement** by drawing an arrow from the subject to its verb. All the sentences have more than one set of subjects and verbs.*

1. In the modern world, houses are kept cool by trees and grass, so a house is shaded and surrounded by heat absorbers.
2. An attic keeps hot air moving away, especially if an electric fan blows outward.
3. Thick walls insulate a building since they keep the outside air from coming in.
4. Overhanging eaves prevent direct sunlight from entering the windows, and big porches do the same.
5. Windows on different sides of a house are left open; this allows breezes to circulate through the rooms.
6. Some people prefer to cover windows, which, they say, keeps out the hot air of the day.
7. They point to the basement, which is usually the coolest spot in a house.
8. But the basement, which has few if any windows, is insulated by being underground.
9. Heat also rises, so the attic is often the hottest place even when the windows are shaded.
10. The top floor in a building is typically the hottest in both summer and winter, demonstrating that heat goes up.

Exercise 19.2   Correcting Subject-Verb Agreement Errors

*Correct the **one subject-verb agreement error** in each sentence by crossing out the error and replacing it with a correct verb.*

are
Example   The books on the shelf ~~is~~ mine.

1. Space-age inventions, used for insulation, has helped.

2. For example, Mylar is one of those inventions that has insulating abilities.

3. Typically, runners after a race wears Mylar to keep from cooling down too fast.

4. Two hours with a Mylar cape are enough to help muscles adjust.

5. Mylar window shades that work like conventional ones is used to keep out the sun.

6. Air that moves around are almost always cooler than still air.

7. Ceiling fans often seen in a tropical setting is good for circulating air.

8. Small, handheld, battery-operated fans, although not very efficient, keeps a steady stream of air around the face.

9. There is romantic ideas connected with bamboo or cloth fans fluttering in a Southern lady's hand.

10. The energy necessary to wave the fan generate body heat.

Exercise 19.3   Correcting Subject-Verb Agreement Errors

Correct the **one subject-verb agreement error** *in each sentence by crossing out the error and replacing it with a correct verb.*

1. In my third grade class, every student are seated before the bell rings.

2. After it sounds, they stand up and greets me politely.

3. This week, Rebecca, Ayla, and John is the board monitors.

4. That means they are in charge of making sure that each of the erasers are clean and free of chalk.

5. The class vote on who will take attendance.

6. They keep their school supplies in their desks, but scissors is off limits.

7. All of the students has learned to respect their neighbors.

8. Mathematics seem to be the subject students have the most trouble with.

9. One girl, Julie, along with the boys, always like to write stories about dinosaurs.

10. Arissa, the one with the ponytail, are the class clown and tries to be funny in her papers.

11. The rest of the girls, who tend to be slightly tomboyish, writes adventure stories.

12. Caleb is the only one of the children who write stories based on current events.

13. His mother and brothers says he reads the paper while eating his cereal in the morning.

14. I think he, of all my students, are the smartest.

15. Of all the classes I've taught, this class are my favorite.

Exercise 19.4   Correcting Subject-Verb Agreement Errors

*Each paragraph has **one error of subject-verb agreement**. Correct it by crossing out the error and replacing it.*

Example   Entomology ~~are~~ is the study of insects.

1. Now our houses don't need porches, eaves, attics, and basements. What have revolutionized many aspects of our society is air conditioning. We can easily stay cool.

2. The first residential air conditioner appeared in 1929. It was huge and heavy, but two-hundred pounds were not too much for hot people even if only the rich could afford one.

3. House decorators were not pleased with the refrigerator-size air conditioners in the living room. But newer houses, along with the apartment building, was revolutionized also.

4. Thin walls and huge windows replaced the insulating walls and small windows. The physics of cooling from the inside were changing how we live and breathe.

5. The craze for summer movies also owe a debt to air conditioning. Formerly, movie houses closed in the sweltering summer months. The heat was just too much to bear.

6. Hot states, such as California, Nevada, and Arizona, is indebted to the air conditioner. Why would anyone choose to be among those who swelter in the desert heat?

7. Florida, too, has become a vacationland even in the summer. Disney World have to run a business year round, counting on these summer vacationers in addition to all the others.

8. Even governments over the summer is more efficient. The legislators have not escaped to the countryside as in former days, leaving bills unpassed and politicking undone.

9. Now 73 percent of American homes has air conditioning, although many people profess to hate it. Air conditioning gives them sore throats, the sniffles, and chills, but they can't do without it.

10. There's now many reasons to air condition. The inexpensive units are small and built-in. What we fear now are brownouts, when too many people use air conditioners at the same time.

Exercise 19.5   Correcting Subject-Verb Agreement Errors

*Each paragraph has **one or more errors of subject-verb agreement.** Correct the verbs by crossing them out and replacing them.*

Example   The dog, as well as the cats, ~~are~~ is hungry.

1. In America, Mother's Day is celebrated on the second Sunday in May. Most Americans give their mothers gifts and cards, a special meal, or help with family chores. But most of us has never stopped to wonder how the holiday originated. Some say the beginnings may be found in the ancient spring festival known as Hilaria, dedicated to the mother goddess Cybele.

2. In medieval England there was a day known as Mothering Sunday. Every fourth Sunday of Lent, children, most of whom were living away from home as apprentices, was sent home to see their mothers. Usually they brought a gift with them. Traditionally, food was the most popular gift, either a "simnel" or a "mothering cake"—a fruitcake with almond paste. All of the cakes was to be eaten on Mid-Lent Sunday.

3. In America, the evolution of Mother's Day began with a series of false starts. In 1890, Miss Mary T. Sasseen of Kentucky suggested to a gathering of teachers that they pays an annual homage to mothers each year on April 20, which happened to be the birthday of her own mother. Nothing came of the suggestion. Then in 1892 Robert K. Cummings, head of the Universalist Church Sunday

School in Baltimore, Maryland, proposed an annual memorial service. It would take place on May 22, which were the date when Emily C. Pullman, mother of the church's pastor, had passed away.

4. This effort was repeated throughout many years, but the idea never really caught on and were eventually discarded. In 1902, Fred E. Hering of Indiana, a member of the Fraternal Order of the Eagles, made another attempt to support a national observance dedicated to mothers. No one seconded his motion. Neither laymen nor clergy was able to gain support. It looked as though a national holiday in recognition of mothers would never come to pass.

5. Finally, however, one person championed the successful crusade for a national holiday. Anna M. Jarvis was unmarried and childless when she decided to create Mother's Day. A seminary graduate, Miss Jarvis had devoted her life to caring for her mother to the exclusion of her own marriage and happiness. Though she taught Sunday School devotedly for two decades, her true devotion and attention was to her mother.

6. Miss Jarvis's mother finally passed away in Philadelphia on May 9, 1905. Needless to say, Miss Jarvis and her sisters was inconsolable. For three years, she grieved the loss and was angered by the thoughtlessness and neglect with which most children treats their mothers. She conceived the idea of an international "Mother's Day" in which all children pays homage to mothers.

7. Her first step was to instigate simultaneous Mother's Day services in Grafton, West Virginia, and Philadelphia. Miss Jarvis invited mourners to the services primarily to honor her own mother. It was her suggestion that the congregation wears white carnations, her mother's favorite flower. Following these memorials, Miss Jarvis began a widespread letter-writing campaign, showering businessmen, congressmen, governors, religious leaders, and journalists with requests to set aside a special holiday for mothers.

8. Gradually she wore down public resistance. By 1910, many governments, including Oklahoma, West Virginia, and Washington was proclaiming official Mother's Day holidays. Within another year, continuing pressure forced every other state in the union to do the same. Encouraged by her success, Miss Jarvis founded the Mother's Day International Association.

9. By 1914, Miss Jarvis's dream had become a reality. Both houses of the U.S. Congress recommended that the president declare a national holiday. On May 8, 1914, President Woodrow Wilson issued a proclamation directing that officials displays the U.S. flag on all government buildings. He encouraged people at home to do the same "as a public expression of our love and reverence for the mothers of our country." In a speech, Miss Jarvis declared that nine years are too long to wait for success.

10. The holiday caught on elsewhere, too. It soon began to be observed in the neighboring countries of Canada and Mexico. From there, the commemoration spread to such distant locations as South America and Japan. The example of Miss Jarvis proves that every person, even if he act alone, are able make a difference and create an international celebration.

11. Still, the creation of her holiday brought her little joy. Sadly, thirty years of her life were primarily unhappy. She occupied herself by nursing her blind sister, teaching Sunday School, staying active in church, and supervising the celebration of Mother's Day. She still considered the day "her holiday."

12. She lived to see the holiday deviate from its original purpose. Mother's Day changed from a primarily religious observance into a predominantly commercial holiday. Florists, greeting card companies, and candy manufacturers was capitalizing on the popularity of the holiday to invade homes with their merchandise. There was nothing Miss Jarvis could do but watch businesses profit from the holiday. In 1944 Miss Jarvis, ailing and penniless, were placed in a Pennsylvania sanitarium where she was supported by friends until her death in 1948.

Exercise 19.6   Filling in Correct Verb Forms

In the following short essay, write in the appropriate **singular** *or* **plural** *form of the* **present tense verb** *in parentheses.*

Example   Insects (be) ___*are*_____ abundant in the summer.

Summer Solutions

As a poor graduate student living in a hot state, Sally, along with her two roommates, (do) _____ not use an air conditioner. There (be)

_____ plenty of reasons not to. Their electric bill, in addition to the water and gas bills, (be) _____ already too high.

Since physics (be) _____ her major, she (have) _____ decided to build a swamp cooler. With some hay, water, and an electric fan, she (have) _____ managed to bring the temperature of their room down by ten degrees. Also her roommates, who (be) _____ less capable at physics, simply (keep) _____ a tub full of water. What (keep) _____ them cool (be) _____ their wet clothing. One of their other methods (be) _____ putting aluminum foil on the windows. Also Sally is one of those people who (be) _____ capable of lying very still. She is the only person who (read) _____ without moving her eyes at all. Fanning herself (have) _____ little benefit since the arm movements (result) _____ in warmth.

Some of the people who (live) _____ in the house (cooperate) _____, but the rest of them (turn) _____ on the air conditioner too often. But everyone (agree) _____ that eight hours at a time (be) _____ enough.

Exercise 19.7   Proofreading

*Find and correct the **five errors of subject-verb agreement** in the following paragraph.*

What have been called a "blue moon" occurs three or four times in a hundred years. There is blue moons when two full moons appear in a single month. Since all months (except February) has thirty or thirty-one days and the moon's cycle take twenty-eight days, this occurrence is possible. The last blue moon occurred in January 1999 and hadn't occurred for over thirty years. Are thirty-odd years too long to wait for the next blue moon? Probably for most people it doesn't matter much since a blue moon doesn't look any different and depends strictly on a quirk of the calendar and nothing else.

Summary

I. Subject-Verb Agreement
   A. Definition: In **subject-verb agreement,** a singular subject takes a singular verb, and a plural subject takes a plural verb.
   B. Types of agreement
      1. Multiple subjects joined by *and* take plural verbs.
         a. Exceptions are single joined units.
            Examples: *peanut butter and jelly, peaches and cream*
         b. Exceptions are subjects that have *each* or *every.*
            Example: *each house and every room is . . .*
      2. Collective nouns are usually singular: *club, committee, couple, group,* etc.
         Examples: *the club has, the couple wants*
      3. Some pronoun subjects can be singular or plural depending on their reference: *all, most, number, rest, some.*
         Examples: *The **rest** of the book **is** interesting.*
                       *The **rest** of the books **are** mine.*
      4. Plural-looking nouns
         a. Some single-item nouns look plural and take plural verbs: *glasses, jeans, pants,* etc.
            Examples: *my glasses are, these pants have*
         b. Some nouns look plural but take singular verbs: *economics, mathematics, measles,* etc.
            Example: *Economics **seems** difficult.*
         c. Units of measure are singular.
            Example: *Six yards **is** enough.*
         d. Titles and company names that look plural are singular.
            Examples: Great Expectations ***is** a good book.*
                          *General Motors **has** many cars.*
   C. Special cases
      1. Ignore intervening phrases and clauses for agreement.
         Example: *This **book,** along with others, **has** a nice cover.*
      2. A verb agrees with its subject even when the subject follows the verb.
         Examples: *Where **are** the **books**? There **are** two **books.** In my house **are** many **books.***
      3. Relative Pronouns
         a. *That, which,* and *who* can be singular or plural depending on the nouns they replace.
            Examples: *the **book that is** mine, the **books that are** mine*
         b. In a *one of those . . . who (that, which) . . .* construction, the relative pronoun agrees with the preceding word.
            Example: *one of those **people who read** books*

Chapter 20

Pronoun-Antecedent Agreement

Indicate **pronoun-antecedent agreement** by drawing an arrow from each pronoun to the previous noun or pronoun it refers to. You should have some long arrows, but don't worry if you can't find all the pronouns.

I was 54 years old before venturing beyond the shores of my native Japan. It was 1953, and Georges Ohsawa and I were leaving on our first world tour. I remember feeling as naive, excited, and hesitant as a young schoolgirl about to embark on her first voyage into a wide and unknown world. I knew that Georges, having previously spent some years abroad, could speak both English and French, and that I, limited to my native language, would have to rely on him to steer our course. So I firmly resolved to accept in silence whatever fate had in store for us. We traveled by ship to Calcutta, arriving in November, and were engulfed by a surging crowd of beggars the moment we stepped ashore. Shocked and bewildered, I wondered to what kind of world my husband was so intent upon introducing me. (Lima Ohsawa, *The Art of Just Cooking*)

Agreement

Agreement in general means that one part of a sentence has the same number, person, gender, or tense as another part that goes with it. In ***pronoun-antecedent agreement,*** a pronoun later in the sentence must agree with the noun or pronoun to which it refers in person, number, and gender.

Person

Person also applies to things and ideas.

	First Person	*Second Person*	*Third Person*
Singular	I, me, my	you, your	he, him, his (masc.) she, her, hers (fem.) it, its (neut.)
Plural	we, us, our	you, your	they, them, their

Person in grammar distinguishes the speaker or writer (***first person***), the person or thing spoken to (***second person***), and the person or thing spoken about (***third person***).

Number: Singular or Plural

In most cases it is clear whether a pronoun is singular or plural. But sometimes the pronoun's reference determines its number. *Who, whom, that,* and *which* can be either singular or plural depending on the reference:

> She, **who is** a musician, enjoys concerts.
> They, **who are** musicians, enjoy concerts.

You also depends on the context of the sentence to determine whether it is singular or plural, and sometimes the number will not be clear:

> You are the best musician. (single musician)
> You are a wonderful orchestra. (many musicians)

Gender: Masculine, Feminine, Neuter

Masculine, feminine, and neuter gender apply only to third person singular pronouns since first and second person, as well as all the plural forms, do not indicate masculine or feminine:

> **Elaine** brought **her** guitar. (3rd person singular, feminine)
> The **chairs** were in **their** places. (3rd person plural)
> My **stool** is missing **its** cushion. (3rd person singular, neuter)
> The **musicians who** came play well. (3rd person plural)
> **He** will play **his** flute. (2nd person singular, masculine)
> **You** should take **your** seats. (2nd person plural)
> **I** want **my** oboe. (1st person singular)

When the antecedents are joined by *and,* use a plural pronoun:

> The chair and stand are in **their** places.

Only when *each* and *every* are used with the antecedent should you use a singular pronoun:

> Each chair and stand has **its** place.
> Every flutist and each oboist is in **his or her** place.

When the antecedents are joined by *or* or *nor,* make the pronoun match the final antecedent:

> The violinists or the **pianist** takes **his or her** seat first.
> The pianist or the **violinists** take **their** seats first.

Use singular for indefinite pronouns:

> **Everybody** plays **his or her** instrument.
> **Anyone** may play **his or her** solo.

Although people often use *their* to refer to a singular noun in speaking (*Everybody plays their instruments*), in writing it is better to observe strict pronoun-antecedent agreement. If the sentence sounds awkward to you, change it to plural (*All of them play their instruments*), or change the sentence (*Everybody plays an instrument*). However, you should not simply use *his* to refer to both males and females. Switching from *his or her* to *her or his* is also a nice variation.

Collective Nouns

Use singular or plural pronouns for collective nouns depending on the sense of the sentence:

The group wants **its** break. (All of them act as one.)

The group play **their** instruments. (Each one was separate.)

The orchestra has **its** schedule. (All of them are together.)

The orchestra take home **their** instruments. (Each acted separately.)

American English speakers often find it awkward to use collective nouns as plurals. In that case, change *orchestra* to *group members* or *musicians* and so forth.

Clarity of Reference

Relative pronouns and demonstrative pronouns (*which, this, that*) should have clear references. Otherwise the sense is unclear:

I played in a rock band for five years during my youth, **which** was wonderful. (Was her youth wonderful or playing in a rock band? BETTER: *I had a wonderful experience playing in a rock band for five years during my youth.*)

The conductor made the trumpet players stand during the finale of the Souza march. **This** was wrong. (Was it wrong for the trumpet players to stand or for them to stand during the finale? BETTER: *The conductor was wrong to make the trumpet players stand for the finale of the Souza march.*)

However, many writers view broad reference as acceptable when the pronoun refers clearly to the sense of an entire clause:

The orchestra members take their instruments home with them, which is normal. (*Which* refers to the whole previous statement but the reference is still clear.)

Make sure that a correct referent follows the antecedent:

The pianist was very good, but **it** was out of tune. (. . . *but the piano was out of tune.*)

The conductor likes the violin section although he never played it (or *one*). (. . . *he never played the violin.*)

Change written sentences that have indefinite *they, you,* and *it says* constructions:

They say the orchestra will play an encore.   CORRECT: *The orchestra was told (was asked) to play an encore.*   OR   *I hear that the orchestra will play an encore.*

The orchestra tunes up before **you** come in.   CORRECT: *The orchestra tunes up before the audience comes in.*

It says in the papers **that** the orchestra is playing tonight.   CORRECT: *The papers report that . . .*

Exercise 20.1   Finding Pronoun-Antecedent Agreement

*Indicate **pronoun-antecedent agreement** by drawing an arrow from the **one** pronoun with an antecedent back to its antecedent.*

Example   Bruce took his piano to Maine.

1. My brother lived for a year in Nepal and found its people fascinating.
2. He lived in a small village outside of the capital, Katmandu, which was a tremendous experience for him.
3. Nepalis don't allow people to wear shoes in their houses.
4. So everybody in my brother's house had his or her own slippers for indoor wear.
5. Once someone wanted to borrow the house for a wedding, and the housemates voted to let strangers into their house.
6. It was a fantastic time and everyone had the time of his or her life.
7. His roommate, Dorje, married a girl he had never seen before.
8. My brother says his nervousness showed itself in Dorje's knocking knees.
9. The married couple went to spend their first married night in a hotel.
10. My brother and his housemates cleaned up the mess until every cushion and piece of furniture was back in its proper place.

Exercise 20.2   Finding Pronoun-Antecedent Agreement

A. *Indicate **pronoun-antecedent agreement** by drawing an arrow from the **one** pronoun with an antecedent back to its antecedent.*

Example   Jill belongs to her college orchestra.

1. Gustave Alexandre Eiffel was a French civil engineer who wanted to use wrought iron.

2. In 1889, Eiffel built the tower that bears his name.
3. The tower has four huge legs that stand on concrete bases.
4. These legs curve inward until they meet to form a central tower.
5. The tower's three levels have observation decks and restaurants on them.
6. Most tourists use the elevator, but they can climb the stairs, too.
7. Before the tower was built, many people objected to its construction.
8. These people thought the lacy black iron construction did not fit their beautiful white stone city.
9. Now many Parisians feel that the Eiffel Tower is a symbol of their city.
10. Paris owes much of its identity to Monsieur Eiffel.

B. In the following essay, indicate **pronoun-antecedent agreement** *by drawing arrows from the pronouns with antecedents back to their antecedents. Many antecedents will be in earlier sentences.*

Example   Tom played "Amazing Grace," which he learned by himself.

He performed it really well.

Frugality

My Uncle Tibor and Aunt Shirley are very frugal people. They say their immigrant experiences have shaped them. When they first came to this country, they had almost nothing to call their own. Now they are middle class, but they still count their pennies.

At home they economize in lots of ways. Both Uncle Tibor and Aunt Shirley always cut their own hair; they would not pay someone else to cut it. They buy their clothes at the Salvation Army, Goodwill, and garage sales. They know when all the supermarkets near them have their sales on remainders and day-old bread. They do bulk buying, which is cheaper, so they have stocks of pasta and dry goods. They use cloth towels and napkins that they got at garage sales rather than paper ones, which cost more in the long run.

For entertainment, they frequent the local library. They can check out their favorite books, of course, but they also get videos of movies that they haven't seen at movie theaters. Also bookstores have their schedules of poetry readings that Uncle Tibor enjoys. Aunt Shirley really likes band concerts in the park, but Uncle Tibor prefers using it for jogging as his entertainment.

They have traveled quite a lot by joining a home exchange club, which helps match up people who want to go to each other's locations. They have spent time in Miami and San Diego recently where they had to pay only for their car expenses and for some of their meals. They could have cooked all the time at their home-away-from-home, but eating out was their one big extravagance.

I would rather do things my way, but I see that my uncle and aunt have carved out their lives in a way that is very satisfying to them. I hope I can be as happy as they are.

Exercise 20.3   Correcting Pronoun-Antecedent Agreement Errors

*Correct the **pronoun-antecedent agreement error** by removing the error and/or writing in other words. You may have to change additional words also.*

Example   The piano needs ~~their~~ keys tuned.
                                           its

1. The penguin originally was a flightless bird characterized by their upright stance.

2. The name "penguin" was first applied to the great North Atlantic auk. They are now extinct.

3. A similar flightless, upright bird was found in Antarctica, so they were also called penguins.

4. Penguins are classified as birds even though it is flightless, eats sea animals, and swims.

5. It has winglike appendages that act like flippers, which they use in swimming.

6. The penguin's feathers are scaly, and it molts all at once, unlike most birds.

7. A young molting penguin is larger than their parents because of the inflated, loose feathers all around it.

8. While it is molting, penguins cannot go in the water.

9. The parents of the penguin must feed them for those few weeks.

10. The exhausted parents must be happy when the molting season has seen their end.

11. Emperor penguins, which is the tallest of all penguins of the Antarctic, can reach four feet.

12. King penguins can also reach great heights, but it is not as tall as the emperor.

13. This king penguin also makes their home in Antarctica, as well as other places in the southern hemisphere.

14. The blue, or fairy, penguins of Australia are the smallest one, being under sixteen inches tall.

15. All penguins live in cold climates and have frigid oceans as its natural habitat.

16. They are insulated from the cold by three layers of dense feathers, which is helpful.

17. They also have a heavy layer of fat under its feathers.

18. Its wings, used as paddles, allow them to swim rapidly and efficiently.

19. A penguin's webbed feet and their tail act as rudders to guide it through the water.

20. It is well adapted for their environment, although it does not breathe under water.

Exercise 20.4   Correcting Pronoun-Antecedent Agreement Errors

*Correct the **one error of pronoun-antecedent agreement** in each paragraph. Use the blank space to write the corrected sentence.*

1. There are eighteen species of penguins, and every one of them knows their own kind. However, many of them mix and live together. Some even breed together. _____

2. Penguins tend to live in colonies, called rookeries, sometimes composed of millions of individual birds. They swim together in large groups to find food and fend off enemies, which is helpful. _____

3. The penguin's worst enemy is the skua, which eats their young chicks and eggs. Also large seals and killer whales may eat penguins, but penguins are naturally protected. _____

4. They are protected by its huge numbers and also by the inaccessibility of their habitat. They often live in icebound, rocky, and extremely isolated places.

5. During the mating season, penguins return to its previous home and gather together in enormous numbers. They travel along rock paths worn smooth by them in past centuries. _____

_____

6. Penguins travel along the exact paths of their ancestors, even when topographical changes have made the route many miles from the ocean. It knows exactly where they're going. _____

_____

7. A male penguin usually selects a spot to call their home. Then he may "decorate" it with small stones and sticks. Small penguins burrow into nests; larger ones live in the open. _____

_____

8. Each species has their own special posture and call to attract one another. Some flap their flippers, others call with strange sounds, and some bow and dip. _____

_____

9. One kind of male penguin must search high and low for a nice gift, usually a good-looking stone. Then he places it at a female's feet, which might or might not accept it. _____

_____

10. Females are sometimes quite choosy about her mate. They visit different "homes," look at the decor, evaluate the male displays, and finally picks one with whom to mate. _____

_____

Exercise 20.5   Filling in Pronouns

*Fill in the blanks with appropriate **pronouns**.*

Example   Pete did not take __his_____ oboe with __him_____.

1. Once a female penguin has laid _____ eggs, both males and

females take _____ turn at incubation.

2. Burrowing small penguins protect _____ eggs from the cold by

filling the whole burrow with _____ body warmth.

3. The emperor penguin in the open covers _____ one egg with stomach flaps that extend over _____ feet.

4. Large males sometimes fast for weeks while _____ build _____ nest, court, and incubate.

5. Incubation takes place when Antarctica is at _____ coldest time when _____ temperature might reach –80 degrees.

6. After laying _____ eggs, the female swims out to feed and then returns to take _____ turn at tending the eggs.

7. Depending on _____ distance from the water, penguins feed _____ several times a day or once every several weeks.

8. When the eggs hatch, parents must feed _____ chicks through constant trips to find food for _____.

9. Thousands of chicks gather in nurseries awaiting both _____ parents' return from _____ trip to the sea.

10. When a chick gets _____ first plumage, _____ is ready to fend for _____.

Exercise 20.6   Filling in Pronouns

*Fill in the blanks with the appropriate **pronouns**.*

Example   Sheila wants ___*her*___ piano tuned.

1. Most people have no idea whether or not _____ heart is a healthy heart.

2. A healthy heart can pump out an increased volume of blood to meet _____ increased demand.

3. Healthy hearts contract strongly, _____ arteries are clear, and _____ valves function smoothly when blood makes _____ journey through the chambers.

4. You can make sure _____ heart is a healthy heart by exercising and sticking to a low-fat diet.

5. Americans are lazy; many don't want to leave _____ homes even to improve _____ own health.

6. Professors at top universities claim that exercise has _____ benefits, be they physical or emotional.

7. For example, a man who has just run five miles basks in the glow of endorphins released through exercise, _____ emotions more in keeping with a meditation period than a jog.

8. People who exercise regularly have a reduced risk of diabetes and cut down on _____ risk of cancer, obesity, and heart disease.

9. Osteoporosis is a particular danger to women; they can delay _____ onset with regular exercise.

10. If you've never exercised before, start with realistic expectations; otherwise, you won't reach _____ goal.

11. If after a month you feel ready to increase _____ efforts, make sure to keep your efforts within _____ and _____ heart's capabilities.

12. Anyone can start exercising _____ or _____ way to a healthy heart.

Exercise 20.7   Proofreading

*Cross out and correct the **four errors of pronoun-antecedent agreement** in the following paragraph.*

Drunk driving has been on the decline in the past twenty years even though they have increased by 15 percent. Several factors have contributed to this phenomenon. Mothers Against Drunk Driving (MADD) and Students Against Drunk Driving (SADD) maintain vigorous campaigns to educate drivers. A majority of people now use the designated driver idea when they are out with friends. Others simply don't drive because their car might be confiscated for good. For those reasons, they say that there are fewer drunk-driving arrests. Still, 50 percent of deaths from drunk driving are committed by just 1 percent of drivers, which means it is still a problem.

Mandatory treatment for alcoholics and preventive devices on cars are two possible solutions. You can't tell how these systems will work, however.

Summary

I. Pronoun-Antecedent Agreement
  A. Definition: **Pronoun-antecedent agreement** means that a pronoun must match its antecedent in person, number, and gender.
  B. Types of agreement
    1. Pronouns and antecedents must agree in person.
       Example: *I took **my** turn.*
    2. Pronouns and antecedents must agree in number.
       Example: ***They** had **their** plans.*
    3. Pronouns and antecedents must agree in gender.
       Example: ***She** has **her** way.*
  C. Special cases
    1. Indefinite antecedents take third person singular, masculine and feminine pronouns.
       Example: ***Everybody** likes **his or her** instrument.*
       a. Alternatives
         i. Change to a plural subject.
            Example: ***They** all like **their** instruments.*
         ii. Change the sentence.
            Example: *The **students** like **their** own instruments.*
    2. Collective nouns take third person singular, neutral pronouns.
       Example: *The **group** decides **its** direction.*
  D. Clarity of references
    1. Relative and demonstrative pronouns (*which, this, that*) should have a clear reference.
       Example: *Here is **the plan that** I like.*
    2. An entire previous statement may be a reference if it is clear (called **broad reference**).
       Example: *I took fencing lessons for a year, which was terrific.*
    3. Avoid indefinite *they, you, it says.*
       Example: *They say we should eat soy.*
       BETTER: *I have heard that we should eat soy.*   OR   *Reports state that we should eat soy.*

Punctuation

Chapter 21

Commas

Decide why the **commas** are used in each of the following sentences and write in the reason using this list: date, direct address, series of adjectives, introductory word, introductory phrase, introductory clause, title after a name, appositive, compound sentence with coordinating conjunction.

1. Alina, I am writing this letter to congratulate you on your graduation.
   _____

2. You have succeeded, and you have made us proud. _____
   _____

3. This date, May 20, 2001, should be your proudest. _____

4. Now the words "Alina Martin, M.D.," will always have a special meaning for
   me. _____

5. You are diligent, hard working, motivated, and compassionate. _____
   _____

6. As you continue in life, you will always remember this special day when you
   started. _____

7. After studying so much, you should find medical practice relatively easy. _____
   _____

8. However, I hope you will not forget the loving family that now counts on you.
   _____

9. In addition, remember the sacrifices that they made for you. _____
   _____

10. My niece, the doctor, will always make me proud. _____
    _____

Our most common piece of punctuation by far is the **comma** (,) because it has so many different uses.

Compound Sentences with Coordinating Conjunctions

Two independent clauses are joined by a comma and a coordinating conjunction (*for, and, nor, but, or, yet, so*):

I have many pairs of gloves, and I keep buying more.
I don't like cold hands, nor do I like calloused hands.
Gloves have many uses, so I have many pairs.

These commas joining the parts of a compound sentence could be replaced by periods, making the compound sentence into two simple sentences, so the function of the comma here is to join the two (or more) parts of a compound sentence.

Introductory Words and Phrases

These types of words and phrases at the beginning of sentences are usually followed by a comma:

Exclamations (also called **interjections**) (*well; darn; oh, boy*)
Yes, you could say I'm obsessed with gloves.

Transitions (*however, moreover, in addition*)
Nevertheless, it could be worse.

Direct address (*Maria, Students, Mrs. Romero*)
Dad, I need money for another pair.

Prepositional phrases (*at home, before the game*)
After work, I'm buying new gloves.

Adjective phrases (*taken by surprise, having no choice*)
Needing new gloves, I went to a specialty shop.

Infinitive phrases (*to err, to be human*)
To influence my father, I wore my gloves.

Absolute phrases (*time having passed, the book put aside*)
Money being scarce, I couldn't afford that new pair.

When the introductory part is very short and cannot be misunderstood, the comma may sometimes be omitted, but it is never wrong to put the comma in:

With lunch she had tea.   OR   With lunch, she had tea.

Nonrestrictive Phrases and Clauses

Phrases that are not essential to the sense of a sentence (also called **interrupters**) should be set off with commas:

My brother, **wearing expensive leather gloves,** changed a tire.

My brother changed a tire, **flattened by a nail.**

Adjective dependent clauses that do not change the sense of the sentence but that give additional information need commas:

My sister, **who rarely wears gloves,** doesn't like them.

She has only a few pairs, **which she always loses.**

An adverb dependent clause at the beginning of a sentence usually takes a comma after it:

Because I love gloves, I have many pairs.

If you want to give me a gift, consider gloves.

An adverb dependent clause at the end of a sentence only takes a comma after it if it shows contrast or hesitation:

Buy me gloves, **even though I already have ten pairs.**

You may pay for my new gloves, **if you don't mind.**

A Series of Words, Phrases, or Clauses

Any series of items of three or more usually takes a comma *after* each item in the series except the last one. The series may be words, phrases, or clauses:

She bought lacy, elbow-length, skin-tight evening gloves. (coordinate adjectives)

We shopped for gloves, ate lunch, and wrapped our gifts.

She works in the kitchen, at the office, and out in the yard.

He likes gloves, she likes mittens, and I like bare hands.

Although many journalists and some writers omit the comma between the last two items in a series, this omission can be misleading. It also eliminates a valuable distinction:

My preferred sandwiches are tuna, cheese, and peanut butter and jelly. (Peanut butter and jelly form a unit.)

My preferred sandwiches are tuna, cheese, peanut butter, and jelly. (All are separate items.)

Dates, Addresses, and Personal Titles

The American method of writing dates has a comma after the date and the year:

April 3, 1968, was the day Martin Luther King, Jr., was shot.

However, *no* comma is necessary for just the month and day (April 3), for just the month and year (April 1968) unless some other reason calls for a comma, or for the international date-writing method: 3 April 1968.

American addresses call for commas after each major division of street, city, state and zip code, and country:

He lives at 88 Sunset Drive, Palm Beach, FL 30001, U.S.A., and wants to move to Miami next year.

The post office prefers the official two-letter designations for states, but writing out the complete name (Florida) does not change the punctuation.

Titles that come after a person's name have commas:

Peter Smith, **Jr.,** sells gloves.
Sandra Smith, **M.D.,** wears sterilized gloves.
Frederico Smith, **Ph.D.,** experiments on synthetics.
Mingli Smith, **Esq.,** litigates for small businesses.

Emphasis and Reversed Order of Words and Phrases

When a phrase emphasizes something contrary to what is stated, it has a comma to separate it:

My cold and chapped hands need gloves, **not pockets.**
I need gloves, **don't I?**

When words (often adjectives) or phrases are out of normal order for emphasis or variety, they take commas:

Cold and chapped, my hands need gloves.
My hands, **cold and chapped,** need gloves.
I need gloves for my hands, **cold and chapped.**

In normal order, no commas are needed: *My cold and chapped hands need gloves.*

Appositives

Appositives rename or mean the same as the preceding word. Most appositives have commas that set them off from the main sentence:

My cousin, **Melissa,** likes gloves.
Melissa, **my cousin,** likes gloves.
My cousin likes gloves, **the leather kind.**

When the appositive is not surrounded by commas, it indicates that there is more than one of that kind. So *my cousin, Melissa,* means that I have just one cousin, and her name is Melissa. But *my cousin Melissa* indicates that I have more than one cousin, one of whom is named Melissa. However, this distinction is not always followed, especially with proper names.

Avoiding Misunderstanding

Sometimes a comma is needed to prevent misreading:

After washing, the gloves shrank.
Long before, he had bought the gloves.

These sentences would seem ungrammatical or incomplete without these commas.

Exercise 21.1   Identifying Comma Use

A. Decide which of the following uses each **comma** *has and write one of these abbreviations in the space:*
   TR   *transitional word or phrase*
   ADC   *adverb dependent clause*
   SER   *series of words, phrases, or clauses*

Example   Moreover, I prefer gloves as a gift. __TR__

  1. Because the facts are lost in antiquity, the origins of some foods are a mystery.

   ____

  2. For example, ice cream has been around for centuries. ____

  3. Ice cream possibly started in China, Mongolia, Greece, or somewhere else. ____

  4. Accordingly, some Chinese farmer spilled milk in the snow. ____

  5. Since adult Chinese rarely drink milk, it seems unlikely that the farmer ate

      this accidental ice cream. ____

  6. More likely, a Mongolian did the same and drank it. ____

  7. As Mongolians have very little water, milk seems a possible substitute.

   ____

8. Mongolians are known for raising vast herds of yaks, goats, and other milk-producing animals. _____

9. Mongolia is also a very cold place, so snow is everywhere. _____

10. On the other hand, Greece is a relatively warm place. _____

B. *Decide which of the following uses each* **comma** *has:*
    CD   *compound sentence with a coordinating conjunction*
    REVL   *reversal of previous statement*
    APP   *appositive*

1. The Greeks wanted a cool drink on a hot summer day, so they poured a little wine over crushed ice. _____

2. This concoction is the classic slush, not ice cream. _____

3. The Sicilians, a southern people, possibly added more snow than flavoring and invented the sorbet. _____

4. The Arab residents of Sicily claim the sorbet was originally theirs, not the Sicilians'. _____

5. The Italian word *sorbetto* may have come from the Arab word *sharbat*, a slush-like fruit dessert. _____

6. These desserts were thick, so they were no longer drinks. _____

7. Normally they were eaten with a spoon, not sipped. _____

8. Alexander the Great apparently liked snow or ice with honey and nectar, a true *gelato*. _____

9. Catherine de Medici brought pasta to France, and she brought *gelato* too. _____

10. Many other countries may also have invented similar treats, for these foods did not have to begin in just one place. _____

C. *Decide which of the following uses each* **comma** *has:*
    PP   *introductory prepositional phrase*
    INTRO   *introductory adjective or infinitive phrase*
    ABS   *absolute phrase*

1. In the beginning, ice cream or *gelato* was just ice and flavoring. _____

2. After a while, whether milk or ice was used didn't matter. _____

3. Creamy or icy, *gelato* was a favorite dessert. _____

4. Chocolate, vanilla, and strawberry are common flavors, vanilla being the favorite. _____

5. To go with pies and cakes, vanilla ice cream probably is the best choice. _____

6. Not to be outdone, strawberry and chocolate also appear everywhere. _____

7. The public wanting variety, several companies started a number of mixtures.

    _____

8. Variety being the spice of life, companies started adding cookies and candy bars. _____

9. At the August garlic festival, vendors make and sell garlic ice cream. _____

10. Feeling inventive, chefs now add such ingredients as curry and beets to ice cream. _____

Exercise 21.2   Adding Commas

*Add one or more **commas** in the following sentences and then identify the reason as follows:*

MIS	*misunderstanding*	**REVL**	*reversal of statement*
CD	*compound sentence*	**ADC**	*adjective dependent clause*
INF	*infinitive phrase*	**ADJ**	*adjective phrase*
TITLE	*personal title*	**SER**	*series of words or phrases*

1. Studying to be a doctor takes many years not months of hard work and sleepless nights. _____

2. To be successful a future doctor should start early. _____

3. She or he should study biology chemistry and anatomy. _____

4. Having graduated from college the future doctor is just beginning. _____

5. Premed students must go to medical school and then they must do an internship at a hospital. _____

6. The internship usually means long days many sleepless nights and lots of unglamorous cases. _____

7. To prepare really well an intern also must continue taking notes and studying.

    _____

8. A doctor who may already know all about medicine must also study ethics and bedside manners. _____

9. Deciding on a specialty the future doctor must learn even more than basic medicine. _____

10. After deciding entering the field is usually difficult. _____

11. Many women prefer obstetrics pediatrics gynecology and geriatrics. _____

12. Maybe they prefer to have women patients not men. _____

13. Cosmetic surgery might seem frivolous to some people but it is an important field. _____

14. Birth defects mutilating injuries or disfiguring diseases make a cosmetic surgeon necessary. _____

15. Being a general practitioner which is not very fashionable these days can be the most rewarding choice. _____

16. Seeing a variety of cases the G.P. can treat whole families and see diverse maladies. _____

17. Specializing the doctor can develop a real expertise in one area. _____

18. Sports injuries has become an important specialization and geriatrics keeps growing with more and more patients. _____

19. To choose one field each future doctor must think long and hard. _____

20. Becoming John or Jane Doe M.D. must be a proud moment in any doctor's life. _____

Exercise 21.3   Adding Commas

*Add the **thirty commas** necessary in the following essay.*

Life Choices

Life has not been easy for my family. My parents worked very hard but made very little money. They saved as much as they could and finally we left and came here. Oh that was a wonderful and fearful day.

My first address in this new country was 123 West Sunrise Road Oakland CA 90005 where we lived for three years. My father my mother my sister Andie and my brother Lu and I lived in just three rooms. Then my grandma asked us to move and live with her in Houston Texas after my grandpa died. The house was the same size as our apartment but we had a yard where my parents built an addition. On December 31 2000 we celebrated by moving Andie Lu and me into our new rooms.

We still don't have much money. Without any complaint Grandma takes care of all the cooking cleaning and shopping. All the rest of us work. Andie is in junior high Lu is in high school and I am in college. After I work and study sleeping is usually the best "recreation" I can think of not going out or dating.

Well who knows what the future will bring? I hope to have a nice job managing a restaurant. My sister will be Andie Esq. someday, but I'll just be Kim Jr. although I'll be able to treat my family to some nice meals.

Exercise 21.4   Adding Commas

*Add the **twenty commas** necessary in the following essay.*

Many people think my obsession with the art of Tarot divination is misguided uneducated and downright weird. I however beg to differ. Tarot has been linked with and influenced the formation of religion and psychology as we know it today and we owe much of our spiritual development to its guidance.

Tarot began in Renaissance Europe where the art of using pictorial memory systems was adapted from ancient Greece. Tarot has been linked to respected religious institutions such as Hebrew Kabala astrology and gnosticism.

Much modern Tarot interpretation is influenced by Carl Gustav Jung Sigmund Freud's famous pupil who broke away from Freudian psychology to found his own richly symbolic system. Jung's concern with spirituality and dreams as well as astrology and oracles was in many ways closer to ancient occult teachings than to psychology. In his writings he divulges several personal psychic experiences including telepathy prophetic dreams visions and even a ghost sighting.

The dreamlike images of the Tarot cards help bring unconscious knowledge to the surface. They emerge in a pattern meaningful to the inquirer and reflect the deeply hidden underlying motives fears and desires which mold individual destiny. So Tarot is more than just a deck of cards; it can be a powerful tool for introspection.

Exercise 21.5   Adding Commas

*Find and correct the **ten comma errors** in the following essay.*

The Last Bareknuckle Prizefight

In 1889 the reigning champion of bareknuckle boxing was John L. Sullivan. A devastating two-handed hitter, Sullivan had completed a tour of the United States during which he would take on anyone who offered to fight awarding $1,000 to any man who lasted four rounds. Even through his typical haze of bourbon, Sullivan bested fifty-nine men in a row. It was this love of the bottle that gave his last opponent, Jake Kilrain of Baltimore even odds.

The men came to scratch at 10 A.M. at Richburg Missouri. There were three thousand spectators assembled, most having taken the train from New, Orleans to the secret ring (bareknuckle boxing was illegal in all of the thirty-eight states). It was a brutal day; the thermometer registered 100 degrees even in the shade. And though, Sullivan had dressed for the role of champion, most people figured that his alcohol-soaked legs would only last him 20 minutes before the formidable Kilrain.

With $10,000 at stake the men fought hard. Kilrain tried to dance around Sullivan, but to everyone's surprise, Sullivan withstood the exertion. Still he was furious with Kilrain's avoidance tactics. Before the application of the Queensbury rules, rounds lasted until a man went down, and in this bout, the fourth round lasted a full fifteen minutes. Kilrain drew blood from Sullivan's ear as the men clinched in the seventh round which prompted an exchange of money amidst the spectators. The fight wore on; both men were scorched crimson from the sun, and Kilrain showed signs of tiring. His eyes were glassy and his head lolled around on his neck like a rag doll's. Finally, in the seventy-fifth round, a doctor declared Kilrain unfit to continue fighting.

The last bareknuckle fight in prizefighting history lasted 2 hours, and 16 minutes. A far different, gorier and bloodier sport than we know today in our era of padded gloves and three-minute rounds bareknuckle fighting lost way to more "civilized" rules. Sullivan lost his crown barely three years later in a glove fight. Kilrain, who seemed close to death after his grueling seventy-five rounds, lived to be a pallbearer at Sullivan's funeral in 1918.

Exercise 21.6   Writing with Commas

Write sentences using the topic indicated and the type of comma indicated.

Example   Gloves

(Compound sentence) ___*I like these gloves, but I hate the price.*___

(Reversal) ___*I like these gloves, not those hats.*___

1. House

   (Date) _____

   (Address) _____

2. Apartment

   (Prepositional phrase) _____

   (Transitional phrase) _____

3. School

   (Personal title) _____

   (Appositive) _____

4. Street

   (Compound sentence) _____

   (Exclamation) _____

5. Store

   (Reversal) _____

   (Nonrestrictive dependent clause) _____

6. Supermarket

   (Series of adjectives) _____

   (Introductory adverb clause) _____

7. Dog

   (Direct address) _____

   (Reverse order) _____

8. Baby

   (Date) _____

   (Appositive) _____

9. Parents

   (Compound sentence) _____

   (Transitional word) _____

10. Playground

    (Exclamation) _____

    (Series of phrases) _____

Exercise 21.7   Proofreading

*Add the **five commas** needed in this paragraph.*

Almost everyone has eaten M&Ms but hardly anyone knows what those two Ms stand for: Mars and Murrie. Although Forrest Mars inherited an already vast candy empire from his father he expanded it. While in Europe during the Spanish Civil War, he saw soldiers eating small round, candy-coated chocolates. Because of sugar and chocolate rationing during World War II he knew he could not manufacture these chocolates by himself. Approaching the head of Hershey, William F. R. Murrie, he proposed a joint venture. Thus, the M&M brand was born. Improvements continued over the years with new flavors and a coating that melted in your mouth not in your hand.

Summary

  I. **Commas**
    A. Use a comma between the parts of a compound sentence containing a coordinating conjunction: *for, and, nor, but, or, yet, so* (FANBOYS).
        Examples: *The storm passed, and the sun came out.*|
                I won't go out, nor will you.
    B. Use a comma after introductory words and phrases.
      1. Use a comma after interjections (exclamations).
        Example: *Well, I'll go if you will.*
      2. Set off transitional words and phrases with commas.
        Examples: *On the other hand, I will go.*
              Besides, you're right.
              I'm not wrong, however.
      3. Use a comma after direct address.
        Examples: *Professor Davis, I need more time.*
              Mom, can you help me?
      4. Use a comma after prepositional phrases.
        Example: *Before returning, he'll buy it.*
      5. Use a comma after verbal phrases.
        Examples: *Seeing him, we stopped.* (adjective)
              To see him, we stopped. (infinitive)
      6. Use a comma after absolute phrases.
        Example: *The storm having come, we stayed inside.*
    C. Use commas for nonrestrictive elements.
      1. Use commas around adjective verbal phrases.
        Example: *The storm, which lasted an hour, is over.*
      2. Use commas for adverb dependent clauses at the beginning of sentences and around them in the middle of sentences.
        Examples: *Because I went out, I got wet.*
               My motive, if you must know, is honorable.
      3. Use commas before adverb dependent clauses at the end of sentences only to show contrast or hesitation.
        Examples: *I went, although I didn't enjoy it.*
               I'll go to school, if you insist.

D. Use commas between items in a series.
   1. Use commas for a series of words.
        Examples: *I danced, ate, and talked.*
                Peter, Paul, and Mary sang.
   2. Use commas for a series of phrases.
        Examples: *I have books on the floor, in the closet, and on the bed.*
                We drank milk, ate pizza, and listened to CDs.
   3. Use commas for a series of clauses.
        Example: *Bob cooked dinner, Sue washed the dishes, and I dumped*
                the garbage.
E. Use commas around dates, addresses, and personal titles.
        Examples: *They got married on June 12, 2001, at 4:00.*
                Their address is 123 North Street, Spring, NY.
                Susan Jones, M.D., is here.
F. Use commas to indicate reversals and reversed order.
        Example: *Take the table away, not the chairs.*
G. Use commas around appositives unless they are restrictive.
        Example: *Susan Jones, the doctor, is arriving soon.*
H. Use commas to avoid misunderstandings.
        Examples: *After cleaning up, Dad took us out.*
                Because they bite, mosquitoes are bothersome.

Chapter 22

Semicolons and Colons

Circle the **semicolons** and **colons** in the following paragraphs and note in the margin why they are used.

Wisdom is better than possessions and an advantage to all who see the sun. Better have wisdom behind you than money; wisdom profits men by giving life to those who know her.

Consider God's handiwork; who can straighten what He has made crooked? When things go well, be glad; but when things go ill, consider this: God has set the one alongside the other in such a way that no one can find out what is to happen next. (Ecclesiastes 7:11–19, *The New English Bible*)

A *semicolon (;)* indicates a greater separation than a comma but not as great a separation as a period. A *colon (:)* indicates further details about the preceding statement. A colon also has a number of other uses.

Semicolons (;)

Use a semicolon between two or more independent clauses when no coordinating conjunction (*for, and, nor, but, or, yet, so*) has been used:

Rollerblading is fun; it is also cheap.

I rollerblade; my sister swims; my parents loaf.

Use a semicolon even if a conjunctive adverb or a transitional phrase comes between the independent clauses:

Wear a helmet and pads for rollerblading; otherwise, you might get hurt.

Wear a helmet; in addition, wear knee and elbow pads.

Here is a list of common conjunctive adverbs and transitional phrases:

accordingly	consequently	furthermore
after all	even so	hence
also	finally	however
besides	for example	in addition

in any case	nevertheless	then
in fact	on the contrary	therefore
instead	on the other hand	thus
meanwhile	otherwise	
moreover	still	

You can place the semicolon to allow the conjunctive adverb or transitional phrase to modify whichever clause you want:

Rollerblading is fun; however, it isn't for everyone.

It has dangers, however; precautions should be taken.

Be cautious; after all, rollerblading has hazards.

Don't dwell on the dangers, after all; you want to have fun.

If a compound sentence with a coordinating conjunction has commas in either or both independent clauses, use a semicolon between the clauses for clarity's sake:

Rollerblading, despite its dangers, should be fun; but you should wear a helmet, knee pads, and elbow pads.

When a list of items is presented in a sentence, semicolons are needed to avoid misunderstandings. Consider this sentence: *I went skating with Max, my aunt, Jun, a classmate, and Kim.* Did I go with five, four, or three people? The sentence indicates five people, but, if that is not the case, use semicolons to clear up the ambiguities:

I went skating with Max; my aunt, Jun; a classmate; and Kim. (Four people: Max, Aunt Jun, unnamed classmate, Kim)

I went skating with Max, my aunt; Jun; a classmate; and Kim. (Four people: Aunt Max, Jun, unnamed classmate, Kim)

I went skating with Max, my aunt; Jun, a classmate; and Kim. (Three people: Aunt Max, classmate Jun, Kim)

Thus semicolons are used in compound sentences and also in other types of sentences to avoid ambiguities.

Colons (:)

A colon at the end of a sentence announces that further details will follow in the form of a single word, a phrase, a series of items, or a complete sentence:

I love one sport: rollerblading. (word)

I want one thing: to rollerblade with you. (phrase)

I like these sports: rollerblading, skating, and skiing. (series of words)

I like these sports: rollerblading in the park, ice skating at the rink, and skiing at Snow Mountain. (series of phrases)

He had an idea: he would rollerblade down the hill. (sentence) (A capital letter can begin a sentence after a colon; usage varies.)

I get plenty of exercise: I rollerblade in the park; I ice skate at a local rink; I ski during the winter. (series of sentences) (Notice that semicolons are used to separate these sentences.)

Make sure that the parts after the colon are parallel; that is, they should all be nouns or all infinitive phrases or all prepositional phrases or all sentences, etc. They need not have the same number of words in each or be precisely the same, but grammatically they should have the same structure.

Usually a complete sentence precedes the colon, but occasionally you will see a fragment used effectively:

I like sports. Among them: ice skating, hockey, skiing.

Be careful, however, not to use a colon preceding a list when the list should be part of the sentence:

My favorite sports are rollerblading, hockey, and skiing. (Do *not* add a colon after *are.*)

I like sports such as hockey and skiing. (Do *not* add a colon after *such as.*)

The colon could be avoided altogether by rewriting a sentence, but often a colon is the simplest and most economical way to present material:

UNNECESSARY WORDS: I have three favorite sports. They are skiing, skating, and swimming.

ECONOMICAL: I have three favorite sports: skiing, skating, (and) swimming.

Colons have various other uses:

Setting off a quotation (*He wrote in his diary: "I can't go on."*)

Separating hours, minutes, and seconds (*11:31:04*)

Citing Bible chapter and verse (*Ecclesiastes 7:19*)

Following a salutation in formal letters (*Dear Madam:*)

Heading memos (*To: Food Staff*
       From: Manager
       Re: Service)

Indicating letter writer and typist by initials (*KCD:ez*)

Noting a subtitle with a title (*Mission: A Personal Story*) (Add the colon even when not written on the title page.)

Citing a city in a footnote (*New York: Macmillan*)

Numbering a list (*No. 1: Call first*) but not with numerals alone (1. Call first.)

Exercise 22.1   Identifying Uses of Semicolons and Colons

A. Identify the use of the **semicolon(s)** *in each sentence as follows:*
  1   *independent clauses without coordinating conjunction*
  2   *independent clauses with conjunctive adverb or transition*
  3   *for clarity with independent clauses having commas*
  4   *avoiding ambiguities*

Example   I skate all year round; it's the best exercise. __1__

1. The wombat is a burrowing animal; it has long claws and sharp, chisellike teeth. _____
2. It is native only to Australia and Tasmania, a nearby island; therefore, it is not a well-known animal. _____
3. The wombat, being nocturnal, emerges only at night to find food; and during the day, it sleeps, hidden from sight in a burrow. _____
4. It is rarely seen; only zoos have specimens for the public to see. _____
5. The wombat could easily be mistaken for a small bear; after all, it is stocky, has a stubby tail, and has thick fur. _____
6. The thick fur, usually quite coarse, varies from light brown to black; and, on the average, it measures around three feet long. _____
7. An herbivore, the wombat prefers eating grasses and other plants; it holds little danger to other animals or humans. _____
8. It is a docile animal; nevertheless, it has been nearly exterminated because of its damage to crops. _____
9. The wombat's burrows allow rabbits, another pest, to hide; and the burrows present hazards to other livestock. _____
10. The people of Canberra, Australia; Christchurch, New Zealand; and all of Borneo are interested in animals on the list of endangered species. _____

B. Identify **colon** *use in each sentence as follows:*
  1   *further details after a sentence*
  2   *letter information (salutation, memo address, typist)*
  3   *time*
  4   *book citations (subtitle, city of publication, Bible verse)*
  5   *formal quotation*
  6   *numbered list*

Example   We skate everywhere: the rink, the streets, the park. __1__

1. To: The Staff at Our Business _____

2. From: Ms. Singh _____

3. Subject: Important information missing _____

4. Please route this memo as follows: Mr. Pak, Ms. Allen, Mr. Yee _____

5. The time is exactly 20:27:10. _____

6. Our ship carries these people: 1,000 passengers, 300 crew. _____

7. Please fax me the following information: name and address of our contact in the Tokyo office. _____

8. Follow my rules. No. 1: Consult Ms. Smith, No. 2: Get the company directory, No. 3: Copy the correct reference. _____

9. Also look in *World Directory: A Guide to Business.* _____

10. The title page should say New York: Directory Publs., 2000. _____

11. Look for this quotation: "Your people shall be my people." _____

12. It is our password from Ruth 1:17. _____

13. Send the information to me at this address: World Meeting, Sakura Hotel, Tokyo, Japan. _____

14. Remember to include the following information: the contact person, the address, and the password. _____

15. As the Japanese say: "Sayonara." _____

Exercise 22.2   Adding Semicolons and Colons

*A. Change **one** or **two commas** to **semicolons** in the appropriate places in each of the following sentences.*

Example   Rollerbladers should wear a helmet; they need protection.

1. Everybody wants to visit Niagara Falls, it's one of the top attractions in North America.

2. Along with Honolulu, Hawaii, Disney World, Florida, and San Francisco, California, it ranks as a top vacation spot.

3. Over twelve million people visit every year, consequently, it gets very crowded, especially in the summer.

4. The waterfall spans the Niagara River, which flows between Ontario, Canada, and New York, U.S.A., so the two countries, both having a claim to part of the falls, have exploited it.

5. Horseshoe Falls is on the Canadian side, American Falls is on the U.S. side.

6. An observation area where the falls descends has a great view, furthermore, it is free and always open.

7. Other observation points abound, thus the falls can be viewed from almost all angles.

8. A boat, *Maid of the Mist*, goes up to the falls from below, however, the tremendous roar and the drenching mist are difficult.

9. People can also rent waterproof ponchos and walk down a narrow tunnel behind the falls, it's very wet but worth it.

10. Various people have ridden over the falls in kayaks, barrels, and open boats, a few have lived to tell about it.

B. *Add* **one** *or* **two colons** *in the appropriate places in the following sentences.*

1. I am reading a guidebook called *Canada A Travel Survival Kit* (Melbourne Lonely Planet Publications, 1992).

2. Although the United States is smaller and divided into fifty states, Canada has much larger divisions ten provinces and two territories.

3. Most of Canada is divided into ten provinces, but it also has two so-called territories the Northwest Territories and the Yukon.

4. Canada has six time zones Pacific, Mountain, Central, Eastern, Atlantic, and Newfoundland.

5. Only one part does not observe Daylight Saving Time Eastern Saskatchewan.

6. One province is different from all the rest Newfoundland.

7. When it is 400 P.M. in the Atlantic time zone, it is 430 P.M. in Newfoundland.

8. Canada has something for everyone big cities, small towns, mountains, untamed wildernesses, and the great Yukon.

9. Canada has a great mixture of people Europeans, Asians, Africans, and native Inuits.

10. This mixture means one important thing everyone will fit in.

Exercise 22.3   Adding Semicolons and Colons

In the following essay, add **six semicolons** *and* **four colons.** *Other punctuation is correct.*

Before starting college, a friend and I took the trip of a lifetime. We planned on seeing two places Nepal and the Himalayas. First we would visit the main city for a week then we would spend a few days trekking in the mountains.

We flew to Katmandu, the capital of Nepal, after stopping in Tokyo and Calcutta for a few hours but, given such an arduous journey, we hardly saw anything. We passed the international dateline at exactly 10 35 A.M. and skipped a whole day. I took a short nap, falling asleep on Thursday and waking up on Saturday! In Katmandu we saw the temples, Freak Street, and marketplaces and, outside the city, we saw the Himalayas. We did a four-day trek with some really nice people Prasad, our guide a British woman, Sandra an Australian student two porters, Mohan and Bahadur.

Our bus ride from Katmandu to the border of India was truly hair raising, but fun. We thought we had to run for the train to Calcutta, but we were early because Nepal time is fifteen minutes ahead of India time. On our return trip we got back our one lost day Friday.

Exercise 22.4   Adding Semicolons and Colons

Find and correct the **colon** *and* **semicolon errors** *in the following sentences.*

Example   I like petunias; he doesn't.

1. I am definitely not a chef let me say that right off the bat.
2. The first time I tried to cook, I figured I had all I needed chicken, vegetables, and fruit for dessert.
3. But of course I forgot the bread in addition I didn't even think about appetizers.
4. I was a little nervous I had important company coming over.
5. Mostly, they were friends from out of town Patricia a friend from Spain her boyfriend Max a banker and his cousin Juliet who is a food critic for the local paper.
6. My hands were sweating so much I could hardly hold the spatula globules of sweat dripped down onto the pan.

7. At 700 I still hadn't finished the sauce.

8. Everyone arrived punctually at 830.

9. I considered leaving a note on the door "I've been kidnapped by aliens. Please go elsewhere for dinner."

10. But I did what I always do in this situation I called my mom.

11. She really calmed me down after all, she has years of experience.

12. Basically she told me that a good cook is one who cooks with love ingredients and ability don't matter.

13. I'm not sure she's right nevertheless, I felt much better.

14. Everyone was very sweet and ate my food in fact, we were laughing so much it didn't taste too bad.

15. I'll say this about cooking with the right company any meal can be enjoyable.

Exercise 22.5 Adding Semicolons and Colons

In the following essay, add **semicolons** *and* **colons** *where necessary.*

1. Homesteading is central to our national experience. On every frontier families faced the tasks of clearing the fields only then could they begin the process of farming, raising livestock, and building shelter. It was difficult, but essential after all with the harsh New England winters, having a roof over your head made the difference between life and death.

2. Homesteaders built several kinds of dwellings temporary shanties and lean-tos, rough cabins, simple frame houses, and more substantial and permanent brick and timber homes. These three phases of building occurred everywhere every sodbuster, gold miner, planter, and cattle raiser struggled to move from subsistence to success.

3. In Massachusetts, however, archeologists found something unusual. New Englanders rebuilt their temporary clapboard homes into sturdy timbered dwellings on the other hand in the south around the Chesapeake Bay settlers continued to construct rickety buildings.

4. The William Boardman house, built in 1687 is a good example of New England architecture. Its floor plan shows a typical spatial arrangement the hall, used for cooking, eating, working, and socializing the parlor a sleeping room for the

parents and a lean-to for kitchen chores and activities such as dairying. Up-stairs was used for storage and sleeping.

5. Archeologists contrasted this house with a typical reconstructed Chesapeake to-bacco planter's house. Both houses were built around the same time hence they have many similarities. But there are also many differences between the two.

6. In the Chesapeake house, the chimney is not built of brick but of mud and wood there is no window glass, only small shutters. The exterior is rough with unfinished planking the placement the interior has only one small room down-stairs with a loft above. In short, the Chesapeake family obviously did not live as comfortably or with as much privacy as the Boardmans did.

7. Historians have puzzled over the reasons for the difference in techniques and approaches toward building between the northern and southern colonies. They developed several theories the different climatic conditions, the different im-migration patterns, slavery, and gender imbalance.

8. In the colonial south, disease killed people at a greater rate than in New En-gland this left a population accustomed to an unstable family life. It simply didn't make sense to make a substantial investment in permanent homes. So-ciologists suggest a different reason stable houses are a result of the Puritan work ethic that compelled New Englanders to build solid homes.

9. Slavery, too, can account for the housing difference. Slaves meant money after all, they could work more land and harvest more tobacco. It appears that planters economized on everything possible to buy as many indentured ser-vants and slaves as they could. Better to live in a shanty than to have a large house and no one to cultivate the fields.

10. Of course, we all remember the large plantations of *Gone with the Wind*. Once the Chesapeake region left behind its problems of mortality and economic in-stability (around 1720), farmers began building the large mansions we know today nevertheless, the differences in housing between the two regions reflect the different economic situations, weather, philosophies, and social pressures that existed in America's early history.

Exercise 22.6   Writing with Semicolons and Colons

A. Write sentences using **semicolons** about the subject mentioned.

Example   Skating ___I love to skate; Peter does not.___

1. Your college

    _____

    _____

2. Your major

    _____

    _____

3. Your courses

    _____

    _____

4. Your best and worst course

    _____

    _____

5. Your professors

    _____

    _____

6. What you enjoy and don't enjoy in your courses

    _____

    _____

7. Your classmates

    _____

    _____

8. Some things you do between classes

    _____

    _____

9. The places where you study

    _____

    _____

10. Who you study with

    _____

    _____

B. *Write sentences with* **colons** *about the following subjects.*

1. The books you like

   _____

   _____

2. A particular book you like

   _____

   _____

3. The title and subtitle of the book

   _____

   _____

4. The city, publisher, and date

   _____

   _____

5. The people you recommended the book to

   _____

   _____

6. One thing you liked about the book

   _____

   _____

7. The names of the people or events in the book

   _____

   _____

8. Why you read this book

   _____

   _____

9. A quotation from the book

   _____

   _____

10. At what time you read your books

    _____

    _____

Exercise 22.7   Proofreading

Find and correct the **three semicolon errors** *and* **three colon errors.** *Some are misused and others are replaced erroneously by a comma.*

Georgia O'Keeffe

Georgia O'Keeffe (1887–1986) was: a teacher, a model, and a well-known painter. Above all, however, she was essentially a painter. She had studied art in New York City and then became an art teacher in Texas, among other places. By chance, a friend took some of her drawings to a gallery in New York. The owner was very impressed and exhibited them. Later, they met, she became the model for many of his photographs. After many years together, they married.

She lived in a number of different places, such as: Texas, New York City, Lake George, and New Mexico. Each place influenced her immensely, so she painted buildings in New York, trees and flowers in Lake George, and skulls and deserts in New Mexico.

She was particularly influenced by: Alfred Stieglitz, a photographer, Arthur Dove, a painter, and many others. Though feeling the influence of places and people around her, she was always essentially her own person.

Summary

I. **Semicolons**
   A. Use semicolons between independent clauses without a coordinating conjunction.
      Example: *Miami is hot; San Francisco is cool.*
   B. Use semicolons between independent clauses connected with a conjunctive adverb or transitional phrase.
      Example: *Miami is hot; however, San Francisco is cool.*
   C. Use semicolons for clarity when independent clauses have commas for various reasons.
      Example: *Tom left, taking hat, scarf, and boots; but despite the weather, he climbed to the top.*
   D. Use semicolons for misunderstandings in a list that could be ambiguous.
      Example: *I packed my hat, the blue panama; the green and yellow striped swimsuit; and suntan lotion; and I left for the beach.*
II. **Colons**
   A. Use colons after statements announcing further details.
      Example: *Three of us went: Charlotte, Mimi, and David.*

B. Use colons before a quotation.
    Example: *She stated: "So be it."*
C. Use colons to tell hours, minutes, seconds.
    Example: *21:16:59*
D. Use colons to cite Bible chapters and verses.
    Example: *Galatians 4:7–12*
E. Use colons for salutations in formal letters.
    Example: *Dear Sir:*
F. Use colons at the headings of memos.
    Example: *To: Staff*
G. Use colons to indicate the letter writer and typist by initials.
    Example: *KCD:ez*
H. Use colons for noting subtitles with titles.
    Example: *Forgery: How It's Done*
I. Use colons to cite a city in a footnote.
    Example: *London: Oxford UP*
J. Use colons for numbering a list.
    Example: *Rule no. 1: Do no harm.*

Chapter 23

Quotation Marks and Italics

Write above each quotation the reason the **quotation marks** are used in the following paragraph.

A twelve-inch gold-plated disk containing twenty-seven musical selections had been placed in the Voyager 2 spacecraft and by 1990 had already left the solar system. The contents of the record were selected for NASA by a committee chaired by Dr. Carl Sagan. Among the selections, which included a Pygmy girls' initiation song, "Melancholy Blues" performed by Louis Armstrong and his Hot Seven, and the Sacrificial Dance from Stravinsky's *Rite of Spring*, the committee had chosen the cavatina from Beethoven's "String Quartet no. 13 in B flat, Opus 130." . . . As Sagan noted, "The spacecraft will be encountered and the record played only if there are advanced spacefaring civilizations in interstellar space." . . . And how will they react to the middle section marked *Beklemmt*, which we of the human race find so moving? *Beklemmt* translates loosely into "oppressed" or "anguished." Will the aliens find it so? (Arnold Steinhardt, *Indivisible by Four*)

Quotation marks (", ") come in pairs. The first opens the quoted material; the second closes it. Quotation marks have a number of different uses.

Quoted Words

Most frequently, quotation marks enclose the exact words spoken or written by someone. In quoting formally, as in an essay or research paper, use a colon before the quoted material:

> Ralph Waldo Emerson wrote: "A foolish consistency is the hobgoblin of little minds."

Make sure the quoted material is a complete sentence. Or run the quotation into your sentence, making sure that the whole sentence is grammatical:

> Some people think "consistency is the hobgoblin of little minds" (Emerson), but I don't.

With a quotation that is not a complete sentence, running it into your sentence is usually the easiest:

> Emerson's comment about "hobgoblin of little minds" probably was a criticism of his critics.

For **dialogue,** use commas around the quoted material, but omit the first comma if the quoted material starts the sentence and the final comma if it ends the sentence. Start the quotation with a capital letter:

> **She said,** "You are consistently late."
> "Be glad I'm consistent," **he replied;** "that helps a lot."
> "You should study Emerson," **she retorted.**

Punctuate the sentence with a comma or a semicolon as you normally would do. In American usage, commas and periods go before the closing quotation marks (see examples above). Semicolons and colons go after the closing quotation marks:

> Emerson wrote about "a foolish consistency"; I am referring to a general consistency.
> Here is an example of your "foolish consistency": you are late for everything.

Question marks and exclamation points go before the ending quotation marks if they apply only to the quoted material:

> "For heaven's sake!" she yelled, "Why are you so late?"

They go after the quotation marks if they apply to the whole sentence:

> Why did she continue with her "foolish consistency"?

Use quotation marks around short quotations of up to two lines of prose and two or three lines of poetry (use space-slash-space between lines of poetry when more than one line is quoted):

> Emerson wrote "I am not wiser for my age, / Nor skilful by my grief" to express his continued doubts.

For long quotations, indent the whole quotation and omit quotation marks.
Use single quotation marks (', ') for a quotation within a quotation:

> "Why discuss 'a foolish consistency' with me?" he asked.

Do not use quotation marks for indirect quotations since you are not using exact words:

> INDIRECT QUOTATION: She said he was foolishly consistent.
> DIRECT QUOTATION: She said, "You are foolishly consistent."

Also do not put quotation marks around the title of your own piece of writing.

Divisions within a Work

The general rule is to use quotation marks when citing parts of larger works such as the following:

Chapters, divisions, parts, short stories, essays, and articles within books, newspapers, and collections

Titles of musical pieces and speeches within albums, cassettes, or CDs

Episodes within radio or TV series

Otherwise, titles of books, newspapers, magazines, record albums, cassettes, CDs, movies, radio and TV shows, plays, and musicals usually take italics (underlining in handwriting).

Words Cited as Words

Specialized words that may not be familiar to everyone can take italics:

He had perfected a *retro-waif* look.

Words used sarcastically or ironically, intending the opposite of their meaning, can take quotation marks in informal writing:

Their child's "masterpiece" was shown to everyone.

Use these types of words rarely, however. Instead, take the time to find the right words and the right tone.

In a discussion of words (or numbers or letters) as themselves, use quotation marks or italics to avoid misunderstanding:

What does "hobgoblin" mean anyway?

I was late because your "1" looked like "7."

Dot the "i" and cross the "t" in your name.

Italics (underlining in handwriting) should be used to write *8s* or *ts*, for example, to avoid the awkwardness of "8"s or "t"s.

Translations

Translations (when necessary) of foreign words take quotation marks, but use italics (underlining in handwriting) for the foreign words themselves:

Consistency goes against *chacun à son gout* ("each to his own taste").

Nicknames or Titles

Nicknames or titles given to people also take quotation marks. They may be inserted in the complete name if short (Leo "The Lip" Durocher) or added after the name (Kate Smith, "Songbird of the South").

Exercise 23.1   Identifying the Purpose of Quotation Marks or Italics

Write the purpose for each italicized word or set of quotation marks using these numbers:
  1   *exact words written or said by someone*
  2   *music piece, speech*
  3   *specialized words*
  4   *nicknames and titles given to people*

Example   Charlie "Bird" Parker was a great trumpeter. ___4___

1. Jazz probably was born in New Orleans with the so-called "New Orleans style." _____

2. This style owed much to piano *rags,* particularly those of Scott Joplin. _____

3. It continued northward to Chicago and made Louis "Satchmo" Armstrong famous. _____

4. *Swing* was big-band improvised music that was created by playing melodies that alternately came together and separated. _____

5. Improvisational music reached a peak in *bebop* in the 1950s. _____

6. Ella Fitzgerald, one of America's foremost jazz singers, made *scat* famous. _____

7. She used scat in her rendition of "Mack the Knife." _____

8. She herself wrote "Oh, But I Do" and "You Showed Me the Way." _____

9. Often known as "America's First Lady of Song," she moved easily from jazz to popular music. _____

10. Fitzgerald expressed her love of music succinctly: "The only thing better than singing is more singing." _____

11. "She doesn't know how good she is" sums up her extraordinary talent. _____

12. Edward Kennedy Ellington, always known as "Duke" because of his elegant ways, started early as a musician. _____

13. At the Cotton Club in New York City, he performed "Black and Tan Fantasy" and "Mood Indigo" with his orchestra. _____

14. The orchestra became known for its unique "voice." _____

15. The trombonist Joe "Tricky Sam" Nanton and trumpeter James "Bubber" Miley used plunger mutes on their instruments for this sound. _____

16. "Take the 'A' Train" became Duke Ellington's signature piece. _____

17. When he said, "It don't mean a thing if it ain't got that swing," that line turned into his signature song. _____

18. Billie Holiday, "Lady Day," sang with many musicians and had a great influence on the jazz and blues scene. _____

19. Many jazz musicians *jazzed the classics.* _____

20. George Gershwin composed symphonic pieces, such as "Rhapsody in Blue," that had definite jazz influences. _____

Exercise 23.2   Adding Quotation Marks

*In the following sentences, add **quotation marks** where necessary.*

Example   "Out of my way," he yelled.

1. Where's my favorite coffee cup? Bob wondered silently.
2. Then he asked out loud, Patricia? Have you seen my coffee cup?
3. Which one's that? Patricia answered.
4. Bob sighed. The one I always drink from. The one that has Globetrotters printed on it.
5. You mean that ugly orange coffee cup? The one with the crack in it? Patricia asked.
6. Yes, that one, Bob said. I don't mind the crack. I like that cup because it has a three-fingered handle.
7. We could afford to get a new coffee cup, Patricia thought. Out loud she said, Well, I wouldn't check the dishwasher because you never put anything there.
8. Let's not start on that again, Bob warned.
9. Then Bob thought to himself, no need to get worked up over a coffee cup. It'll turn up somewhere sooner or later.
10. Honey? Patricia said, looking up at him. I'm so sorry: I threw it away.

Exercise 23.3   Adding Quotation Marks and Italics

In the following sentences, add appropriate **quotation marks** *(more than one set might be needed) and underlinings. Write why they were needed according to this list:*
1   *chapter, short story, essay, or article*
2   *radio or TV series episode*
3   *words, letters, or numbers as themselves*
4   *translation of foreign words*

Example   En retard means "late" in French. __4__

1. A program on the radio called Asia/America tried to explain to its listeners what Asia really means. _____

2. One episode was called Asians in America. _____

3. An actor read Zia Jaffrey's The Monkeyman, published in Polygraph, about a surreal childhood experience. _____

4. An excerpt from the White Tigers chapter of The Woman Warrior by Maxine Hong Kingston told about what she called living with ghosts. _____

5. One time, a linguist explained why many Chinese and Japanese mixed the letters l and r, while Filipinos mixed p and f. _____

6. An interior decorator explained the concept of feng shui, literally wind-water, and how it applied to room design. _____

7. One really interesting segment was called Japanese Look at the West. _____

8. The host read excerpts from the chapter Diary of a Voyage to America kept by a Japanese diplomat in the mid-nineteenth century. _____

9. This diplomat never got used to what he called kogaku (barbarian music), which greeted him everywhere. _____

10. A cook said that dim sum meant a dot on the heart and explained how to order and eat it. _____

Exercise 23.4   Adding Quotation Marks and Italics

In the following essay, add **quotation marks** *and* **underlining (italics)** *where necessary.*

Example   "He's always late," she told me. "He's been reading Be Your Own Boss again."

You are such a snob, Maria exclaimed; you pretend to like Virginia Woolf when you don't understand a word she wrote. She tossed aside Orlando and Mrs. Dalloway as if these volumes were garbage. But, my dear Maria, you just haven't learned the donné of Woolf's work, Ty exclaimed. But Ty knew in his heart that he hadn't understood Woolf's stream of consciousness style either until Professor Smith had explained it. When Professor Smith had used donné (given), she meant we had to know that Woolf did not write in a linear way. He considered recommending A Room of One's Own, Woolf's essay about women's rights, or the movie Orlando. But being fed up with Maria, he said, Since you are such an intellectual, why don't you watch Sesame Street, especially the Big Bird Learns to Read episode. It's probably your favorite. Maria stomped out.

Exercise 23.5   Adding Quotation Marks and Italics

*In the following essay, add **quotation marks** and **underlining (italics)** where necessary.*

It seems like no matter how many conveniences are invented, people still want their lives to be easier and faster. The other day at the office when I was getting some water, my secretary complained about having to wait in line at the post office. I mean, she said, it takes them so long to weigh and stamp your package. I wish there were some robot that could just take care of it. I suggested to her that she could get a robot to stand in line for her, and her face lit up.

Joe from accounting chimed in, saying that he'd like a robot to watch The Wizard of Oz with his kids for the 158th time. Georgia finished her photocopying and laughed. I'd like someone to chop up onions for me. My eyes get so teary when I have to cook. Or wait—better yet, I could get a robot to cook for me. Andrew the mail guy said that he agreed that chopping onions was the worst part of cooking, and there was an acquiescent murmur from the crowd. At this point, the gathering around the water cooler was getting to be a mob.

I'd like a fashion robot, someone shouted, so I wouldn't be so unhip, as they say. Someone else wanted a robot to do their taxes, while another person said she'd like a replica to go visit her in-laws on Sundays. A robot to do the ironing. One to go to traffic court, another to remember to pick up the dry cleaning and to return the rented video by ten.

At this point I held up my hand. Hey, wait, people, I said. Tell me, what would you do with all this free time on your hands? Everyone stared at me blankly. I remembered what my mother used to say: you can't get to Heaven by taking the elevator. But I held my silence. They moved away from the cooler, shouts of one to shovel the walk! One to fix the plumbing! echoing down the hall.

Exercise 23.6   Writing with Quotation Marks and Italics

Use quotation marks and underlining (italics) to write the following paragraphs:

1. Write a dialogue between two people arguing about deer hunting.

2. Discuss the meaning of foreign words you know.

3. Tell your favorite episodes of a TV show (make up the episode title if you want).

4. Give the title of a short story or newspaper article and summarize it.

5. Discuss your (or a friend's) favorite slang words.

6. Write sarcastically about a friend's inability at a sport.

7. Write about your favorite pieces of music.

8. Quote a line from a song and tell about it.

9. Make up nicknames for your best friends.

10. Write about your two favorite chapters in this textbook.

Exercise 23.7   Proofreading

Add **two sets of quotation marks** *and* **three underlinings** *(italics) to the following paragraph.*

Susan Cheever, the daughter of the well-known writer, John Cheever, writes about her battle with alcoholism in Note Found in a Bottle, a moving memoir of her life as an alcoholic. In particular the first chapter, Drinking with Daddy, tells of her family's addiction. She tells of her father's stories that he called crypto-autobiographical: they were fiction, but they were true. Many of his short stories, for example, The Sorrows of Gin, depicted middle- and upper-class people who loved to drink. She herself started at an early age. After many battles with herself, she overcame alcoholism and has remained sober for years. Cheever has written many books, in particular the novel Looking for Work and a memoir about her father called Home before Dark.

Summary

I. **Quotation Marks and Italics**
  A. Use quotation marks to signify exact words spoken or written by someone.
    Example: *Grandma calls the VCR "that gosh darn thing."*
  B. Use quotation marks to enclose titles of parts of a whole work. (Use italics or underlines for the title of the whole work.)
    1. Chapters, divisions, parts, short stories, essays, articles
        Example: *I like the story "Gooseberries" by Chekhov.*
    2. Musical pieces, speeches
        Example: *"Un Bel Di" is my favorite aria.*
    3. Episodes of radio or television series
        Examples: *Did you see "The Ministry of Funny Walks" episode of* Monty Python's Flying Circus?
    4. Sarcastic and ironic uses of words
        Example: *The robbers "borrowed" from the bank.*
    5. Words, letters, and numbers as themselves
        Example: *In Europe, the "7" is crossed.*
    6. Translations
        Example: Hasta la vista *means "until we meet again."*
    7. Nicknames and titles given to people
        Example: *Bruce Springsteen, "the Boss," is here.*
II. Punctuation with Quotation Marks
  A. Commas and periods go inside the closing quotation marks.
    Example: *I read Joyce's short story "The Dead," but I didn't read "Araby."*
  B. Semicolons and colons go outside the closing quotation marks.
    Examples: *I read "The Dead"; you didn't.*
        I liked these characters in "The Dead": the husband, the wife, and the dead boy.
  C. Location of question marks and exclamation points
    1. Question marks and exclamation points go inside the quotation marks if they are part of the quoted material.
        Examples: *I want to read that article "Why Work?"*
        Don't yell "help!" unless you mean it.

2. Question marks and exclamation points go outside the quotation marks
   if they apply to the whole sentence.
   Examples: *Did you read that article "How to Win"?*
   Stop saying "yadda, yadda, yadda"!

Chapter 24

Apostrophes

In the following paragraph, circle the words with apostrophes and explain why each apostrophe was used.

Innovative architectural response to domestic change was especially strong in and around Los Angeles, where it had been led, since the 1930s, by the Austrian emigrés Rudolph Schindler and Richard Neutra. California's climate was perfect for the modernist ideal of thin-skinned houses, with a steel or wood frame and plentiful glass. But Schindler, Neutra, and others warmed up the International Style with brick hearths, wooden beams and built-ins, appealing to American ideals of tradition. They revolutionized American housing while responding to its context and history. These architects' most widely imitated visual change was the flat roof. By the late '40s, the flat-roofed, single-story house had become an affordable deus ex machina, not only for down-sized households, but also for thousands of G.I.s returning to a severe housing shortage. (Lisa Zeiger, "Natural Selection," *New York Times Magazine*)

Probably in about one hundred years we will no longer use **apostrophes** (') since they are already so widely misused or omitted. But until then, apostrophes have two uses:

1. To indicate missing letters (and numbers) in contractions
2. To show possession (something belongs to something or someone)

Contractions

In grammar, **contractions,** as the name implies, are shortened forms of words that omit a letter or letters; the missing letters (or in a few cases, numbers) are indicated by apostrophes. Usually two words are made into one (*don't* for *do not*). Notice that the apostrophe appears where the letter or letters are missing, *not* between the two words. Here are some common contractions:

aren't (*are not*)	don't (*do not*)	haven't (*have not*)
can't (*cannot*)	'40s (*1940s*)	he'd (*he would, he had*)

he's (*he is, he has*)	it's (*it is, it has*)	there's (*there is, there has*)
I'd (*I would, I had*)	let's (*let us*)	we'd (*we would, we had*)
I'm (*I am*)	she'd (*she would, she had*)	won't (*will not*)
isn't (*is not*)	she's (*she is, she has*)	you've (*you have*)

Although contractions have always been very common in speech, in the past they were generally considered too informal for serious writing; now, however, more and more formal writing has begun to include some contractions. Try not to use them unless the sentence sounds too stiff or artificial without them, but a few contractions in written work are all right.

Although the general trend is to omit apostrophes as the contractions establish themselves (we no longer write *'phone* or *'bus*, for example), some contracted words simply have no other accepted form: *jack o'lantern, o'clock, O'Casey, rock 'n' roll, tam o'shanter*. In order to imitate the sounds of a dialect, some writers use such contractions as *goin'* or *'fraid* or *so's* (*so as*). As you can see, contractions have a time-honored tradition in English.

Possessive Nouns and Possessive Indefinite Pronouns

When something belongs to something else or someone, we use an apostrophe to indicate that fact: *Mary's computer* (the computer that belongs to Mary), *the man's shirts* (the shirts that belong to the man), *the ladies' room* (the room that belongs to the ladies), *someone's chair* (the chair that belongs to someone). This rule applies also to things and ideas: *today's weather* (the weather that belongs to today), *the world's rivers* (the rivers that belong to the world), *time's passage* (the passage that belongs to time), *the thing's colors* (the colors of the thing). Notice that *all* these apostrophes for possession are added to **nouns** or **indefinite pronouns** (*anything, anybody, someone, a few,* etc.).

To decide when to use the possessive case, try the *". . . that belongs to . . ."* test. Then add the apostrophe to the last word.

To know where to put the apostrophe, follow these steps:

1. Do the apostrophe test (*cat's paws* = the paws that belong to the cat; *cat* needs apostrophe)
2. Add the apostrophe to the **end** of the word (*cat'*)
3. Add *s* after the apostrophe if there is no *s* already (*cat's*)
4. If the noun is singular and ends in *s*, add an apostrophe and another *s: Morris's bowl, Camus's novel*. (Because pronunciation is sometimes awkward with the added *s*, some writers use only the apostrophe: *Mary Jones' book*.) Greek and Latin proper names do not add the *s: Sophocles' plays, Jesus' teachings*. Otherwise, correct usage calls for adding the *s*.
5. If the noun is plural and ends in *s*, add only an apostrophe: *cats' paws*.

You may think that *'s* is for singular possessive nouns and *s'* is for plural possessive nouns, but this is *not* the rule. Consider, for example, *men's room, women's jobs, children's menu*; they are plural possessives with the apostrophe before the *s*.

The possessive noun does not always have to be followed immediately by the noun it goes with. Sometimes modifiers come between the two words: the **cat's** *sharp-clawed* **paws, Morris's** *very empty* **bowl.** Or sometimes the order is reversed: *the computer is* **Mary's** [*computer*], **that weather forecast is today's** [*forecast*], *those shirts are that* **man's** [*shirts*].

Plurals of Abbreviations, Numerals, and Letters

Apostrophes should not be used to make a word plural. Plurals of abbreviations, numerals, and letters should be treated like other plurals. Write plurals of abbreviations simply by adding an *s:* M.A.s, MBAs. Do the same with the plurals of numerals: 7s, 10s, 1980s, '80s (year). For letters, use underlining (italics in print) to avoid the appearance of typographical errors: *t*s, *h*s. Such plurals do not occur very frequently but do have their uses:

Many students dropped out of school in the turbulent '60s.

In the 1940s, my mother told me to mind my *p*s and *q*s.

How many M.D.s are in the teaching hospital?

Last semester I received As and Bs in my courses.

Omitting the apostrophe in these plurals could cause some confusion in meaning—for example, *90s* could refer to the temperature, the decade, or an amount of money—so be sure that your context makes clear what you are talking about.

Although you may see *'s* in plurals of abbreviations, numerals, and letters in writing from earlier periods, modern usage now calls for eliminating this use of the apostrophe. Unless a boss or professor insists on your adding the apostrophe, do not add it.

Knowing When to Use an Apostrophe

Many words often end in *s*, so be sure you have a possessive or a contraction before adding an apostrophe. Words end in *s* for these reasons:

1. Plurals (*cats, houses, students,* etc.)
2. Some contractions (*he's, it's, let's, she's, that's,* etc.)
3. Third-person singular present-tense verbs (*he sees, she runs, it goes,* etc.)
4. Possessive personal pronouns (*yours, his, hers, its, ours, theirs*)
5. Spelling (*always, dress, kiss, octopus,* etc.)
6. Possessive nouns and possessive indefinite pronouns (*girl's shoes, America's food, books' covers; nobody's business, anyone's guess*)

Notice that only contractions, possessive nouns, and possessive indefinite pronouns take apostrophes:

spelling	*third-person singular verb*		*possessive noun*	*plural*
Ellis	needs	to feed	**Brandon's**	cats.

contraction		possessive pronoun	contraction	possessive pronoun
That's	not	yours;	**it's**	hers.

In any normal piece of writing, simple plurals of nouns usually outnumber all the other kinds of words that end in *s*, and third-person singular present-tense verbs also are common, but neither of these takes an apostrophe. So realize that you need apostrophes, but not for all words that end in *s*.

Exercise 24.1   Identifying Possessive Nouns, Possessive Pronouns, and Contractions

A. *Identify* **apostrophes** *in this paragraph by writing one of these abbreviations above the word:*
  CONT *contractions*
  POSS *possessive nouns and indefinite pronouns*

Example   The dog's collar won't have Xs all around it.

(POSS above "dog's"; CONT above "won't")

1. The world's first "typing machines" were big, clumsy things used by people called "typewriters." They used the "qwerty" keyboard because the layout of the letters kept the keys from jamming while they were typing. For example, the *e* and *o* had to be far from each other because they often fell close to each other in words. The letter's frequency of use wasn't a factor.

2. Because these early typing machines and later ones too were manual, the clarity of the letters depended on the strength of individual fingers. A weak pinky made *q*s look like *o*s, or *a*s look like *u*s. The typist's touch was very important. An uneven touch could cause the page to look unprofessional.

3. My father's typewriter, a manual Royal, stayed with him his entire life; he couldn't live without it, he said. He got it in the 1930s and used it until the 1970s. He couldn't get the hang of an electric's light touch. So when he was in his eighties, he continued to peck away with two fingers on his Royal.

4. Times have really changed for students and office workers. Back in the 1970s, people typed on an electric typewriter called a Selectric that used a little ball with letters on it instead of individual keys. The Selectric's spe-

cial feature meant the keys wouldn't jam and the balls could be changed for different alphabets.

5. Then electronic typewriters with daisy wheels and memory were invented. With memory, a line of type would scroll across the keyboard's front and could be corrected before it went on the paper. Typing was slower until one adjusted to the new method. Soon the personal computer's debut eclipsed the electronic typewriter.

6. Although computers had been around since the 1940s, the public's awareness of them was very low. Early computers were huge, weighed three tons, and needed an expert's assistance to operate. They ate piles of IBM cards, and hundreds of vacuum tubes constantly required time-consuming adjustment and repairs.

7. The computers' temperature rose very high because these machines gave off a lot of heat. Air conditioners with high btus had to run continuously to keep the temperature around 70 degrees. Offices couldn't meet that special requirement, nor did they want the expense of specialists' salaries.

8. Now the computer's size has gone the other way. It's small enough to fit into a person's pocket. That's about as small as practicable since our fingers can't use too tiny a keyboard. But for functions that don't require a keyboard, the sky's the limit where smallness is concerned.

9. The fax's days are numbered since scanners will soon send documents to a computer screen, allowing documents to be printed easily. That'll be much easier than waiting for the fax machine, and it means we won't need a relatively large space for one dedicated use. A scanning slot right in the monitor doesn't seem like a farfetched possibility.

10. When's the next revolution in computers? Probably they'll be streamlined and replace the television set altogether. We'll watch movies, play games, send messages, write novels, talk, listen to music, get information, and learn Spanish all on the same machine. Most of it we're doing already.

Exercise 24.2   Identifying Words Ending in *s*

Above each word ending in **s,** *write one of the following:*
   PL   *plurals (cats, houses, students, etc.)*
   CON   *contractions (he's, it's, let's, she's, that's, etc.)*
   3RD   *third-person singular verbs (he sees, she runs)*
   PP   *possessive pronouns (yours, his, hers, its, ours, theirs)*
   SP   *spelling (always, dress, kiss, octopus, etc.)*
   POSS   *possessive nouns and indefinite pronouns (America's food, book's cover, somebody's house)*

1. Keisha's computer has a virus; she's worried that it's serious.

2. She always thinks that's hers alone, but it's everyone's.

3. Chris lets the bugs stay in; the computer has its own worries.

4. It's anyone's guess when someone's coming to fix the computers.

5. The fuss over the problems appears not worth the stress.

6. The lab technicians' equipment seems out of date.

7. Ellis's CD-ROMs have her worried because they're not hers.

8. Chris fixes Ellis's computer but feels it's useless.

9. "What's the next step if this doesn't work?" cries Ellis.

10. "Chris," says Keisha, "it's all yours; I hate computers."

Exercise 24.3   Adding and Identifying Apostrophes

In the following sentences, all the apostrophes have been left out. Put in the correct apostrophes for contractions, possessive nouns, and possessive indefinite pronouns. You might have to add an **s** *to some words. Some sentences may not need any apostrophes.*

1. Music Impressionisms true representative can be found in French composer Claude Debussy.
2. Born in 1862, he was Mme. Montè de Fleurvilles (Chopins disciple) pupil.
3. Debussy entered the Paris Conservatory but wouldnt have received any notice had it not been for his aptitude for a type of singing called *solfeggio*; he won the Conservatorys competition three years in a row.
4. After graduation he was employed by Tchaikovskys patroness, playing Tchaikovskys music for her, although its lyricism never really appealed to him.

5. In 1884 he won the Grand Prix de Rome, but, in the jurys opinion, his composi-torial skills were insufficient.
6. Meanwhile, in the early 1880s, the French poets created a Symbolist school; Debussys introduction into this group would prove to be the turning point in his musical career.
7. In 1888, he traveled to Bayreuth to hear Wagners *Parsifal*, but it wasnt all that hed expected.
8. More influential were Javanese gamelan music and Parisian painters works.
9. In the first years of the 1890s, Debussy developed his individual style of Im-pressionism around the three subjects of mood, atmosphere, and color.
10. His unique Impressionistic style is first heard in 1894s "Prélude à l'après-midi d'un faune."
11. It was only later in his career that his music took on Neo-Classicisms tinge of austerity.
12. Debussys Impressionistic opera *Pelléas et Mélisande* is the one great opera of its kind.
13. Written without arias or ensemble numbers, the composers matching of fanci-ful characters with his musics free-flowing nature is a major accomplishment.
14. He borrowed many of the Symbolists poems and fashioned them into music so that the poems almost ceased to be theirs.
15. Cancer took Debussys life during the Germans shelling of Paris in 1918.

Exercise 24.4   Correcting Possessive Nouns and Contractions

In the following paragraphs, all the apostrophes have been left out. Put in the cor-rect apostrophes for

1. *Contractions*
2. *Possessive nouns and indefinite pronouns*

   You might have to add **s** *to some words. Not all the paragraphs need apostro-phes in them.*

1. This book must be someones. If its not yours, it might be Alexis, and if not Alexis, then Jess. But he knows its not his because its cover looks red, and his is violet.
2. Peters handwriting looks sloppy. His letters and numbers are hardly readable, so he uses a computer to do all his writing. Luckily he has computers at home and at school. But when hes out and wants to leave a note to someone, he has problems.

3. His dress pants have designs on them. A cactus with thorns goes up one leg; a walrus lies along the other leg. The legs match though with greens and grays on both.

4. Sis report card has three As. But my parents know that she also has Ds in math and English. I think the As are for recess, giggling, and eating lunch. Shes proud anyway.

5. My grandparents house in Texas really has class. Its antebellum style seems authentic, but its only five years old. Also its three acres of grounds include a pond and lots of trees.

6. Bangkoks temperature is always hot. In the winter the days are in the nineties, usually around 95. The summers always have temperatures in the 100s. And the humidity is high also.

7. My two best friends cars are both Hondas. One wants to sell hers, but the other loves his and wants to keep it forever. Id buy hers if she didnt want lots of dollars for it.

8. In theaters, the ladies room always has a long line while the mens room line is very short. Whats the solution? Shouldnt womens rooms be larger since women take longer?

9. Smokers not only harm their own lungs but also the lungs of people around them. Childrens lungs are particularly susceptible, so parents really shouldnt smoke around children.

10. A cherry trees trunk is distinctive. Its bark seems to run sideways and looks smooth and shiny. Its also slightly reddish, so it looks different from most other trees.

Exercise 24.5   Writing with Possessive Nouns and Contractions

Write paragraphs using the words listed.

1. Write a paragraph about a lost book using these words:
   Chris's, couldn't, that's, it's

2. Write a paragraph about weather using these words:
    United States's, Canada's, the tropics', the coasts'

3. Write a paragraph about hair style using these words:
    Terry's, Jocelyn's, Cass's, Willis's

4. Write a paragraph about homes using these words:
    Sylvester's, grandparents', parents', cousin's

5. Write a paragraph about pets' names using these words:
    dog's, cat's, hamster's, parrot's

Exercise 24.6   Writing with Apostrophes

Write paragraphs using the listed words.

1. Write paragraphs about what Peter used to do on Sundays when he was a child.
    he'd   lamps'   Grandma's   they'd

2. Write a paragraph about going on a trip.
    Florida's   it's   beach's   condo's

3. Write a paragraph about finding buried treasure.
    pirates'   '30s   X's   didn't

4. Write a paragraph about fixing up an old car.
   '50s   Bart's   nobody's   won't

5. Write a paragraph about a canoe trip.
   hadn't   canoe's   o'clock   water's

6. Write a paragraph about a child's birthday party.
   Laurel's   cake's   she's   let's

7. Write a paragraph about what makes a good Western.
   horses'   cowboy's   you've   hats'

8. Write a paragraph about why blue is your favorite color.
   sky's   oceans'   isn't   my husband's (wife's)

9. Write a paragraph about your first day in school.
   couldn't   playground's   pencil sharpener's   children's

10. Write a paragraph about what children do on Halloween.
    jack o'lantern   10 o'clock   bells'   Woody's

11. Write a paragraph in which you apologize for hurting someone.
    I'm   you're   stupidity's   can't

Exercise 24.7   Proofreading

Delete any apostrophes used incorrectly in this paragraph and add any missing apostrophes. If you find no errors, do nothing.

I was born in the early 1950s, so I've measured my life's progress with the passing decades. The 50s scared everyone: the Cold War, air raid practice, bomb shelters, communism, the Korean War. Fear haunted my early years, too. Then the 60s brought "flower power," Woodstock, and hippies. Like other teenagers, I heard freedom's call: beads, fringes, bellbottoms, and sandals. In my twenties I experienced the 70s with long hair, long tokes, and long philosophical discussions deep into the night. The prosperous 80s belonged to me too; I'd joined the corporate world's rat race and made a bundle. I mellowed in my forties during the 90s watching the wonder that is my family's. Now that I'm in the 00s, I want to watch life's passage and hope I'll make it far into the twenty-first century.

Summary

I. **Apostrophes**
   A. Uses
      1. Use apostrophes to indicate the missing letter(s) or number(s) in contractions.
         Examples: *she's, he'd, '50s*
      2. Use apostrophes (and sometimes *s*) to make possessive nouns and possessive indefinite pronouns.
         Examples: *Alan's dog, anybody's guess*
   B. Where to place apostrophes in possessives
      1. Do the apostrophe test.
         Example: *He has the cars' engines* = the engines that belong to the cars. *Cars* needs an apostrophe.
      2. Add an apostrophe to the end of the word.
         Examples: *cars', car'*
      3. Then add *s* to the end of the word if it does not already end with an *s*.
         Example: *car's*
      4. If the noun is singular and ends in *s*, add an apostrophe and another *s*.
         Examples: *dress's hem, news's impact*
   C. When to use an apostrophe with words ending in *s*
      1. Words end in *s* without apostrophes for various reasons.
         a. Plurals often end in *s*.
            Examples: *dogs, houses, reasons*

      b. Third-person singular verbs end in *s.*
         Examples: *he has, she walks, the chair sits*
      c. Most possessive personal pronouns end in *s: yours, his, hers, its, ours, theirs.*
         Example: *The book is yours.*
      d. Some words are just spelled that way.
         Examples: *always, cactus*

2. Words end in *s* with apostrophes for two reasons.
      a. Some contractions end in *s.*
         Examples: *she's, it's*
      b. Possessive nouns and possessive indefinite pronouns end in *s.*
         Examples: *Pete's chair, everybody's trust*

Chapter 25

Dashes, Parentheses, Brackets, Slashes, Hyphens, *, . . . , &, %, #, @

Note after each sentence why the **punctuation** (aside from commas and periods) is being used in the following sentences.

1. Our modern world—the twenty-first century—has become reliant on symbols for identification instead of words. _____

2. Our world includes pictures (logos, icons) that we recognize instantly. _____

3. This symbol-laden world is not new, however. _____

4. Before literacy was widespread, all communication (stores, products, rulers, routes) was based on recognition of symbols. _____

5. A seller and/or buyer knew the pawnshop by the three hanging balls over door. _____

6. A would-be political leader would choose a sun or cow or hat to iden' or herself. _____

7. So that people could swear their allegiance—an absolute nece leader—they could just follow the symbol. _____

8. The alphabet (in itself a series of symbols) made written c᷍ ier, but we continued to use other symbols. _____

9. One boss recently wrote this note to an employee: ⁗ a 10% discount.* _____

10. *Buy 12 @$7.00 w/o discount." _____

Dashes, Parentheses, and Brackets

These three punctuation marks are used to add information within a sentence.
The **dash** (—), two hyphens without spaces before, between, or after them, interrupts a sentence and calls attention to added information, an explanation, or a definition, which may be in the middle or at the end of a sentence:

> That hat—the one with red and yellow flowers—is beautiful.
> He bought a beret—to look Basque—and a baseball cap.
> She is wearing a cloche—a bell-shaped, close-fitting hat.

Place the set off words as near as possible to the word(s) they explain in order to avoid confusion. Material set off by dashes seems informal but is an effective way to add variety, as well as to emphasize, reinforce, or elaborate. Use them sparingly, however.

Parentheses (( )) (*parenthesis* = singular) also interrupt a sentence. They add information, an explanation, or a definition that is not very important to the sentence:

> His hat (a panama) kept the sun off.
> She is wearing a cloche (a bell-shaped, close-fitting hat).

The context and your intentions will dictate whether you should choose dashes or parentheses in a piece of writing.

In addition, use parentheses to add an "aside" (your own comment), to enclose ~rs in a list, and to repeat spelled numbers:

> d the striped fedora (**I didn't**). (aside)
> is cowboy hat (!) to drink water. (aside)
> to (1) bring a sun hat, (2) use suntan lotion, and (3) drink plenty of ᵇered list)
> for three hundred forty dollars ($340.00). (numerals after spelled

Se used for making an editorial change or inserting your own
(info You make the change for grammatical reasons or to add in-

Another use is M]aybe I will run again." (grammatical)
Well, maybe I will [run again], but I haven't decided."

Senator Jones
If a quotation has an er, information within parentheses:
cate that you are quoting witching only once [1999]) on the gun issue.

"I'm throwing my hat in dity, use *[sic]*—meaning "thus" or "so"—to indi-
xactly:

the
k *[sic]*," said Senator Jones.

Slashes and Hyphens

Both the slash (/) and the hyphen (-) link words to each other.

The **slash** (/) has become increasingly popular as a shortcut: *singer/songwriter, actor/writer/producer, his/her, there is/are, was/were, and/or.* Overuse can be annoying, especially when simply adding *and* or *or* will suffice (*singer and songwriter, his or her*), but sometimes changing will require recasting the sentence, as with *and/or.* For example, to change *Her sister and/or her brother will go,* you must write, *Her sister or her brother or both will go.* However, try to avoid *and/or* when you can.

Use the slash also to indicate a new line of poetry when you are quoting two or more lines in the text:

One of Basho's haiku reads: "Your song caresses / the depths of loneliness, / high mountain bird."

Leave a space before and after the slash to differentiate this slash from other uses. Also it can be used for fractions (3/4) if many will occur in your essay: if not, write the fraction out. The **backward slash** (\) has its computer uses.

Hyphens (-) (often erroneously called dashes) connect words or parts of words:

Prefixes and suffixes to main words (*mid-July, anti-war, self-esteem, president-elect, school-aged*)

Words in phrases to form adjectives (*on-the-job training, back-to-school sale, high-school diploma*)

Compound names and titles (*Juan Lopez-Jones, ambassador-at-large, mother-in-law*)

Noun or adjective from a two-part verb (*a follow-up on the report, a follow-up report*)

Compound phrases used as nouns (*mother-daughter, forget-me-not*)

Units of measure and numbers (*light-years, eighty-four, nine-tenths, 555-9876*)

Partial words to be connected with a later word (*him- or herself, pre- or postwar, full- and part-time*)

You can use a hyphen to divide a word at the end of a line of type (called **syllabification**), but the tendency today is to avoid such divisions. If you are using a word processor, word wrap automatically eliminates end-of-line divisions. If you must divide a word, break it only at a syllable. Check a dictionary for accurate syllable breaks, and never leave a single letter at the end or beginning of a line.

Asterisks (*) and Ellipses (. . .)

Both the **asterisk** (*) (sometimes called the *star key* on the telephone) and the **ellipsis** (. . .) indicate that words are missing. The asterisk signals that further information is given, usually at the bottom of the page. The *ellipsis* (*ellipses* = plural) indicates that words have been omitted in a quotation:

> ORIGINAL: The senator was open about her use of campaign funds and candid about her past financial indiscretions.
>
> WITH ELLIPSIS: Senator Jones seemed "open . . . and candid" in her remarks.

Make sure that you still have a complete and grammatical sentence with the ellipsis. An ellipsis also indicates an interruption, a trailing off, or a hesitation in dialogue:

> REPORTER: And you . . . (interrupted)
>
> SENATOR JONES: Yes! I want to run for office. . . . (trailing off)
>
> REPORTER: But you're not sure you have the votes?
>
> SENATOR JONES: Well, I think I have the votes . . . , but I'm still unsure of financial backing. (hesitation)

As shown, form the ellipsis with three spaced dots, but add a fourth dot to indicate a period if one is necessary, or add a comma after the three dots if one is needed for the whole sentence.

Ampersand (&), Percent (%), Number (#), and Each (@)

In general, these symbols should be written out in a piece of writing. Some companies use the ***ampersand*** instead of *and* in their titles (e.g., Allyn & Bacon). Write *percent* instead of % except for data or lists. Instead of # (also called the *pound sign*), use "No." (Nos. = plural) if you must abbreviate; otherwise write "Number One." @ means *each* (or *per*) on lists and invoices and *at* in e-mail addresses; it has little or no use in pieces of writing.

Exercise 25.1   Identifying Uses of Dashes and Parentheses

*In the following sentences, identify the use the **dashes** and **parentheses** have, according to this list:*
   1   *to call attention to information*
   2   *to add some less important information*
   3   *to give an "aside"*

Example   My sister (a born athlete) can play jai alai. __3__

   1. Most American Buddhists are converts—rarely being born into the religion. _____

   2. The most popular book in America about Tibetan Buddhism is *The Tibetan Book of the Dead*—a book very few Buddhist monks encounter in their studies.

   _____

3. In reality, it is an obscure text read to the recently departed about the peaceful and wrathful deities the dying can expect to encounter in the afterlife (Buddhists believe in life after death). ____

4. *The Tibetan Book of the Dead* was first introduced to the west by W. Y. Evans-Wentz—an Oxford-educated "eccentric" who lived in San Diego. ____

5. In 1927 he published a commentary based on Theosophy (an occult religion founded in New York in 1875). ____

6. The introductions and commentaries surrounding the text—which are often longer than the original text itself—have little to do with traditional Tibetan Buddhism. ____

7. Other versions include a Jungian rendition (by D. I. Lauf) and a simulated, eight-hour acid-trip-like version by former Harvard professor turned counter-culture guru Timothy Leary, called *The Psychedelic Experience.* ____

8. This elaboration of Buddhism—a far cry from the original religion—has even affected traditional Buddhists, changing their patterns and conceptions of worship. ____

9. Westerners love the idea of a kinder, gentler religion—simple, peaceful, positively Zen-like. ____

10. After all, that which is furthest from us (and what's farther than Tibet?) often seems the most exotic. ____

Exercise 25.2   Identifying Uses of Dashes, Parentheses, and Brackets

*In the following sentences, identify the use the **dashes, parentheses,** or **brackets** have, according to this list:*

  1 *to call attention to information*
  2 *to add some less important information*
  3 *to give an "aside"*
  4 *to insert own words in a quotation*

Example   He always removes his hat indoors (what a gentleman). __3__

1. Zora Neale Hurston (1891–1960) grew up in a family of eight children in Florida. ____

340   *Part V | Punctuation*

2. Her early gifts—writing, research, story telling—were stifled, however, because of poverty. _____

3. She finally received an associates degree from Howard University (a predominantly black school in Washington, D.C.). _____

4. Hurston continued her education at Barnard College and graduated in 1928 (already thirty-seven years old but claiming to be twenty-seven). _____

5. She went on to publish seven books—four novels, two folklore anthologies, and her autobiography—and numerous short stories and essays. _____

6. Henry Louis Gates, Jr. (a renowned professor and writer), wrote incisively about Hurston's novel, *Their Eyes Were Watching God.* _____

7. He noted that the "charting of [the main female character's] fulfillment as an autonomous imagination" revealed a different perspective. _____

8. Hurston had her characters speak in black dialect, which (wrongly) caused many writers to criticize her. _____

9. "This use of the [black] vernacular became the fundamental framework" for most of her work, stated Gates. _____

10. Her concentration on female characters and de-emphasis of the "black experience" (subjugation, racism, injustice) put her out of the mainstream of black writers. _____

Exercise 25.3   Identifying Slashes, Hyphens, Asterisks, and Ellipses

*A. In the following sentences, identify the use the **slashes, asterisks,** and **ellipses** have, according to this list:*
  1 *shortcut for* and *or* or
  2 *lines of poetry*
  3 *signifying that further information follows later*
  4 *words omitted in quotation*

1. As a novelist/essayist/anthropologist, Zora Neale Hurston had a full career.

   _____

2. Hired by Franz Boas,* she gathered folklore in the South. _____

   *World-famous anthropologist at Barnard College, New York.

3. She published articles/essays/reports in the *Saturday Evening Post*, the *Journal of Negro History*, the *Pittsburgh Courier*, and the *Journal of American Folklore.* _____

4. Her novels show a "questing hero as woman, . . . giving a woman character such power and such daring" (Mary Helen Washington). _____

5. *Their Eyes Were Watching God* has been called "a bold feminist novel . . . in the Afro-American tradition." _____

6. This novel depicts good times in the South as shown by a character's singing these racy lyrics, "Yo' mama don't wear no Draws / Ah seen her when she took 'em off." _____

7. But Hurston did write of the black experience in her essay, "How It Feels to Be Colored Me."* _____

   World Tomorrow, 1928.

8. In his biography of Hurston, Robert Hemenway concluded that "Zora lived a difficult life . . . obsessed with a book she could not finish." _____

9. Her troubles might well be embodied in the old spiritual, "Nobody knows the trouble I've seen; / Nobody knows my sorrow." _____

10. Jobless, penniless, accused of child molestation,* she died alone and was buried in an unmarked pauper's grave. _____

    *Hurston was acquitted of the charges, but her reputation was ruined.

B. *In the following sentences, identify the use the* **hyphens** *have, according to this list:*
   1 *prefix or suffix attached to main word*
   2 *combined phrase to form adjective*
   3 *compound name, title, phrase*
   4 *partial word to be connected to later word*

   1. Sarah Johnson-Smith hadn't planned to, but she became an alcoholic. _____
   2. Although a college-bound student, she liked having a good time. _____
   3. She mixed with the offbeat crowd and took up drinking and smoking. _____
   4. At the graduation ceremony, she reached for her high-school diploma and missed because she was so drunk. _____

5. After one semester of a less-than-sterling college career, she dropped out to get married. _____

6. Her husband-to-be also liked drinking, so the two of them went on long binges. _____

7. Luckily her future father-in-law, experienced with his son's troubles, saw that together they might overcome alcoholism. _____

8. He sent them to a rehab center for a month-long stay. _____

9. Sarah and her fiancé helped each other, but finally each had to depend on her- or himself to get through. _____

10. Newly sober, attending AA meetings daily, Sarah hopes finally to get that community-college degree. _____

Exercise 25.4   Correcting Errors in Using &, %, #, @, and Numbers

*In the following essay, change the **symbols** to words.*

Although the fax (short for "facsimile") machine seems like an interim machine between the telephone & the scanner, it has become essential for over 50% of businesses. The fax has been around since the 1960s, but at that time it took 6 minutes to send 1 page of copy. By the 1980s that time had been cut to 30 seconds@page, a 200% improvement. However, the # of pages that businesses send has increased to over 5 pages. So now it still takes a long time to send a fax & the expenses mount up too. Although costs have gotten cheaper, a typical long-distance transmission runs to $.15@minute, which can be rather high, especially for a long document. At least the #1 complaint has been solved: not many menus & ads come over the fax anymore.

Exercise 25.5   Writing with Dashes, Parentheses, Brackets, Slashes, Hyphens, and Ellipses

A. *Write sentences using the indicated **punctuation** and subject.*

Example   Slash (Hats)

_____ My cowboy hat/water bowl really comes in handy.

1. Dash (kinds of dogs)

    _____

2. Parentheses (your dog [hypothetical or real])

    _____

3. Brackets (what you tell your dog)

    _____

4. Slash (the names you call your dog)

    _____

5. Hyphen (what you are to your dog)

    _____

6. Ellipsis (what you have yelled at your dog)

    _____

7. Dash (others who care for your dog)

    _____

8. Parentheses (who else love[s] your dog)

    _____

9. Hyphen (your dog's attitude toward life)

    _____

10. Dash (dogs you have had)

    _____

*B. In each of the following sentences, add **dashes** and material that **emphasizes, reinforces,** or **elaborates.** Choose any part of the sentence that seems logical to you:*

Example   *—wanting to make a good impression—*
Senator Jones͜talked forcefully about financial reform.

1. Almost everyone I know sends e-mail.
2. I see my colleagues almost every day, but we still send e-mail.
3. I keep in closer touch with my relatives through e-mail.
4. Sometimes all of us just exchange insignificant stuff.
5. Sometimes long lists of jokes pass from person to person.
6. But organizing a family reunion among relatives from many states was much easier.

7. Only my grandmother in Florida had to be telephoned.

8. Everyone could have input and could see what everyone else said.

9. We narrowed down our reunion to just two states and just one season.

10. I'm in charge of finding Idaho facilities for this event.

Exercise 25.6   Adding Dashes

*In each of the following sentences, add **dashes** and material that **emphasizes, reinforces,** or **elaborates.***

—a play by Shakespeare—
Example   Reading *A Winter's Tale* is difficult.

1. Everyone in Josephine's family eats something different for breakfast.

2. Mornings at her house are like rush hour at a roadside diner.

3. Josephine likes cereal, but only if it's healthful.

4. Her brother, a marathon runner, likes to eat eggs in bulk.

5. Her father is a junk food addict who likes doughnuts, especially the kind with sprinkles.

6. Josephine has twin younger brothers, one who will eat only cinnamon toast and one who will eat only oatmeal, and that only if it's made from scratch.

7. Last year, Josephine's mother went on strike and refused to be her family's short-order cook.

8. The five of them sat around the breakfast table, looking at each other as the minute hand wound around the clock, making them late for work and school.

9. Finally, Josephine's father got up and all of them helped make wheat toast.

10. Then they took a tray of orange juice, toast, and jam up to their mother in bed.

Exercise 25.7   Proofreading

*Find the **four errors** in the use of **dashes, parentheses,** and **brackets,** and correct them.*

Poison ivy, poison oak, and poison sumac (genus name: Toxicodendron) contain urushiol, an oil that easily penetrates the skin and causes an allergic reaction.

Urushiol can be found in all parts of the plants—roots, stems, leaves, flowers, and berries, so it cannot be avoided. But you don't have to be in contact with a plant to be poisoned by it. Touching anything outdoors (a garden tool, pet, clothing, sports equipment, shoes—can trigger a reaction. Burning leaves or logs can send urushiol into the air. And it is long lasting—fall clothing or tools can contaminate you the following year. "Leaves of three, let [it] be" applies to poison ivy; poison oak and poison sumac have more leaves and are hard to recognize. To treat a bad case of poison ivy (mild cases do not need treatment), wash everything that came in contact with the plant. Then apply calamine lotion and compresses with Epsom salts (or other astringent. A very severe case needs the care of a doctor and prescriptions. The symptoms can be treated, but as any doctor will say, "There is no cure [despite its prevalence."

Summary

I. **Dashes** (—)
   A. Dashes add information, explanations, or definitions.
      Example: *Anton Chekhov—a precursor of Raymond Carver—wrote many short stories.*
   B. Dashes emphasize, reinforce, and elaborate by interrupting the sentence.
      Example: *Her grave—unmarked and neglected—was forgotten for many years.*
II. **Parentheses** (())
   A. Parentheses add information, explanations, or definitions considered not important to the sentence.
      Example: *Peruvian women wear Borsalinos (bowler hats).*
   B. Parentheses add "asides," the writer's comment.
      Example: *He paid for dinner (what a guy).*
   C. Parentheses enclose numbers in a list within a sentence.
      Example: *Your instructions are (1) to buy bread, (2) to order a chicken, and (3) to learn how to grill.*
   D. Parentheses enclose numerical sums after written sums.
      Example: *Enclosed is a check for twenty-four dollars ($24.00).*
III. **Brackets** ([])
   A. Brackets make editorial changes for correct grammar or clarity.
      Example: *"I want to [take a vacation], but I have many other commitments."*
   B. Brackets insert the writer's own words in a quotation.
      Example: *The senator stated, "I have been deeply interested in gun control [he is against it] and will continue to be."*

IV. **Slash (/)**

A. Slashes are shortcuts replacing *and* and *or.*
    Examples: *and/or, writer/actor, producer/director*

B. Slashes indicate a new line of poetry in quotations of more than one line.
    Example: *Roses are red; / Violets are blue. / Sugar is sweet, / And so are you.*

C. Slashes indicate fractions if many are being used in one text (otherwise write out the fractions).
    Examples: *3/4, 1/10*

V. **Hyphen (-)**

A. Hyphens attach prefixes and suffixes to main words.
    Examples: *self-help, school-aged*

B. Hyphens combine phrases to form adjectives.
    Examples: *high-tech industry, middle-aged parents*

C. Hyphens attach compound names or titles.
    Examples: *Smith-Jones, ambassador-at-large*

D. Hyphens make nouns and adjectives from two-part verbs.
    Examples: *follow-up report, walk-in closet*

E. Hyphens connect words in compound phrases used as nouns.
    Examples: *mother-to-be, father-in-law*

F. Hyphens connect units of measure and numbers.
    Examples: *light-years, forty-six, one-fifth, 123-4567*

G. Hyphens indicate that a partial word is to be connected with a later word.
    Examples: *him- or herself, pre- or post-game*

H. Hyphens syllabicate words.
    Example: *es-tab-lish-ment*

VI. **Asterisk (*)**

A. Asterisks indicate further information follows.
    Example: *Only $2.* *With $50 purchase*

B. Asterisks are sometimes called the "star" key.

VII. **Ellipses (. . .)**

A. Ellipses indicate omitted words in a quotation.
    Examples: *"The movie has superior visuals and engrossing portrayals of characters."*
    The movie is "superior . . . and engrossing."

B. Ellipses indicate an interruption or a trailing off in written dialogue.
    Example: *"But that's not . . . ."*

VIII. **Ampersand (&)**, **Percent (%)**, **Number (#)**, **Each (@)**

A. & should be written *and* except for some company titles and logos.
    Examples: *Allyn & Bacon, Barnes & Noble*

B. % should be written *percent*, except in invoices and lists.
    Example: *They charge 5 percent interest.*

C. # should be written *number* or *no.*
    Example: *Give me a no. 2 pencil.*

D. @ should be written *each* or *per*, except for e-mail addresses.
    Example: *These hats cost ten dollars each.*

Errors

Chapter 26

Sentence Fragments

Each of the following advertisements has one or more **sentence fragments.** Underline the fragments you find.

Want to lose weight? Have friends? Get a good job? Find that special someone? Join the TopNotch Health and Sports Club and make all your dreams come true. It's a proven fact that thinner people have more fun and go further in life. Sign up today! Join now and get the first month free. Also a tee shirt with our logo. And two free passes for anyone you know. A great bargain!

The perfect jacket for all occasions. Dressy with a tie. Casual with a polo shirt. Stain resistant. Waterproof. Inside and outside pockets. Secret pocket for important documents. Roomy. Hand-turned lapels. Five-button cuffs. Comes in charcoal or black. Order now while supplies last. One per customer, please!

Here is the famous Palm Light you've been hearing about. It fits into the palm of your hand and lights with a touch of a finger. Invaluable in hotel rooms. Perfect for the theater. Makes dark staircases safer. Read maps in the dark. Order one for everyone in your family. Each $3.95. Special for a limited time only: Five for only $17.95. Big savings. Free shipping and handling. Don't wait until you're stuck in the dark.

Subscribe to *Computer Casuals.* The only magazine that tells you what to wear while you work at your computer. You'll feel better knowing you look right for Games. Chats. Surfing.

Types of Fragments

A *fragment* is part of a sentence or independent clause that has been punctuated as if it were a sentence. Professional writers often use intentional fragments for emphasis and variety since they want to attract and maintain their audience. However, the writing that you do for school and business will probably be in complete sentences, so you want to avoid unintentional fragments.

Most fragments fall into a few types:

1. A dependent clause cannot stand alone, so either remove a word to make the dependent clause an independent clause or attach it to a nearby independent clause. For example, *although I like pizza* is a fragment; it can be changed by removing the subordinating word *although*, but this change probably alters the meaning. Attaching it to an independent clause usually works better: *Although I like pizza, I prefer spaghetti.*
2. Another type has an incomplete verb, such as *Pizza being the best.* Here the verb may be changed (*Pizza is the best*), or the fragment may be attached to a previous sentence (*I like many kinds of snacks, pizza being the best*).
3. Some fragments lack a subject and verb although the rest of the sentence is there. For example, in *I love pizza. The best of all foods and my personal favorite of all times,* the second part needs both a subject and verb. Adding *It is* will work, or this second part may be attached to the first part with a comma.
4. Some fragments are phrases. They also lack a subject and verb, but usually just attaching them to an independent clause that comes before or after will avoid a fragment. In *During my college years. I ate pizza almost every day*, just attaching the prepositional phrase with a comma to the next sentence will work. Additional words probably will not be necessary.

Some fragments, however, cannot be salvaged and must be rewritten completely. If you find that many of your fragments seem uncorrectable by these methods, you should study sentence structure carefully.

Intentional Fragments

Advertisements often contain fragments to catch readers' attention by featuring short strings of words that are easy to read. So now and then well-placed fragments can be effective when you want to call attention to a point. Use them sparingly. Here are a few possibilities:

1. You can use a **word** all by itself for emphasis. For example, if you write, *Everyone knows the best food in the world,* you could continue with, *It is pizza.* But writing a complete sentence hardly seems necessary. Just write, *Pizza.* Use this type of fragment no more than two or three times in a piece of writing so as not to lose the effect.
2. **Exclamations** (*Wow! Oh, boy! Wonderful! Great!*) can be used sometimes to make your writing more colorful and exciting. Don't overdo this usage or you will sound like an inarticulate teenager.
3. **Phrases** (*So what? What a day. How come? Why me?*) are also colorful and exciting a few times in a piece of writing.
4. **Dependent clauses** are rarely acceptable. In some cases, however, when *which* (a pronoun) is used to refer to a complete idea before it, it sometimes is written as a separate sentence. For example, in *Pizza delivery often means cold pizza.*

Which isn't the worst thing in the world, the *which* serves as the pronoun subject of the sentence and refers to the entire previous sentence. Normally, however, *which* should refer to a specific word and be part of an independent clause.

Exercise 26.1   Finding Fragments

*Underline the **five fragments** in each of these paragraphs.*

1. We owe potatoes to Peru and Ecuador. Still their national dish. Lots of varieties, from tiny thumb-sized ones to huge breadloaf size. And colors ranging from white to purple. Although sweet potatoes and yams belong to an entirely different botanical family. One of the staples of many countries in South America, Europe, and Africa.

2. Potato chips, everyone's favorite snack. They may have been invented in the United States. A rich summer resident of Saratoga, New York, possibly Cornelius Vanderbilt, criticizing the potato made by the cook. Who, to get even, sliced the next batch too thinly, fried them too much, and oversalted them. And called them "Saratoga potatoes." Instant success.

3. Europeans not as enthusiastic at first. England had meat and bread. Did not want to ruin the soil with this new crop. Ireland seeing them grow well. France thinking they were poisonous. But finally found them nutritious, easy to grow, and quite delicious.

4. Became the food that saved Ireland. When all else failed. Luckily potatoes were nutritious. Although poor people rarely had much variety in their potatoes. Eating them boiled, skin and all. Kept everybody alive.

Exercise 26.2   Correcting Fragments

*Change the punctuation so that the **five fragments** are attached to independent clauses.*

1. People are crazy about lobster. Although they taste bland. And need lots of melted butter or a flavorful sauce. They look like giant insects. Since that's what they are with their wavy antennae, curly tails, and huge claws. They are related to other exoskeletal insects. That crunch when we squash them. People like the high price. Because they think they are getting something special for so much money.

2. A real dish for the intellectual set is brains. Calf brains or lamb brains being the most common. Fry them for a short time. With just a little butter or olive oil, a touch of garlic, a light sprinkle of parsley. And a squeeze of lemon juice. Having lots of protein and very little fat. Brains could help even the nonintellectual set.

3. Not long ago chicken wings ranked low. As the preferred part of the chicken. With the neck and back. They usually went into making chicken stock or were thrown away. Considered cheap and unworthy. Only poor people bought them. Now everyone loves chicken wings. And orders them all by themselves. Or fights at the dinner table for them.

4. Always considered the best part by Asians. And served at banquets and to special guests. Chicken wings were the tastiest and daintiest part. With wings having lots of bones. And since the meat closest to the bone is considered the best. Wings were especially prized. For that reason, wings cost the most. Unlike in Western countries.

Exercise 26.3   Changing Fragments into Sentences

*Turn these **fragments** into complete sentences. Then use them in paragraphs that make sense. Finally, use the space on the next page to turn them into a short essay. Use additional paper if necessary.*

1. Insomnia, which is a terrible affliction.

2. Unless experienced, never know how frustrating it is to lie in bed awake all night.

3. My college roommate, who never slept more than three hours a night.

4. Although she was very tired and her eyes drooped heavily all day.

5. Even falling asleep in her classes!

6. My poor roommate, being exhausted all the time, pale and irritable.

7. Along with her grades falling, her failing performance in soccer, and an inability to concentrate.

8. Affecting me, too!

9. Every time she got up at night to turn on the light, waking me up.

10. Finally, my roommate agreeing to go to the doctor.

11. Got a diagnosis of chronic insomnia and a pamphlet on techniques for falling asleep.

12. Americans moving beyond the days of counting sheep.

13. After taking a warm bath every night and wearing socks and a sleep mask to bed.

14. With occasional use of sleeping pills, too.

15. Finally, rest for both of us.

Exercise 26.4   Correcting Fragments

*Correct the **ten fragments** in the following essay.*

Born on May 23, 1734, in Germany, Franz Anton Mesmer the father of the modern practice of hypnotism. Dr. Mesmer was educated at the University of Vienna. Where he discovered and developed the theories of British physician Richard Mead. Mead believed that the gravitational attraction of the planets affected human health. By influencing an invisible fluid found in the human body. Mesmer revised this theory into the notion of "animal magnetism" wherein the laws of magnetism, not gravity, affected this mystery fluid, and any trained person could manipulate that influence.

Mesmer then reasoned that disease was the outcome of obstacles to the flow of fluid in the body. The dislodging of these obstacles was executed through "crises." Trance states which often ended in delirium or convulsions. Mesmer developed many forms of treatments to restore the proper flow of fluid. He, of course, a very active participant in these treatments.

In 1778, Dr. Mesmer was accused of fraud by a group of Viennese physicians, so he settled in France. Where he continued to enjoy a successful practice. Still, he came under suspicion from King Louis XVI. Who appointed a committee of physicians and scientists (which included, among others, American statesman Benjamin Franklin). The committee decided that Mesmer was unable to prove his "scientific breakthrough." The Mesmerist movement lost popularity.

Though Mesmerism and its accompanying theory of the mysterious invisible body fluid has gone the way of many scientific "mis-discoveries." It is undeniable that Mesmer did develop a close relationship with his patients and alleviated many of their nervous disorders. Much in the same way psychiatry would a century later. Followers of Mesmer would continue to investigate the trance state. Leading to the modern development of legitimate applications of hypnotism.

Exercise 26.5   Correcting Fragments

*Correct the **ten fragments** by using these methods: attach it to an independent clause; complete the verb; and give it a subject and/or a complete verb.*

There is much more food in the sea than we Americans are willing to eat. Although recently we have started eating more fish. Formerly, canned tuna, fish sticks, and breaded fried shrimp about the only seafood we liked. People in the south had always eaten catfish. Considered a lowly food for poor people. On the opposite side, only rich people ate raw oysters and lobster. Because of the health benefits. Some people eating fish that was not fried. Salmon, halibut, bluefish, and other varieties. Squid and octopus too. Using the Italian words *calamari* and *scungilli* for these two foods. Made a big difference. The words had snob appeal, too. For the same reason, shark called *mako*.

Exercise 26.6   Changing Fragments into Sentences

*Turn these **fragments** into complete sentences, expand them into paragraphs that make sense, and then turn them into a short essay with transitions to connect the paragraphs. Use additional paper as needed.*

1. Because nobody likes to waste food

    Probably a Neapolitan cook coming upon some leftover dough

    Flattened out and spread a little leftover tomato sauce and mozzarella

    After baking in a wood-burning oven, the only kind around

    Invented the first pizza

2. Pizza, which means "pie" in Italian

   A traditional dish in Naples, Italy

   During World War II, discovered by American soldiers

   Became popular in America

   Branched out into many styles and varieties

3. Pizza having a style depending on the region and crust

   Chicago style being thick-crusted

   New York style having a thin, crisp crust

   Sicilian style having rectangular-shaped, bread dough

   Neapolitan style made smaller with a soft, breadlike crust

4. Pizza also depending on the ingredients

   Neapolitan style using buffalo mozzarella, special tomatoes, and flour, and baking in a wood-burning oven

   New Haven style having whole clams, garlic, olive oil, and oregano

California style combining ham and pineapple, goat cheese and sun-dried tomatoes, or other odd mixtures

Nobody claiming anchovies as his or her own idea

Exercise 26.7   Proofreading

*Find and correct the **twenty fragments** in this short essay. Either attach them to an independent clause, complete the verb, or add a subject and/or a verb.*

Watermelon

Who doesn't love a big slice of watermelon on a hot summer day? The perfect snack or dessert at a picnic, at the beach, in the back yard, or just in the kitchen. Everybody loves it.

Watermelon cultivated over four thousand years ago in the deserts of Africa. Where the dry climate made it an important source of water. People in Europe, the Middle East, and Asia also ate watermelon. The American colonists liked watermelon also and did not let a bit of it go to waste. Ate the pulp, drank the liquid, pickled the rind, and roasted the seeds. As did most other people.

They knew why they were eating it. Although watermelon has over 90 percent water. But also full of vitamins, such as A and C. In addition to some iron and potassium. And no fat at all. Although containing lots of sugar. It is not botanically a fruit. But is a vegetable, particularly of the gourd family. So not just for dessert but also eaten as a staple.

Along with red pulp, also white, yellow, and pink. Seeds sometimes white or green. In addition to the usual brown and black. The outside dark green sometimes with yellow or white patches.

Every summer at my house, we buy a really big one. And soak it in a tub of ice water. Then invite the neighbors and friends. Everyone getting a big slice or two and sitting on the grass to eat it. Spitting seeds on the ground and dripping all over the place. That's the best way to eat it.

Summary

I. Sentence Fragments
  A. Definition: A **sentence fragment** is a word, phrase, or dependent clause punctuated as a sentence.
  B. Types of fragments
    1. A dependent clause is used without an independent clause.
      Example: *Because it was true.*
    2. The verb is not complete.
      Example: *The dog having no collar.*
    3. A subject and/or a verb is lacking.
      Example: *Whatever truth in the story.*
    4. A phrase is used alone.
      Example: *Singing his head off.*
  C. Intentional fragments
    1. A word or phrase can be used for emphasis.
      Example: *He plays his guitar. In the shower.*
    2. Exclamations can express emotion.
      Example: *What gall. For Pete's sake!*
    3. A *which* clause sometimes can be used to emphasize a point (but usually should be avoided).
      Example: *I drank cold coffee. Which was terrible.*

Chapter 27

Run-Together Sentences

Underline the five **run-together sentences** in this paragraph and correct them using punctuation. Don't worry if you can't find them all.

Brazilians say that God created the world in six days on the seventh day he made Rio. Rio de Janeiro is one of the most beautiful cities in the world it has a wonderful setting. The city consists of a long beachfront, rocky islands jutting out of the water, forested mountains rising inland, and a tropical rainforest within the city limits. The world-famous beaches include Copacabana, Ipanema, and Leblon. One rocky peak is Sugar Loaf, the other is Corcovado. Both rise spectacularly over the city. The Tijuca National Park has hilly areas with lush tropical vegetation. The climate is generally very healthful trade winds keep the air relatively cool. The coolest time is June, July, and August, the hottest times are in the winter when temperatures go over 100 degrees. Being south of the equator, the seasons are reversed.

Run-Together Sentences

A *run-together sentence* consists of two (or more) sentences that have been put together either with no punctuation or with insufficient or misleading punctuation. Sometimes these sentences are also called *run-on* sentences, but many people think that a run-on sentence is a long sentence. Run-together sentences can be either long or short.

Usually a run-together sentence has one of two problems:

1. It has no punctuation between the two sentences.
2. It has insufficient or misleading punctuation.

When no punctuation divides the two sentences (sometimes called a *fused sentence* or run-on sentence), the problem can be corrected by one of these methods:

1. A semicolon between the two sentences
2. A comma and coordinating conjunction (*for, and, nor, but, or, yet, so* [use FAN-BOYS to remember])
3. A subordinating word (*because, if, since,* etc.)
4. A period and a capital letter

Notice how the run-together sentence can be corrected by the various methods:

*The house is solid it is stone. (run-together sentence)
The house is solid; it is stone. (semicolon)
The house is solid, for it is stone. (comma + FANBOYS)
The house is solid since it is stone. (subordinating word)
The house is solid. It is stone. (period)

All the choices are correct, but in any given context one or some will sound better to you.

Sometimes the two or more parts of the run-together sentence are divided by a comma that is not strong enough to divide the two parts (sometimes called a **comma splice** error):

*Wooden houses look nice, they are quaint. (comma splice)

In this case, the writer displays a good sense of sentence structure since he or she senses a division or pause, but the sentence has insufficient punctuation. Between the two sentences use either a semicolon, a comma + FANBOYS, a subordinating word, or a period:

Wooden houses look nice; they are quaint.
Wooden houses look nice, and they are quaint.
Wooden houses look nice because they are quaint.
Wooden houses look nice. They are quaint.

Be careful when using conjunctive adverbs such as *consequently, hence, however, nevertheless, then, therefore,* and *thus.* These words do not replace either a FANBOYS (for, and, nor, but, or, yet, so) or subordinating words (because, if, since, etc.). They are not connectors; they are modifiers and can be placed in more than one place in a sentence, unlike the others. For example, we can write

I like brick; however, I prefer stone.   OR
I like brick; I prefer stone, however.

When a run-together sentence has one of these adverbs, be sure to punctuate it correctly.

Exercise 27.1   Finding Run-Together Sentences

*Find and underline the **one run-together sentence** in these pairs of sentences.*

1. Gertrude Stein was born in 1874 to a well-to-do family living in Philadelphia. She had a brother his name was Leo.
2. Young Gertrude was always interested in the arts she herself liked to write. As a young woman she moved to Paris with her brother.

3. They lived on the Left Bank and had a number of friends who later became famous. She entertained often she enjoyed meeting artists and writers.

4. She often entertained Ernest Hemingway and F. Scott Fitzgerald, James Joyce also visited. She particularly liked Pablo Picasso.

5. Her brother left Paris, Gertrude Stein became friends with Alice B. Toklas. Toklas became her companion for life.

6. Picasso painted a portrait of Stein, she sat many hours for him. But he painted her face only after he had not seen her for a long time, using just his memory of her.

7. She did not think the portrait looked like her, he said it would. Now this painting is the most famous image of Gertrude Stein.

8. During World War I, Stein and Toklas worked very hard for the troops. She was recognized by the French government they gave her the Medal of Honor.

9. Stein wrote *The Autobiography of Alice B. Toklas.* The title is a joke the book was by Stein and about Stein.

10. Stein's most famous line is "a rose is a rose is a rose." This line is frequently quoted, nobody knows what it really means.

Exercise 27.2   Correcting Run-Together Sentences

*Combine these sentences by using one of the four methods to avoid **run-together sentences:***
   semicolon,
   comma + FANBOYS
   subordinating word
   period
Use more than one of these four methods.

Example   I like stone houses __;__ they are solid.

1. Many cities in the world have subway systems _____ one of the oldest is New York City's.

2. The system had several lines with names such as the IND and the IRT _____ some people still call them by these names.

3. These days the lines have numbers or letters such as the 1, 2, E, F, and N _____ this allows for more lines and trains.

4. Formerly the subway lines did not always connect easily with each other _____ it was better to know which station to use.

5. The old vaudeville line, "You can't get there from here," was almost true _____ sometimes it was a long ride.

6. Nowadays underground tunnels and short lines connect all the lines _____ the system is more convenient.

7. The shuttle goes only from East 42nd Street to West 34th Street and back _____ the distance is less than a mile.

8. The shuttle connects Grand Central Station with Penn Station, however _____ these are important junctions that connect with other subway and railroad lines.

9. People can transfer from the subways to buses _____ they don't have to pay extra within a certain time limit.

10. The subway is definitely the fastest, cheapest, and most convenient way to go _____ it beats slow buses and expensive cabs.

Exercise 27.3   Correcting Run-Together Sentences

Combine these sentences by using one of the four methods to avoid **run-together sentences:**
   semicolon
   comma + FANBOYS
   subordinating word
   period
Use more than one of these four methods.

Example   The shoes cost too much‸I didn't buy them.

, so

1. Johann's favorite sport is rock climbing he does it every chance he gets.

2. He lives in New York City, however, he does manage to climb once or twice a week.

3. He belongs to a gym, it's down the street from his apartment.

4. Sometimes, after he puts in a long day at work, he's too tired he has to force himself to go.

5. Usually he's glad he went the climbing instructor is a woman he's had his eyes on for a while.

6. What he loves about her is her hair it is long, and she lets it hang loose down her back.

7. Her name, he thinks, is Andrea he's never gotten up the courage to ask.

8. He doesn't know her very well, therefore they've never seen each other outside the gym.

9. Today when he's climbing he wonders what would happen if he got injured then she'd have to visit him in the hospital.

10. Johann imagines the flowers she would bring, they would be carnations or lilies or daisies.

11. She'd sit at the edge of his bed and tell him stories about the time she climbed in Yosemite, she'd sing campfire songs softly in his ear.

12. Then maybe after he got better, they would still be friends, he'd work later on becoming something more.

13. It was important to be friends first on this he was firm.

14. At this point in the climb Johann realizes how far up the wall he has gone he panics.

15. He falls, and she catches him when he arrives at the bottom he'll ask her out.

Exercise 27.4   Finding and Correcting Run-Together Sentences

Find and correct the **one run-together sentence** *in each of the following paragraphs. Use either a semicolon, a comma + FANBOYS, a subordinating word, or a period.*

1. The beach called Copacabana in Rio de Janeiro, Brazil, is one of the most famous in the world. The strip of white sand along the Atlantic Ocean is rimmed by a long decorated walk divided into stations staffed by lifeguards. Stands sell cold drinks they are inexpensive.

2. One of the best snacks is a freshly opened coconut it is delicious cold. A waiter expertly holds the coconut and hacks off the top with a large machete, not losing a drop of the coconut milk inside. Then he chops a small piece of the shell to make a spoon for scooping out the flesh when you have drunk the milk.

3. Each station (or *posto*) has its own character. Some are for families others are for young people. Gays may gather at one, artists at another. Fitness enthusiasts are sure to gather where there is outdoor exercise apparatus, such as parallel bars, slant boards, and chinning bars.

4. Skyscraper apartment houses line the beach also, along with a number of major hotels. Just behind the tall buildings are many shops some are very stylish and expensive. Also excellent restaurants and night clubs can be found here. Copacabana has a very lively, glamorous, and popular nightlife.

5. Beyond Copa (as the natives call it) the beaches of Ipanema and Leblon are less built up and consequently have cleaner water. They also have tall apartment buildings, numerous shops, and lots of nightlife. Here many people like to bicycle and roller skate, at one end of Ipanema many surfers find challenging waves.

6. Although Brazilians all knew Ipanema, it became internationally famous through a song by Carlos Antonio Joabim called "The Girl from Ipanema." This was just a song about a pretty girl walking along the beach, but it had a nice melody many singers gave their version of it. Ipanema became as famous as Copacabana.

7. Other areas beyond Leblon have also been built up, they are thriving residential communities. It is perhaps surprising that besides the beach culture with all the day visitors are families and retired people who simply live along the beach. They make up small cities within the bigger city of Rio.

8. Very near the middle-class and rich people of Rio live the poor people in large and small shanty towns called *favelas.* A *favela* (fah-VEL-la) is usually built on a hillside, the poorer the people are the higher up the hill they live. Their homes range from cinder-block constructions to makeshift shacks.

9. Some *favela* homes seem poor but decent others lack the basic amenities of water and electricity. Self-help projects and government programs are trying to improve the life of these people, but a lack of education, large families, and a history of poverty make the task very difficult.

10. Schools have been built *favela* children will have some education. But most of them will probably be unemployed for most of their lives and never have the income to move out of the *favela.* Although a sense of community no doubt exists in the *favelas,* moving out must be the dream of most.

Exercise 27.5   Finding and Correcting Run-Together Sentences

Find and correct the **one or more run-together sentences** *in the following para-graphs. Use either a semicolon, a comma + FANBOYS, a subordinating word, or a period.*

1. Cigarette smoking is a controversial topic it has ardent supporters on both sides. One side says that smoking is a right, the other side says it harms people. People have smoked for centuries, no one thought about stopping them. Women learned to evaluate and prepare cigars for men it was part of a proper lady's education.

2. Men got together to drink and smoke it was normal behavior. Rich men smoked expensive Cuban cigars poor men smoked hand-rolled cigarettes. Even so, better homes with nice furnishings and properly behaved people did not care for the smoke and smell of cigars and cigarettes men had to go outside or to a separate room. The rich went to fancy salons the poor went to bars.

3. In the nineteenth century, very few women smoked only brazen women or those in hardy jobs like cowpunching smoked. A few movie stars (brazen women) flaunted such manly behavior in the early part of the twentieth cen-tury. In the 1920s, many women chose to show their independence by smok-ing. These "flappers" wanted to prove they were modern and independent.

4. From that time on, American women continued to prove their modernity and independence until much later in that century. They did not receive equal pay for equal work or have the right to go to the most prestigious universities in the country, but they could smoke. Even so, far fewer women smoked than men they did not like bad breath and smelly clothes.

5. Most Americans stopped smoking in the latter half of the twentieth century. Reports of the negative health effects of smoking were widely publicized even though smoking's bad effects have been known for centuries. Emphysema, lung cancer, throat and mouth cancer, even facial wrinkles were caused by smoking, not to mention stained teeth and fingers.

6. Tobacco companies received much unfavorable publicity they ruthlessly pur-sued minorities and youths through advertising. They also were accused of

increasing the levels of nicotine in cigarettes so that more people would become addicted to smoking. Certainly lying about their knowledge of the addictive qualities of cigarette smoking did not help their image.

7. At the beginning of the twenty-first century, only about 25 percent of Americans still smoke some states have gone down to 18 percent. Many of those smokers are teenagers still pursuing what women pursued at the start of the twentieth century, modernity and independence. However, if a teenager does not start smoking by age twenty-one, he or she will have a 90 percent chance of not starting at all.

8. Smoking has gone from a rich man's luxury to a teenager's cry for freedom. And as people grow up, become educated, and raise their incomes, they also stop, so smoking has become the pursuit of the poor and uneducated. Drunken bums on skid row are usually seen with a bottle in one hand and a cigarette dangling from dirty lips. This isn't what we aspire to, it isn't glamorous or high class.

9. Paradoxically, teenagers, often poor and not yet educated, start smoking to seem cool, classy, and grown-up. Yet they are doing what proves they are still children, they form the largest group of smokers. They see movie stars smoking in films, but these films are neither real nor realistic portrayals of real life they don't show characters coughing or getting sick.

10. Television stopped advertising cigarettes a long time ago, billboard advertising stopped a short time ago. Even so, teenagers see other teenagers smoking and desperately copy them in order to fit in. It hardly seems like the best way to make friends, but if that's the only way, they will start. It doesn't say much for friendship it is very sad.

Exercise 27.6   Finding and Correcting Run-Together Sentences

*Find and correct the **four run-together sentences** in this essay.*

America's fascination with violence is not a new development. We have been enthralled by those who challenge and avoid the law since the early days of American society. A prime example of this addiction to blood and gore is the popularity of the James brothers Frank and Jesse James are two of the most notorious siblings the American West has ever known. Who could have guessed that from their humble and quiet beginnings in Missouri, they would become famous American outlaws and the stars of a thousand motion-picture Westerns?

Jesse and Frank were born in 1847 and 1843, respectively. When the Civil War broke out, the brothers joined on the Southern side. Jesse was injured when his troop surrendered it is rumored that he was shot while standing under the white flag of truce. Having been trained in weaponry and marauding, the brothers and eight of their friends committed their first robbery of a Missouri bank on February 13, 1866. This act led to a string of crimes, including bank robberies from Iowa to Alabama to Texas. They began holding up trains in 1873, followed by stagecoaches, stores, and individuals.

It was at this time the press got hold of the story, exaggerating the exploits of the James brothers for public consumption. Writers exaggerated the facts to gain Eastern readers, whose appetite for Western bloodbaths and body counts knew no limits. To the Ozark people of Missouri, Jesse was a romantic figure, an example of a Southerner who was hounded by the authorities who never forgot his loyalty to the South during the war. Frank and Jesse often tried to justify their actions on the grounds of persecution and harassment.

The beginning of the end occurred on September 7, 1876, the gang was nearly destroyed trying to rob the First National Bank in Northfield, Minnesota. The James brothers were the only members of the eight-person gang to escape injury, capture, or death. They recruited new members and began robbing again, until Missouri governor Thomas T. Crittenden offered a $10,000 reward to anyone who could capture the James brothers, dead or alive. Jesse escaped to St. Joseph and was living peacefully under a pseudonym when a member of his own gang shot him in the back of the head to collect the reward Frank James surrendered to the authorities, but at each of his three trials he was found not guilty and lived quietly on his family's farm until his death in 1915. The James brothers live on, of course, in the series of Western movies, books, and television programs that have been created in their honor and in the myriad modern American crime sprees that find their roots in the James brothers' violence.

Exercise 27.7   Proofreading

Find and correct the **run-together sentences** *in the following paragraph. Use either a semicolon, a comma + FANBOYS, a subordinating word, or a period. Use more than one of these four methods and consider which one best fits the sentence.*

Certainly the biggest event in Rio de Janeiro is carnival it takes place every year and lasts officially five days. Samba schools start many months in advance making costumes and rehearsing for their particular event. During carnival week many people dance in the streets at designated spots big hotels also hold masquerade balls thousands of people participate. One huge parade is held on Rio's main downtown street, the Avenida Rio Branco. The parade is free to everyone. The really important parade is held in the huge Sambodromo, it lasts around twelve hours and costs up to $1,000 a seat. All the important samba schools compete they have a theme, an original samba, costumes, rhythmic music, and floats. Each school performs for about an hour and tries to whip everyone into a frenzy of dancing. It is the exhausting but exhilarating highlight to life in Rio de Janeiro.

Summary

I. Run-Together Sentences
    A. Definition: A **run-together sentence** is two or more sentences made into one sentence having either no punctuation or insufficient, misleading punctuation.
    B. Correcting run-together sentences
        1. Use a semicolon between the two or more sentences.
            Example: *You like baseball I don't.*
                     You like baseball; I don't.
        2. Use a comma and a coordinating conjunction: *for, and, nor, but, or, yet, so* (FANBOYS).
            Example: *We went home they went to the movies.*
                     We went home, but they went to the movies.
        3. Use a subordinating word: *because, if, since,* etc.
            Example: *The day is long, I need a nap.*
                     Because the day is long, I need a nap.
        4. Use a period and a capital letter.
            Example: *The computer is nice, it does many things.*
                     The computer is nice. It does many things.

Chapter 28

Words Often Confused

In the following sentences, circle the correct choice among **words often confused.**

1. There are many ways to (*raise, rays, raze, rise*) children.
2. The parents should decide (*weather, whether*) they want a large or small family.
3. The (*amount of, number of*) children in a family makes a big difference.
4. Parents must decide (*who's, whose*) in charge.
5. (*Some, Sum*) parents believe in strict discipline.
6. (*There, Their, They're*) are parents who believe that children should be left alone.
7. Others think parents should (*all ways, always*) be there.
8. They believe in (*fewer, less*) rules.
9. If (*your, you're*) thinking of starting a family, think hard about (*your, you're*) child-rearing philosophy.
10. But mostly you need to give (*a lot, allot*) of love.

English has a large number of ***words often confused*** in writing because the same sound in English can be spelled in a number of different ways. Some of the words sound alike or almost alike but are written differently (*coarse, course; throne, thrown; their, there, they're*). Some words look alike or almost alike (*affect, effect; accept, except*). Some words are sometimes written as one word and sometimes as two words (*all ready, already; any way, anyway; some times, sometimes*). Some words look entirely different but their meanings are confused (*amount of, number of*). Others are simply misspelled (*a lot*). Here are some of the most prevalent ones; consult a dictionary for meanings.

List of Words Often Confused

a, an
accept, except
adapt, adopt
advice, advise
affect, effect

a head, ahead
all together, altogether
a long, along
a lot, allot (*alot* is a
   misspelling of *a lot*)

already, all ready
all ways, always
amount of, number of
any way, anyway
are, our

assent, ascent
ate, eight
bare, bear
be, bee
been, being
blew, blue
bought, brought
bread, bred
buy, by, bye
chose, choose
clothes, cloths
coarse, course
complement, compliment
conscious, conscience
counselor, councilor
crowded, crowed
decent, descent
die, dye, dying
difference, deference
do, due, dew
every day, everyday
every one, everyone
father, farther, further
feel, fell, field, fill
fewer, less
flour, flower
friar, fryer
groan, grown
   (*m**oan*** and *groan*)
guessed, guest
hangar, hanger
have, of
heard, herd
higher, hire
hour, our
idle, idol, idyll
its, it's
knew, new, gnu
know, now, no
ladder, latter, later, letter

lay, lie, lye
lead, led
liar, lyre
load, lode
lose, loose (*loose tooth*)
mantel, mantle
may be, maybe
might, mite
mind, mine, mined
moral, morale
morning, mourning
noisy, nosy
not, knot
of, off
one, won
past, passed
patience, patients
pause, paws
peace, piece
  (*piece* of *pie*)
peak, peek, pique
peer, pier, pear, pair
personal, personnel
plain, plane
poor, pour, pore
precede, proceed
principal, principle
  (*-al* = *main*, *-ple* = *rule*)
quiet, quite, quit
rain, reign, rein
raise, rays, raze, rise
real, reel, rile, rail
recent, resent
right, write, rite, wright
road, rode
sail, sale, sell, seal
scene, seen
shoot, chute
shore, sure
sight, site, cite

sleigh, slay
so, sow, sew
soar, sore
some, sum
some one, someone
some times, sometimes
stake, steak
   (*steak* = *eat*)
stare, stair
stationary, stationery
  (*-ary* = *stay*,
  -ery = *paper*)
straight, strait
than, then
there, their, they're
thought, though
threw, through,
  thorough
throne, thrown
to, too, two
tore, tour
troop, troupe
vain, vein, vane
vale, veil, Vail
want, won't
way, weigh, whey
weak, week
wear, were, where,
  we're
weather, whether
went, when
which, witch
while, wile
whole, hole
who's, whose
wind, whined, wined
yield, yelled
yoke, yolk
your, you're

You probably know all or almost all these words and have confused some of them or not known that different spellings existed. The computer spellchecker will not help with these words because they are not misspelled, just misused. If you have trouble with these words often confused, you should take several steps:

Consult a dictionary when you are in doubt.

Keep a personal list; enter words in a small address book to keep them alpha-
betized.

Exercise 28.1   Choosing among Words Often Confused

*Choose the **correct word** and cross out the wrong word or words in the following
sentences.*

Example   I want to (*know, ~~no, now~~*) the reason.

1. In the eleventh century, (*went, when*) the enemy had (*been, being*) chased out
   of England, soldiers happened to find a leftover skull on the ground.
2. They kicked around this skull, but (*some times, sometimes*) (*their, there,
   they're*) toes became sore.
3. (*So, sew, sow*) they used a cow's bladder instead and (*past, passed*) time playing
   this game.
4. (*By, buy*) the twelfth century, the British (*throne, thrown*) banned this new
   game called "football" as a waste of time.
5. But (*every one, everyone*) saw it was in (*vain, vein, vane*).
6. Football, (*who's, whose*) popularity never diminished, continued as (*a, an*) fa-
   vored sport.
7. In the nineteenth century, people (*knew, new, gnu*) several forms of football
   (*may be, maybe*) played.
8. At Rugby College, a player (*adapted, adopted*) a new strategy by picking up the
   ball; no one had (*heard, herd*) of this before.
9. This unorthodox player (*threw, through, thorough*) the ball rather (*than, then*)
   kicking it.
10. Of (*coarse, course*), this game became rugby, (*which, witch*) is still played all
    over the world.
11. (*Than, then*) the Football Association of England codified rules that (*some one,
    someone*) called "association football."
12. "Association football" was (*way, weigh, whey*) (*to, too, two*) long a term, so it
    was shortened to "assoc," which became "soccer."
13. Both games (*wear, were, where, we're*) called "football" until rugby (*yielded,
    yelled*) and soccer is known as football.
14. American football is closer to rugby (*thought, though*) the (*deference, differ-
    ence*) is obvious to everyone.

15. (*While, wile*) rugby and American football (*are, our*) popular, soccer is by far the most popular in the world.

Exercise 28.2   Correcting Words Often Confused

Choose the **correct word** *and cross out the wrong word or words in the following sentences.*

1. (*A, an*) Ethiopian goatherd noticed that (*went, when*) his goats (*ate, eight*) in a particular field, they became energized.
2. After he (*stared, staired*) at them for a while, he (*guessed, guest*) that it was (*do, due, dew*) to some berries.
3. (*Been, being*) brave, the goatherd, no doubt against everyone's (*advice, advise*), had some of the berries and began to (*feel, fell, fill*) energetic (*to, too, two*).
4. The goatherd's (*every day, everyday*) habit of eating berries was (*scene, seen*) by a monk who then (*bought, brought*) some berries back with him.
5. Since he did not (*want, won't*) to (*die, dye, dying*), he (*chose, choose*) to boil them first.
6. He fed them (*to, too, two*) his (*peers, piers, pears, pairs*) so they would remain (*conscious, conscience*) during services.
7. (*Its, it's*) difficult to (*accept, except*) this legend, since another says that a shepherd (*threw, through, thorough*) the berries into a fire.
8. The wonderful aroma (*lead, led*) (*straight, strait*) to grinding and brewing (*real, reel, rile, rail*) coffee.
9. Another legend says that during a forest fire, people gathered some (*lose, loose*) burned berries that smelled (*quiet, quite, quit*) good and (*preceded, proceeded*) to eat them.
10. Only between 1000 and 1300 C.E. did drinking rather (*than, then*) eating coffee (*peak, peek, pique*) any interest in (*any way, anyway*).
11. The famous Arabian philosopher and physician, Avicenna, also (*one, won*) (*knew, new, gnu*) converts to coffee by touting the medicinal (*affects, effects*).
12. (*Know, now, no*) coffee has become a (*pause, paws*) that refreshes and brings (*peace, piece*) and calm.
13. Even (*thought, though*) (*its, it's*) a stimulant, we still (*want, won't*) do without it.
14. It makes us stay awake (*ladder, latter, later, letter*) (*than, then*) we (*want, won't*).
15. (*While, wile*) you (*poor, pour, pore*) over the books (*their, there, they're*) is nothing better as a stimulant.

Exercise 28.3   Correcting Words Often Confused

*Find and correct the **one** or **two words often confused** in the following sentences.*

Example   I want to be ~~shore~~ of your commitment to me.

> sure (written above "shore")

1. All sorts of transportation fascinate me: soring in the clouds on a plain, rumbling down the road on a motorcycle, and floating on the water.
2. Going on a jet threw the sky at the speed of light would bee a really spectacular experience of a lifetime.
3. It would be a new sensation for me to get on the jet in the mourning and be in another country a few hours latter.
4. I don't own a motorcycle, not even a bicycle, but riding won must be alot of fun and full of excitement.
5. I don't get the same felling of excitement from the stationary bicycle at the gym.
6. Of coarse I've ridden in cars, but a car seems just to mundane and ordinary for me to get excited about.
7. Gliding in the ocean on a ship passed frolicking dolphins must have being thrilling for passengers in the open seas.
8. Still, I would need patients too spend several days on the ship and not arrive anywhere quickly.
9. At least, I could take an ocean liner rather than a selling ship that would depend on the wined.
10. But there must be nothing more thrilling then moving a long some passage and getting to a different place; I wish I had the time and money to see the whole world.

Exercise 28.4   Correcting Words Often Confused

*Correct the **three** or **four words often confused** in each paragraph.*

1. The assent of the mountain was more difficult then the descent. The wind blew right threw our clothes. As we came down, the weather posed fewer

obstacles, so we could bare the difficulties. Mountain climbing is a rough sport.

2. Last winter vacation I went to my cousin's farm. We rode a sleigh over the plane covered with snow. I held the rains because the seats were higher than I had expected, so I could see farther over the yolk of the horses. The ride was a perfect idyll.

3. My kitchen skills have improved. Know I now about using the right kind of flour for baking bread. I also know a fryer from a roaster and which one to use. Also I can pick out a decent stake, one that is tender and juicy. I am more sure of myself.

4. Everyone complements me on my driving. I can get a long on a crowded highway at any hour. I could have more patients, but might makes right, so I must mine the road, shoot for openings, avoid the weak drivers, and sail ahead.

5. My little brother was a compulsive lyre and cheat. He has been going regularly to a counselor for five weeks. All ready he has groan mentally. He seems to have morals and principals now, when before he seemed like a loaded gun ready to go off.

6. The resent plane crash was extremely sad. We saw the rescuers lay the salvaged parts in the hanger. The cite was very quiet, not noisy at all. Everything was stationary as if a vail of silence had fallen, and everyone was in mourning.

Exercise 28.5   Correcting Words Often Confused

*Correct the **words often confused** in the following essay.*

The bagel craze is sweeping our nation. Gone are fattening doughnuts; buttery croissants are a thing of the passed. It seems everywhere you turn there's a bagel store— even two on the same corner. A bagel, for the uninitiated, is a doughnut-shaped, yeast-leavened roll. It is characterized by a crisp, shiny crust and a dense, almost chewy interior. Though bagels are traditionally known as a Jewish food, now everyone, no matter what ethnic group he or she belongs to, is eating bagels for food or snack, often complimenting them with cream cheese, jelly, butter, or lox (smoked salmon).

Bagels are made from the same ingredients as other forms of bread: flower, yeast, salt, and sugar. It is the high-gluten flower that gives bagels their spongy texture. Often the doe is lightened by adding eggs, milk, or butter to the batter. Traditionally, the roll is shaped by hand into a ring, boiled briefly in water, then baked. The shiny crust appears when fewer flour is added, and in its place a glaze of egg yolk is applied before baking.

No one nows for sure the origin of the bagel, but food historians suspect that it has its roots in Central Europe. Legend has it that in 1683, John III Sobieski (king of Poland) successfully defended the city of Vienna from a Turkish invasion. To celebrate the victory, a local baker baked a roll in the shape of a stirrup (King John was a superior horseman). Is it merely coincidence that the present day German word for stirrup is *Bügel*? Any way, the bagel remained a popular food item in Europe until the late nineteenth century, when Jewish immigrants imported the bred to America. Of course, Americans have made it their own, mass-producing bagels in machines and steaming instead of boiling them. Americans have also started adding fruits, spices, and vegetables to bagels.

Exercise 28.6   Writing with Words Often Confused

Write one or two sentences using all of the listed words.

Example   (be, bee, of, off)
        Of all things to love, I must be off my rocker to love bees.

1. (wear, were, where, we're) _____

   _____

   _____

2. (ladder, latter, later, letter) _____

   _____

   _____

3. (right, write, rite, wright) _____

   _____

   _____

4. (real, reel, rile, rail) _____

    _____

    _____

5. (chose, choose, clothes, cloths) _____

    _____

    _____

6. (not, knot, sale, sell, sail) _____

    _____

    _____

7. (know, no, now, knew, new) _____

    _____

    _____

8. (their, there, they're, mantel, mantle) _____

    _____

    _____

9. (quiet, quite, quit, road, rode) _____

    _____

    _____

10. (rain, reign, rein, plain, plane) _____

    _____

    _____

11. (advice, advise, threw, through, thorough) _____

    _____

    _____

12. (tore, tour, whined, wind, wined) _____

    _____

    _____

13. (past, passed, raise, rise, rays, raze) _____

    _____

    _____

14. (scene, seen, one, won, lose, loose) _____

_____

_____

15. (personal, personnel, of, off, troop, troupe) _____

_____

_____

Exercise 28.7   Proofreading

*Find and correct the **ten words often confused** in the following paragraph.*

Moving is one of those chores that every one must experience at sometime in a lifetime. Some people may of moved during there childhood, but often the first move in a person's life might be from home to college. What to bring and what to leave behind our not to difficult. Its not permanent. But after college, that succession of shared apartments means a lode of boxes, that clumsy futon, that table with the ugly chairs, and those too-large pictures. Then a long comes that wonderful someone and than the succession of apartments, a house, and a bigger house as children arrive and work becomes more lucrative. As Americans, we move and then we move several more times. Each time we drag more stuff with us.

Summary

I. Words Often Confused
    A. Reasons for words often confused
        1. Some words sound alike or almost alike but are spelled differently.
            Examples: *ate, eight; blew, blue; to, too, two*
        2. Some words look alike or almost alike.
            Examples: *accept, except; bought, brought*
        3. Some words can be one word or two words depending on their use.
            Examples: *any way, anyway; every day, everyday*
        4. Some words look entirely different, but their meanings are confused.
            Example: *amount of, number of*

5. Some words are often misspelled.

   Example: *alot* should be spelled *a lot*

B. Learning words often confused

   1. Consult a dictionary.

   2. Keep a personal list of words often confused.

Chapter 29

Misplaced and Dangling Modifiers

Underline the one **misplaced** or **dangling modifier** in each of the following sentences. Don't worry if you miss some of them.

1. Some people from the western part of France settled in Acadia, now called Nova Scotia in the seventeenth century.
2. When taken over by the British in 1755, the Acadians fled to Louisiana and eastern Texas mostly to settle in French-owned territory.
3. They became known only as "Cajuns" (from "Acadians") after this move.
4. Mostly fishing, trapping, and farming, life was full of problems and difficulties in this isolated land.
5. Already on the land, the Cajuns were not welcomed by the local Creoles, who considered them invaders.
6. Being Cajun country, the culture's uniqueness can be seen and felt in the land, people, food, and shelter.
7. They have their own language that almost sounds like French, but some major differences in vocabulary, pronunciation, and grammar exist.
8. Bridges and highways forced them to assimilate with the rest of the United States built in the early twentieth century.
9. The state of Louisiana mandated that French could not be spoken in the public schools even.
10. Almost eradicated in recent decades, there has been a revival of Cajun language, music, dance, and cuisine.

Misplaced Modifiers

Words or phrases that modify should be placed next to or near the word(s) they modify. If they come elsewhere in the sentence, they risk being misunderstood, so they are called *misplaced modifiers* and need to be placed elsewhere in a sentence.

Words such as *almost, even, hardly, nearly, not, only,* and any number of other adverbs should be placed carefully for the correct meaning. Notice that the difference between these two sentences depends entirely on the placement of *nearly:*

> I nearly won $100. (I won nothing. *Nearly* modifies *won.*)
>
> I won nearly $100. (I won close to $100. *Nearly* modifies *$100.*)

Both of these sentences are grammatically correct, but only one has the meaning that was intended; the other has a misplaced modifier.

Phrases also must be placed carefully, usually next to the word they modify. Although you probably understand the intention of these sentences, you may notice that the parts don't fit together logically:

> The woman got in the taxi with a long skirt.
>
> Lying in the gutter, Hannah found her watch.

Of course, if the taxi indeed had a long skirt or Hannah herself were lying in the gutter and came upon her watch, the sentences would be accurate. But that was probably not the intended meaning of the writers. To make the meaning clear, place the modifying phrase next to the word it modifies:

> The woman **with a long skirt** got in the taxi. (modifies *woman*)
>
> Hannah found her watch **lying in the gutter.** (modifies *watch*)

Sometimes a modifying word or phrase is placed so that it could modify more than one part of the sentence and thus cause ambiguity or confusion (called a ***squinting modifier***):

> He decided **secretly** to take a vacation. (Did he decide secretly, or is he taking a secret vacation?)
>
> He asked her to marry him **in the garden.** (Was the proposal in the garden, or will the wedding be there?)

To clarify these sentences, place the modifier where it will not cause ambiguity; sometimes other words will also need changing:

> Secretly, he decided to take a vacation.   AND
>
> He decided to take a secret vacation.
>
> In the garden, he asked her to marry him.   AND
>
> He asked that their marriage take place in the garden.

The last sentence needs even more words changed to make the meaning clear.

Dangling Modifiers

Dangling modifiers are prepositional phrases, adjective verbal phrases, infinitive verbal phrases, and noun verbal phrases that have nothing to modify in a sentence. Except for the prepositional phrase, the others are verbal phrases and, as is true of verbs, need a subject, usually the nearest one available. If they do not have one, they dangle:

> Having won nearly $100, the dinner did not seem expensive. (The dinner could not win nearly $100.)
>
> To get in the taxi, her long skirt was gathered up. (Her skirt could not decide to get in the taxi.)
>
> I dressed up, looking expensive and shiny. (nothing to modify)
>
> After deciding on a vacation, the location is important. (The location cannot decide on a vacation.)

Notice that in the last sentence the noun verbal phrase is the object of the preposition *after*. Only a noun verbal phrase that is the object of a preposition becomes a dangling modifier since otherwise noun verbal phrases do not modify.

To correct the dangler, you can give the phrase a logical noun or pronoun to modify:

> **Having won nearly $100, he** didn't think the dinner expensive.
>
> **To get in the taxi, the woman** gathered up her long skirt.
>
> I wore my best **suit, looking expensive and shiny.**
>
> **After deciding on a vacation, I** had to decide on the location.

Or you can change the phrase into a clause:

> **After he won nearly $100,** the dinner didn't seem expensive.
>
> **When she got in the taxi,** her long skirt was gathered up.
>
> I wore my best suit, **which looked expensive and shiny.**
>
> **After I decided on a vacation,** the location became important.

Be careful about placing a modifying phrase in front of a sentence that begins with *there, here,* or indefinite *it,* since these words normally will not be logical words to modify:

> Having won $100, there was much to celebrate. (Cannot modify *there.*)
>
> Deciding on a vacation, here is one option. (Cannot modify *here.*)
>
> Getting in a taxi, it was clumsy with a long skirt. (Cannot modify *it.*)

These sentences can be corrected by changing the word being modified:

> Having won $100, **we** had much to celebrate.
>
> Deciding on a vacation, **I** found one option.
>
> Getting in a taxi, **she** found her long skirt clumsy.

Or the dangling phrase can be turned into a clause:

> When I won $100, there was much to celebrate.
>
> When she got in a taxi, it was clumsy with a long skirt.

But sometimes this option does not sound right, so try different solutions to find the best one:

> INSTEAD OF   After I decided on a vacation, here was one option.   WRITE
>
> After I decided on a vacation, one option was possible.   OR
>
> After I decided on a vacation, I found one option.

Dangling modifiers frequently occur as a result of editing and rewriting. Often their meaning is clear despite the dangling modifier, but you should avoid them in any case.

Exercise 29.1   Correcting Misplaced Modifiers

*In the following sentences, the **misplaced modifying word** has been highlighted. Draw an arrow to where it should be placed. Sometimes more than one place is possible.*

Example   Winning $100 **often** makes me happy.

1. Watching television **frequently** makes me very impatient.
2. The commercials arrive just when I am engrossed in the program **often.**
3. When I am not that interested **even** the commercials are annoying.
4. They **just** stay on for a few minutes, but they come so often.
5. I have stopped **almost** watching movies on television because of the frequent interruptions.
6. Public television **nearly** is as bad as commercial television these days.
7. They have fund drives during their best programs **usually.**
8. I know **only** the fund raising comes on three or four times a year, but the drives seem to last a long time.
9. They should realize that everyone will **not** listen, and many will just tune out.
10. I know I have **desperately** started looking for other forms of entertainment.

Exercise 29.2   Correcting Misplaced and Dangling Modifiers

*In the following sentences, the **misplaced** or **dangling phrase** has been highlighted. Correct each one by*
  1. placing it elsewhere
  2. adding words to the phrase
  3. changing some of the words in the main clause

1. **When five years old,** my father brought our first television set into the house.

2. That was when televisions were just appearing for domestic use **in 1948.**

3. **After returning from school,** *Howdy Doody* would be on.

4. We just loved Buffalo Bob, Howdy Doody, and the whole gang **sitting in front of that huge box.**

5. **Dominating the room,** we watched this tall wooden chest with the tiny ten-inch screen.

6. **Having the first television in the neighborhood,** all the local kids came over.

7. **Being rather small,** there was hardly enough room for everyone to squeeze in.

8. **Having made so many friends so quickly,** it was fun.

9. **After eating dinner,** Ed Sullivan, Paul Whiteman, or Milton Berle would entertain us for the evening.

10. **To maximize television viewing,** close track had to be kept of the hours when broadcasts were on.

Exercise 29.3   Finding and Correcting Misplaced and Dangling Modifiers

In the following sentences, find and correct the **one misplaced modifier.**

1. As much as thirty percent of driving accidents are just caused by driver fatigue.

2. When sleepy, car performance is impaired as much as for drunk drivers.

3. Performing on driving simulation tests, drowsiness was as bad as intoxication.

4. To think clearly and react quickly in a car, alertness and fast reflexes are necessary.

5. While driving, there are some warning signs that you should stop for a rest.

6. Keeping your eyes open only is not the sign of fatigue.

7. Having trouble focusing on the road or keeping your head up frequently also mean fatigue.

8. Drifting across lanes often indicates inattention and possibly sleepiness.

9. You would know that you nodded off probably if you have no memory of the last few minutes.

10. You should notice also if you are maintaining not a constant speed.

Exercise 29.4   Finding and Correcting Misplaced and Dangling Modifiers

*Decide whether the following sentences contain **dangling** or **misplaced modifiers** or whether they are correct. Write **C** for correct and **NC** for not correct.*

Example   To arrive on time, Charlotte must leave at 1:00. __C__

1. When first going to college, laundry was not Kristen's primary thought. _____
2. Everything was fine almost for the first two weeks. _____
3. When she ran out of socks, her laundry became important. _____
4. After packing all her dirty clothes into her laundry bag, it was so heavy she could hardly carry it. _____
5. Part of the problem was that she also packed her dry cleaning in the same bag. _____
6. Carrying the heavy bag, Kristen had difficulty walking all the way to the laundromat. _____
7. She had hardly any idea about separating dark and white clothes or using hot or warm water. _____
8. She managed barely to squeeze all the clothes into one washing machine. _____
9. She sat in the waiting area nearly for an hour. _____
10. With such a huge load, the dryer took a very long time. _____
11. The dryer also cost a lot of money for such a long time. _____
12. Ruining all the clothes that needed dry cleaning, her wardrobe became considerably smaller. _____
13. At least she had much more room in her closet than she did before. _____
14. A couple of her maxiskirts had nearly become miniskirts, so they seemed like new clothes. _____
15. To do laundry next time, her clothes were taken home for her mother to wash. _____

Exercise 29.5   Finding and Correcting Misplaced and Dangling Modifiers

*Find and correct the **one** or **two misplaced** or **dangling modifiers** in each of the following paragraphs.*

1. When drowsy, there are several things you should not do at the wheel. Don't try to overcome sleepiness by forcing yourself to keep your eyes open. Don't think

that a rush of fresh air from the open window will wake you up, so speeding won't help.

2. Caffeine only helps for a short time, so don't rely on lots of coffee. Also don't think that loud and lively music on the radio keeps you awake; lots of people sleep through any kind of music. Voices don't help either on the radio.

3. When planning a long car trip, getting plenty of sleep the night before helps a lot. People usually know how much sleep is enough for them. Check that any medication you take does not cause drowsiness; everyone does not react the same way. Also avoid any alcohol before the drive.

4. Drive at the time you are most active; some people prefer the morning, others the evening. Try to avoid the deadly midnight to 6:00 A.M. time or the mid-afternoon. These customarily are sleeping times, so our bodies are attuned to them.

5. Make stops to walk around, drink coffee, or do some light exercise every two hours. Better still, if possible, invite a friend along on the trip. While driving, someone will keep you alert and awake.

Exercise 29.6   Finding and Correcting Misplaced and Dangling Modifiers

*Find and correct **five misplaced** or **dangling modifiers** in this essay.*

What Happened to the Dinosaurs?

For years scientists have argued about what made the dinosaurs extinct exactly. One debate centers around thermoregulation, or control of body temperature. Although all animals exhibit some form of thermoregulation, they fall into two distinct groups: the ectotherms (gaining body heat from external methods, such as lying on warm rocks) and endotherms (gaining body heat by internal methods, such as eating a large quantity of food). Reptiles and amphibians are ectotherms; mammals and birds are endotherms.

Resembling reptiles, early scientists assumed that dinosaurs were ectotherms. For example, dinosaurs almost had reptilian jawbones and scales. But looks can be deceiving, and dinosaurs could not be measured by the usual methods, such as temperature, records of food consumption, and outputs of carbon dioxide and solid waste. The scientists had to look at indirect evidence, lacking direct evidence.

More recent indications show that dinosaurs might have been endotherms. Some dinosaur clans were herbivores, as seen through their well-developed dental equipment, showing they ate a lot. Others stood on two legs with taloned feet, showing that they were probably agile and rapid. Standing upright, the scientists say, demonstrates that dinosaurs had double-pump hearts to pump blood to their elevated brains. These traits are consistent with endotherms.

Just because dinosaurs exhibit endothermic traits, however, does not mean that they were so exclusively. After discussing the topic at length, dinosaurs have been placed somewhere between the two extremes by scientists. If this mystery were solved, the mystery of the extinction of dinosaurs could also be solved.

Exercise 29.7   Proofreading

Find and correct the **three misplaced** *and* **dangling modifiers** *in the following paragraph.*

Most people will say that they are not superstitious, that they don't believe in the magical powers of rituals, talismans, numbers, incantations, and signs. These same people, however, avoid walking under ladders, stepping on cracks in the sidewalk, having thirteen people at a table, and being passed by a black cat. They might say, "The ladder looked like it could fall." Looking in their purse or pockets, there will be a rabbit's foot, beads, or a particular coin. When going on a trip, crossing oneself, praying, and holding a St. Christopher medal seem comforting. When they want to win something often they wear a lucky cap or shirt or cross their fingers. If they don't win, they'll say it's because of that broken mirror or that black cat or that unlucky number. Then the next time they knock over some salt, they'll throw some over their left shoulder. Or was that the right shoulder?

Summary

I. Misplaced Modifiers
   A. Definition: **Misplaced modifiers** are words or phrases that have not been placed next to or near the word or words they modify, causing confusion or misunderstanding.
   B. Types of misplaced modifiers
      1. A word is in the wrong place.
         Example: ***Almost*** *Jo lost the balloon.*
      2. A phrase is in the wrong place.
         Example: *Jo won the game,* ***pleased with herself.***
   C. How to correct misplaced modifiers
      1. Place the misplaced modifier next to or near the word(s) being modified.
         Examples: *Jo* ***almost*** *lost the balloon.*
                   Pleased with herself, Jo won the game.
      2. Rewrite the sentence.
         Example: *Jo was pleased with herself for winning the game.*
II. Dangling Modifiers
   A. Definition: **Dangling modifiers** are modifying phrases that have not been given any word(s) to modify.
   B. Types of dangling modifiers
      1. A prepositional phrase has nothing to modify.
         Example: *After swimming, the salty water still burned my eyes.*
      2. An adjective verbal phrase has nothing to modify.
         Example: *Being the only player, the game was canceled.*
      3. An infinitive verbal phrase has nothing to modify.
         Example: *To have fun, trees should have swings.*
      4. A noun verbal phrase used as the object of the preposition has nothing to modify.
         Example: *Before eating lunch, the table must be set.*
   C. Correcting dangling modifiers
      1. Rewrite the sentence to have a logical modifier.
         Examples: *After swimming, I still felt the salty water burning my eyes.*
                   Being the only player, he had to cancel the game.
                   To have fun, we should put a swing on the tree.
                   Before eating lunch, I set the table.
      2. Change the dangling phrase into a dependent clause.
         Examples: *Since he was the only player, the game was canceled.*
                   If we want to have fun, a swing should be put on the tree.
                   Before I eat lunch, the table must be set.
      3. Recast the sentence entirely.
         Examples: *The salty water still burned my eyes after my swim.*
                   Since only one player came, the game was canceled.
                   We should put a swing on the tree for fun.
                   I'll set the table before lunch.

Chapter 30

Pseudoerrors

In the following sentences, note **pseudoerrors** (constructions that are sometimes considered to be errors but are not) in the space following each sentence. Don't worry if you don't think any of these are errors.

1. Because she seemed to lead a glamorous life, many people envied Frida Kahlo, the Mexican painter.

2. But she really had a life filled with pain and suffering.

3. Kahlo contracted polio as a small child and then was seriously injured in a bus accident that caused her to spend months in the hospital recovering from the effects of a metal shaft that went through her body.

4. Yet she married Diego Rivera, the famous muralist, and participated in an active social and artistic life.

5. Her many self-portraits depict the ills she suffered from.

6. Knowing about her life helps to really understand her portraits.

7. For they show her surrounded by such things as monkeys, gargoyles, and parrots, each symbolizing an aspect of her life.

8. Or she has a stone pillar instead of a spine, showing that she had a spinal fusion operation.

9. To completely recover from her many ills was impossible.

10. She died at the young age of forty-seven because of illnesses that she could not recover from.

Whether from simplified teaching, faulty learning, or changes in taste, students often think that some grammatical constructions should not be used when in fact they are fine. We call these constructions *pseudoerrors.*

Starting Sentences with Coordinating Conjunctions

It is perfectly all right, sometimes even preferable, to start a sentence with *for, and, nor, but, or, yet,* and *so* (coordinating conjunctions remembered by the acronym

FANBOYS). Since these words are conjunctions (connectors), they often follow another sentence that establishes the context and connection:

> Most people drink sodas. **But** I prefer fruit juice.
>
> Fruit juice comes in many flavors. **And** it is good for you.
>
> People drink orange juice in the morning. **Yet** they don't think of it later in the day.

Of course these sentences could be connected to form compound sentences (*Most people drink sodas,* **but** *I prefer fruit juice*), but occasionally starting with a conjunction puts more emphasis on your statement. Just be sure that the sentence starting with a conjunction is a complete sentence.

Starting Sentences with Because

Because is a subordinating conjunction like *if, since, when,* or *while,* so it may start a sentence, which will probably become a complex sentence. *Because of* is a preposition and may also start a sentence:

> Because I drink fruit juice, I get plenty of Vitamin C.
>
> Because of that, I am very healthy.

Be sure, however, to complete the sentence. Just the *because* phrase or clause is not enough by itself. We hear and say *Because I said so* or just *Because* so often that the word, phrase, or clause sounds complete, but it is actually a fragment. Probably a teacher told you not to start a sentence with *because* in order to help you avoid writing fragments.

Ending Sentences with Prepositions

We use many two-part verbs (verb + preposition [particle]), so a preposition at the end of a sentence appears frequently:

> Fresh orange juice is worth waiting **for.**
>
> Here's the juice which I told you **about.**
>
> Canned juice is something I will not put **up with.**

These sentences could avoid the preposition at the end:

> Waiting for fresh orange juice is worth it.
>
> Here's the juice about which I told you.

But *Canned juice is something up with which I will not put* sounds too odd to be taken seriously.

Writing Long Sentences (and Calling Them "Run-Ons")

Long sentences in themselves are welcome and add variety to a piece of writing when mixed with short and medium-length sentences. A **run-on sentence** is one that is not properly punctuated—often using a comma instead of a semicolon or no comma at all—and has nothing to do with length. Certainly long sentences that are improperly punctuated or that lose their clarity should be avoided, but a clear, properly punctuated long sentence shows a sophisticated use of sentences.

Splitting Infinitives

The infinitive of a verb is the base form with *to* in front of it: *to be, to drink, to want.* We often use infinitives in sentences and modify them with adverbs:

I like **to drink slowly.**

But sometimes it sounds better to put the adverb in the middle of the infinitive. For example, *To fully understand my problems takes time* sounds better than

To understand fully my problems takes time.   OR
Fully to understand my problems takes time.

But *To understand my problems fully takes time* sounds all right. Splitting the infinitive is perfectly acceptable. But do not split the infinitive with a long phrase since doing so can cause confusion. Rather than *It is all right to now and then drink a soda,* write, *It is all right now and then to drink a soda, Now and then it is all right to drink a soda,* or *It is all right to drink a soda now and then.*

Exercise 30.1   Identifying Pseudoerrors

*In the following sentences, identify the **pseudoerror** according to these numbers:*
  1   *Starting with a conjunction*
  2   *Starting with* because
  3   *Preposition at end of sentence*
  4   *Long sentence*
  5   *Split infinitive*

Example   He likes orange juice. Yet he rarely drinks it. __1__

  1. Because we see so much grass, Americans think we have always cultivated it.
  ____

  2. But a lawn covered with short grass is fairly modern. ____

3. In the early 1800s, lawns with foot-high waving grasses was what we thought of. _____

4. Only the very rich could afford to highly cultivate carpetlike lawns. _____

5. By the mid-twentieth century, American suburbs began to widely expand. _____

6. New, hybrid grass seeds, effective pesticides, and the powered lawn mower made a well-kept lawn of green grass around a suburban house a status symbol within the reach of the average person. _____

7. Now lawns cover about 50,000 square miles of the United States, an area larger than that required by any other crop and about the size of Pennsylvania. _____

8. Yet growing grass is hardly natural. _____

9. Most grass prefers to naturally grow about one or two feet high, flower, turn brownish, and die or be dormant until the next year. _____

10. Because lawn cultivators want short, green grass most of the year, they subject the grass to unnatural treatment. _____

11. The ground is plowed and gouged, insecticides are applied to kill pests, fertilizer is worked into the soil, chemically treated seeds are planted, and then more chemicals are added to promote rapid growth. _____

12. The grass is supplied with far more than it ever could possibly ask for. _____

13. But the grass is cut as soon as it achieves some minor growth, thus weakening it and promoting disease and insect infestation. _____

14. Strong growth means that hardy crabgrass, dandelions, and clover will also start to quickly invade the lawn. _____

15. Because these "bad" plants are unwelcome, chemical weed killers are applied. _____

16. And certainly war must be waged against such predators as gophers, rabbits, and moles. _____

17. So the lawn is watered, fed, weeded, and pampered to grow as rapidly as it can. _____

18. Then it is tamed to grow only where the suburbanite wants it to. _____

19. It must grow in the area provided, not on the sidewalk, not in the flower beds, not on the front path, not along the fence, not around the bushes, not under the trees, and not against the house. _____

20. No wonder some people have started to seriously challenge this tyranny of perfect grass. _____

Exercise 30.2   Identifying Pseudoerrors

In the following sentences, identify any **pseudoerrors** *according to these numbers:*
  1 *Starting with a coordinating conjunction*
  2 *Starting with* because
  3 *Preposition at end of sentence*
  4 *Long sentence*
  5 *Split infinitive*

1. I remember very distinctly a time when cell phones did not exist; in fact, it was not until I was in my late twenties that cell phones came into existence, sneaking up on us from behind, so to speak. _____

2. Because not everyone had a cell phone, most of us were convinced that they were only for the rich. _____

3. Or, conversely, popular opinion held that cell phones were only for the self-aggrandizing. _____

4. Now everyone has one; it is the perfect accessory to walk down the street with. _____

5. To fully grasp the implications of cell phone infiltration, you need only to be downtown on a busy afternoon. _____

6. I lost my cell phone once, and I felt I was in a boat on a fast river with nothing to steer with. _____

7. Because all of my phone numbers were stored in its memory, I couldn't call anyone; I felt cut off from the world. _____

8. And running out of battery power is much worse than losing your wallet. _____

9. I wonder, sometimes, what cell phones have added to our lives that we didn't have before. _____

10. But then I remember how I felt when my car broke down in a remote area, and how grateful I was to have a cell phone to call a tow truck with. _____

Exercise 30.3   Correcting Misuse of Pseudoerrors

*In the following sentences, find the **true error** and correct it.*

Example   Because orange juice is good, *, I drink it every day.*

1. Istanbul is the largest city in Turkey. But not the capital.

2. Because of its unique position. It straddles Europe and Asia.

3. Formerly its name was Constantinople. And was changed to Istanbul.

4. In the seventh century B.C.E., Istanbul was founded and served as the capital of the Byzantine empire and later the capital of the Ottoman Empire, then it was renamed Constantinople after Constantine the Great but only after Turkey gained its independence in 1930 did the city regain its name.

5. The Bosporous, a narrow river, runs from the Black Sea in the north. And to the Sea of Marmara in the south.

6. Just crossing a short bridge over the river allows a person to in a matter of minutes go from Europe to Asia.

7. They are two different continents. Yet have little difference.

8. The city has its modern and ancient sections mostly on the European side where are located the most popular tourist sights such as Topkapi a palace complex and Hagia Sophia a famous mosque.

9. Uskudar, a village on the Asian side, has a famous hospital. Because Florence Nightingale worked there during the Crimean War.

10. Although the population is officially around seven and a half million, many immigrants from central Turkey continue to secretly or openly arrive.

Exercise 30.4   Editing Uses of Pseudoerrors

In each paragraph, correct **one** *or* **two true errors** *after deciding whether each of these has been correctly used:*
1   *Starting with a coordinating conjunction*
2   *Starting with* because
3   *Preposition at end of sentence*
4   *Long sentence*
5   *Split infinitive*

1. Because a shorter route was needed between the Atlantic Ocean and the Pacific Ocean, the Panama Canal was dug. It allowed vessels to quickly travel from one side to the other in a short time. Because it reduced travel by thousands of miles and many days. Formerly, ships had to go around South America.

2. The canal is only fifty miles long. But includes artificial lakes, channels, and a whole series of locks, water-filled chambers. The water in these locks may be raised or lowered to compensate for differing water levels in the mountainous terrain of central Panama.

3. Building the Panama Canal, which took place between 1904 and 1914, was a major engineering feat that became the largest and the most complex project ever undertaken up to that time. Because it required damming up a major river and digging through a mountain ridge.

4. This project was unlike the digging of the Suez Canal that connected the Mediterranean Sea and the Red Sea. Although twice as long, the Suez Canal did not need huge locks to gradually and slowly adjust the water levels for ships going through. Because the water levels are the same.

5. The Panama Canal runs through a large portion of Panama that was designated the Panama Canal Zone and was controlled by the United States, much to the displeasure of Panama. But the canal has been turned over to Panama, which now has to completely and unilaterally regulate the canal.

6. Oddly enough, to travel from the Atlantic Ocean to the Pacific Ocean through the Panama Canal, a ship must go from west to east. When a ship enters the canal, it waits in a bay for its scheduled passage. Because a canal pilot must guide the ship through the series of twelve locks.

7. After a ship enters a lock, it must wait until the water lowers or fills up. This is done through long pipes and holes in the lock. Then it moves to the next lock and repeats this process through all twelve locks. Large ships sometimes require more than one pilot and tugboats as well.

8. Because of the tremendous amount of water needed (about 52 million gallons per ship), sometimes small ships are grouped two or three at a time to go through. But the canal has been enlarged in recent years to more easily and quickly accommodate larger and larger ships.

9. Near the end of the trip through the canal large cables and mules guide the ship to where it is lowered into a lake and then to more locks and then to a harbor and finally to the Bay of Panama which leads to the Pacific Ocean. So the whole trip takes between eight and ten hours, not counting waiting time.

10. The most common ships going through the canal are carriers for a large variety of goods such as ore, grain, automobiles, liquid gas, and refrigerated products. And passenger ships, fishing boats, barges, and naval vessels.

Exercise 30.5   Correcting Misuse of Pseudoerrors

*Find and correct any **true errors** in the following essay.*

Will Fads Fade?

I remember very clearly when everyone in my fifth grade class wanted plastic gummy bracelets. We wore ten or twelve of them on each wrist. And I saved my allowance up for weeks just to buy them. Where did this fad come from? And how come we all wanted plastic bracelets so badly that we did extra chores just to get them?

Of course, this is a simple example of a fad, but certain trends do make you stop and wonder. One explanation of a fad would be prestige. Prestige is gained by being the first and most adept at a skill. Or the first one on the block to have a new toy that everyone else covets. A fad is known only by its rarity; when it is no longer scarce, it loses its appeal.

If we take the arenas of scientific research and recreation as examples, we can see how fads operate. A scientific fad begins with a "Eureka!"—that is, a sudden discovery (or rediscovery) of a fact or idea. This new idea must be complex enough to suggest a wide range of minor innovations. After discovering a new drug, drug companies rush to test the drug in all kinds of situations. In a different example, people who follow recreation or style fads don't just copy a pattern but strive to significantly improve on its original design, trying out a number of variations and original uses for the object/action. The Hula Hoop is a prime example of a fad that people could make their own; each person could spin the hoop in a way unique only to him or her.

Another reason fads tend to end is the exhaustion of the possible variations. Because a drug has been tested in all possible manners. Because a Hula Hoop has been spun every way imaginable. Also, gradually, faddists notice that they have been neglecting their other usual activities, having been involved with the fad to the exclusion of all else. Once everyone else has caught on, the faddists become aware of the possible dangers in the fad and lose interest. Of course, there's always a new fad to contend with. Me, I'm just waiting for the gummy bracelets to come back in style.

Exercise 30.6   Writing with Pseudoerrors

Write sentences
> *Starting the second one with a coordinating conjunction*
> *Starting with* because
> *Ending with a preposition (particle)*
> *Using many words and phrases or clauses*
> *Using a split infinitive*

Example   Dogs (Start second sentence with a coordinating conjunction)
> _I love dogs. Yet I have never owned one._

1. Your bedroom (Start with *because*)

2. Your bed (Start second sentence with *for, and, nor, but, or, yet, so*)

3. Your dresser (Use a split infinitive)

4. Your bedroom floor (Use a long sentence)

_____

_____

_____

5. Your bedroom window (Start sentence with *because*)

_____

6. Your closet (Start second sentence with *for, and, nor, but, or, yet, so*)

_____

7. Your walls (Use a long sentence)

_____

_____

_____

8. Your door (Start second sentence with *for, and, nor, but, or, yet, so*)

_____

9. Your computer (Start sentence with *because*)

_____

10. Your radio (Start second sentence with *for, and, nor, but, or, yet, so*)

_____

_____

Exercise 30.7   Proofreading

*Correct the **four misuses of pseudoerrors.***

   We can tell countries and people apart by location, language, clothing, appearance, and lots of other ways you might think of. But one way people are different around the world is in what they use to wash with. Because everyone washes. Americans use small squares of thick cloth. Asians tend to use a thinner piece of cloth but one that is longer, about the size and shape of the American dishcloth. But good for washing the back. The French use a small bag that fits like a mitten without a thumb. Some people use sponges, natural and plastic, and a few use a ball of stiff net-like material. Many Scandinavians use a loofah, a type of long sponge. The loofah's rough surface is for those who want to truly and completely rub off surface dirt. Most countries use nothing at all. Because the people just rub soap over the body.

Summary

I. Pseudoerrors
  A. Definition: **Pseudoerrors** are correct constructions that some people mistakenly consider incorrect.
  B. Types of pseudoerrors
    1. A sentence can start with a conjunction: *for, and, nor, but, or, yet, so.*
        Example: *But you didn't ask.*
    2. A sentence can start with *because* if it also contains an independent clause.
        Example: *Because I went, you had to stay.*
    3. A preposition can end a sentence.
        Example: *I had no one to go with.*
    4. A long sentence is acceptable and should not be mislabeled a run-on sentence.
        Example: *Having no one to go with me shopping, I decided to treat myself to a double feature and spend the entire day just watching movies.*
    5. Split infinitives are acceptable unless split by too many words.
        Examples: *I want them to fully understand.*
                  We told them to quietly go away.

Answers to Pretests at Beginning of Each Chapter

Chapter 1   Nouns and Pronouns *(page 3)*

Read the following paragraph and underline the **nouns** *and* **pronouns**.

Edith Wharton was born Edith Jones on January 24, 1862, in New York, New York, and married Boston banker Edward Wharton in 1885. A member of upper-class society, she wrote about her world and criticized its rigid attitudes and customs. Her work has often been compared to that of another critic of social norms, Henry James, with whom she was acquainted. Wharton's first successful writing was a book entitled *The Decoration of Houses* (1897), an attack on upper-class interior decorating. Later she incorporated her interest in decorating and architecture in her fiction, using detailed settings and commenting on the order or disorder in her characters' homes and lives. (Patricia D. Netzley, *Encyclopedia of Social Protest Literature*)

Chapter 2   Verbs *(page 18)*

Read the following paragraph and underline the **verbs** *in it.*

Our beginnings do not foreshadow our ends if one judges by the Hudson River. A few miles east of the Bad Luck Ponds, the Hudson came down between the ridges to race alongside route 28; it was a mountain stream: clear, cold, shallow, noisy. A few miles from its source in Lake Tear-in-the-Clouds a mile up on Mount Marcy (the Indian name for the mountain is better: Tahawus, "Cloud-Splitter") and three hundred river miles from the thousand oily piers of Hoboken, Weehawken, and Manhattan, here it was a canoer's watercourse. Above the little Hudson, spumes of mist rose from the mountains like campfire smoke. (William Least Heat Moon, *Blue Highways: A Journey into America*)

Chapter 3   Adjectives and Adverbs *(page 34)*

*Read the following paragraph and underline the words that modify (describe) other words, that is, the **adjectives** and **adverbs**.*

I feel like a brown bag of miscellany propped against a wall. Against a wall in company with other bags, white, red and yellow. Pour out the contents, and there is discovered a jumble of small things priceless and worthless. A first-water diamond, an empty spool, bits of broken glass, lengths of string, a key to a door long since crumbled away, a rusty knife-blade, old shoes saved for a road that never was and never will be, a nail bent under the weight of things too heavy for any nail, a dried flower or two still a little fragrant. In your hand is the brown bag. On the ground before you is the jumble it held—so much like the jumble in the bags could they be emptied, that all might be dumped in a single heap and the bags refilled without altering the contents of any greatly. A bit of colored glass more or less would not matter. Perhaps that is how the Great Stuffer of Bags filled them in the first place—who knows? (Zora Neale Hurston, "How It Feels to Be Colored Me," from *I Love Myself When I Am Laughing*)

Chapter 4   Prepositions, Conjunctions, and Interjections *(page 48)*

*Read the following paragraph and underline the **prepositions**, double underline the **conjunctions**, and circle the **interjections**.*

Indeed, the facts and consequences of auto congestion are greatly exaggerated in most large cities. During rush hour, I have driven into and out of Dallas, Kansas City, Phoenix, St. Louis, and San Diego without much more than an occasional slowdown. Moreover, despite the massive reliance on cars and a short-term decline in the economic vitality of their downtown areas, most of these cities have restored their central areas. Kansas City is bleak in the old downtown, but the shopping area (built 75 years ago!) called Country Club Plaza is filled with people, stores, and restaurants. San Diego and San Francisco have lively downtowns. Los Angeles even managed to acquire a downtown (actually, several downtowns) after it grew up without much of one—and this in a city allegedly "built around the car." Phoenix is restoring its downtown and San Diego never really lost its center. (James Q. Wilson, "Cars and Their Enemies," *Commentary*)

Chapter 5   *Subjects and Objects* (page 61)

*Underline the **subjects** in the following paragraph.*

Plant <u>communities</u> are not static but are continually modifying their own environment. The <u>accumulation</u> of decaying organic material builds up the soil and increases its ability to support plant life. Gradually dry <u>land</u> is created out of wet land, and sterile <u>soil</u> becomes enriched with humus. For example, a <u>pond</u> will evolve into a swamp, and an open <u>field</u> will eventually become a forest. As each successive plant <u>community</u> gives way to the next, the <u>habitat</u> becomes more stable, and in time supports a climax community, such as a beech-hemlock forest. If there are no major <u>disturbances</u> (natural or manmade), the climax <u>community</u> will remain essentially unchanged. (Lee Peterson, *A Field Guide to Edible Wild Plants*)

Chapter 6   *Other Complements* (page 75)

*Read the following sentences and underline the words you think are the **complements.***

1. My brother always meant to be a <u>surfer</u> in Hawaii.
2. But he got <u>tired</u> of the "endless summer" lifestyle.
3. He became an <u>astrophysicist</u>.
4. But he grew <u>weary</u> of staring into the vast emptiness of space.
5. He did not remain an <u>astrophysicist</u> for very long.
6. Returning to Hawaii, he became an <u>oceanographer</u>.
7. This change might prove <u>difficult</u> for him.
8. But the salt water and waves taste <u>good</u> to him.
9. This move seems <u>right</u>, so the future looks <u>bright</u>.
10. My brother appears to be <u>happy</u>.

Chapter 7   *Prepositional Phrases* (page 91)

*Read the following paragraph and underline the **prepositional phrases.***

While taking a walk <u>in my neighborhood</u> <u>on an early summer evening</u> <u>at twilight</u>, I stopped to chat <u>with a neighbor</u> who was walking his dogs. As we stood, I noticed that the large expanse <u>of yard</u> <u>in front of which</u> we were standing was aglitter with the intermittent flickering of fireflies. I called attention to the sight, remarking on how magical it looked. "It's like the Fourth of July," I said. He agreed, and then told me he had read that the lights of fireflies are mating signals. He then explained to me details of how these signals work—for example, groups of fireflies fly at different elevations and could be seen to cluster in different parts of the yard. (Deborah Tannen, *You Just Don't Understand*)

Chapter 8   Verbal Phrases: Adjective *(page 104)*

*Underline the one **adjective verbal phrase** in each of the following sentences.*

1. In the Greek myth of *Pygmalion and Galatea*, King Pygmalion makes a statue of a woman possessing ideal qualities.
2. Pygmalion falls madly in love with the statue representing perfection in his eyes.
3. Completely taken with the statue, Pygmalion pines away with unrequited love.
4. The goddess of love, Aphrodite, feeling sorry for him, makes the statue come alive; thus Galatea is born.
5. In modern times, George Bernard Shaw wrote *Pygmalion*, a play based on the same story.
6. His Pygmalion is Henry Higgins, known as a linguist.
7. He finds a poor young woman selling violets outdoors.
8. Using all the "modern" methods, Higgins teaches Eliza correct language and proper manners.
9. Once taught proper English, Eliza passes as a high-class lady, even a princess.
10. But Eliza hates the hypocrisy of the upper class; not wanting any part of it, she returns to her old life.

Chapter 9   Verbal Phrases: Infinitive *(page 117)*

*Underline the **infinitive verbal phrases** in each of these sentences:*

1. Canada geese seem to live all year round in the park nearby.
2. They appear to be very happy in this environment.
3. Everyone likes to see them walking around and eating the grass.
4. They don't mean to ruin the park, but they do.

5. They have managed <u>to leave their droppings all over the ground</u>.
6. People can't find a place <u>to walk or to sit on the grass</u>.
7. The town does not have the funds <u>to clean up this mess</u>.
8. <u>To shoot the geese</u> would be a terrible shame.
9. The mayor decided <u>to post two dogs for eight-hour shifts</u>.
10. The geese will learn <u>to avoid the dogs somehow</u>.

Chapter 10   *Verbal Phrases: Noun* (page 133)

*Underline the one **noun verbal phrase** in each of these sentences.*

1. <u>Smoking any substance</u> should be banned in public and in places where the public may go.
2. <u>Harming others either outdoors or indoors</u> is against the law.
3. Passive smoke is a known carcinogen that contributes to <u>hurting people, especially children</u>.
4. We have banned <u>smoking in workplaces</u> because nonsmokers should not be subjected to a smoker.
5. Why should there be an exception for <u>working in restaurants and bars</u>?
6. <u>Letting people indulge in dangerous behavior</u> appears to be a basic human right, but not if it involves others.
7. However, <u>behaving dangerously</u> may land a person in the hospital for costly care that he or she cannot afford.
8. <u>Seeking reimbursement for medical costs</u> has forced states to sue tobacco companies.
9. The equivalent is <u>requiring people to use seatbelts in cars</u>.
10. Although we are allowed to hurt ourselves, <u>putting on seatbelts</u> is required so that we will not cost the state a lot of money.

Chapter 11   *Independent Clauses: Simple and Compound Sentences* (page 147)

*Underline the **simple sentences** and double underline the **compound sentences** in the following paragraph.*

Two challenges face American education today. <u>We must raise overall achieve-ment levels, and we must make opportunities for achievement more equitable</u>. The importance of both derives from the same basic condition—our changing economy. <u>Never before has the pool of developed skill and capability mattered more in our prospects for general economic health</u>. And never before <u>have skill and knowledge mattered as much in the economic prospects for individuals</u>. (Lauren B. Resnick, "From Aptitude to Effort," *American Educator*)

Chapter 12   *Dependent Clauses* (page 160)

*Underline the **dependent clauses** in the following paragraph.*

The invention of the wheel is often held up as the proudest accomplishment of civilization. Many textbooks point out <u>that no animal has evolved wheels</u> and cite the fact as an example of <u>how evolution is often incapable of finding the optimal solution to an engineering problem</u>. But it is not a good example at all. <u>Even if nature *could* have evolved a moose on wheels</u>, it surely would have opted not to. Wheels are good only in a world with roads and rails. They bog down in any terrain <u>that is soft, slippery, steep, or uneven</u>. Legs are better. Wheels have to roll along an unbroken supporting ridge, but legs can be placed on a series of separate footholds, an extreme example being a ladder. Legs can also be placed to minimize lurching and to step over obstacles. (Steven Pinker, *How the Mind Works*)

Chapter 13   *Adjective Dependent Clauses* (page 175)

*Underline the one **adjective dependent clause** in each of the following sentences.*

1. Jai alai, <u>which evolved in the Basque region</u>, is played in many countries in the world.
2. The Basque region is an area <u>that includes parts of southern France and northern Spain</u>.
3. The jai alai court, called a *fronton*, resembles a racquetball or squash court <u>that has been enlarged</u>.
4. Two players <u>who stand side by side</u> toss a ball against a wall.
5. Each player wears a *cesta*, <u>which is a curved basket tied to the wrist</u>.
6. Catching a ball <u>that has bounced off a wall</u> is very tricky.
7. Jai alai is popular in those parts of Asia <u>where there was Spanish influence</u>.
8. Spain, <u>where some of the best Basque players live</u>, loves jai alai.

9. In the United States, several states <u>that had Spanish influence</u> also have jai alai frontons.
10. Sports fans <u>who like gambling</u> have been attracted to jai alai.

Chapter 14 Noun Dependent Clauses *(page 188)*

Underline the **noun dependent clauses** in the following sentences.

1. <u>Whoever has been to an ice skating rink</u> has seen the Zamboni.
2. Ice skaters know <u>that this machine comes out periodically</u>.
3. <u>Whatever needs doing on the ice surface</u> is done by this machine.
4. The fact <u>that the Zamboni does many chores</u> is obvious.
5. <u>How this Zamboni works</u> needs explaining.
6. One cannot tell by <u>how it moves around the ice</u>.
7. Water hoses, a pump, conveyors, a blade, and a towel are <u>what the machine uses on the ice</u>.
8. <u>What the blade and water do</u> is smooth out and fill in the cracks.
9. <u>What the pump and conveyors do</u> is collect excess water and snow.
10. That is <u>why ice skaters should be grateful for the Zamboni</u>.

Chapter 15 Adverb Dependent Clauses *(page 200)*

Underline the **adverb dependent clauses** in the following sentences.

1. <u>Although they were once considered part of the raccoon family</u>, giant pandas are actually bears.
2. <u>Since they have black patches around their eyes and ears</u>, they have a resemblance to racoons.
3. Pandas mostly live <u>where they can find their staple food, bamboo</u>.
4. Unfortunately, bamboo is not very nutritious <u>even if pandas eat vast quantities of it</u>.
5. <u>When bamboo blooms and produces seeds every sixty years or so</u>, it becomes inedible.
6. Many pandas die at this time <u>since they cannot find enough food</u>.
7. Female pandas give birth to one cub a year <u>if they manage to mate during the few days a year of fertility</u>.

8. <u>Because giant pandas live in a small</u> mountainous area of western China and <u>cannot survive elsewhere</u>, they will soon be extinct.
9. Only about a thousand giant pandas still exist, <u>although many efforts have been made to preserve them</u>.
10. <u>Even though pandas have been protected in zoos</u>, they have rarely reproduced successfully.

Chapter 16   *Inverted Sentences and Passive Voice* (page 217)

Underline the **inverted sentence parts** *in the following paragraphs.*

1. Why <u>do so many people</u> study Spanish? <u>Do they</u> think that Spanish is easy? Spanish is not easy to learn, nor <u>does it</u> come easily to most of us. So I will not think it is easy, nor <u>will I</u> assume I'll be speaking Spanish in a few days.
2. <u>Had I</u> gotten a good Spanish teacher, I would have learned much faster. The teacher would drill me on verb forms and give me lots of tests to make sure that I did my work. Why else <u>would anyone</u> want a teacher? Certainly it's not for the fun of it.
3. I won't tell anyone I'm studying Spanish, nor <u>will I</u> try to practice on anyone. Why <u>would I</u> want this kind of embarrassment? I'll just study quietly. Then one day, <u>were someone</u> to say something in Spanish, I would surprise everyone by responding.

Chapter 17   *Parallel Structure* (page 233)

Underline examples of **parallel structure** *in the following paragraphs.*

In my next life, when I am an architect, I always will design houses with kitchens that open to the outdoors. I love stepping out <u>to head and tail</u> my beans while sitting on the stone wall. I <u>set dirty pots out to soak, dry my dishcloths on the wall, empty excess clean water on the arugula, thyme, and rosemary</u> right outside the door. Since the double door is open <u>day and night</u> in summer, the kitchen fills with <u>light and air</u>. A wasp—is it the same one?—<u>flies in every day and drinks from the faucet, then flies right out</u>. . . . <u>The leisure of a summer place, the ease of prime ingredients, and the perfectly casual way of entertaining</u> convince me that this is the kitchen as it's meant to be. (Frances Mayes, *Under the Tuscan Sun*)

Chapter 18   Faithful... *Faulty Predication* (page 243)

*Underline the one sentence that is an example of **faulty predication** in each of the following short paragraphs.*

1. I have great plans for the future. <u>I will be married with children and a pharmacist.</u> We'll live in a nice house in the suburbs, and both my husband and I will work in the city.
2. <u>Happiness is when I am at home playing with my children while my husband barbecues in the backyard.</u> We'll take a swim in our in-ground pool and then sit down for a picnic.
3. My ambitions reveal my personality. <u>I feel a high achievement as well as a dreamer.</u> I want what a lot of people want perhaps, but I won't have to work very hard for it.
4. <u>The reason why I am ambitious is because my parents raised me to aim high.</u> They said I could have anything I really wanted. So I want this life, and I will get it.

Chapter 19   *Subject-Verb Agreement* (page 255)

*Indicate **subject-verb agreement** by drawing an arrow from the subjects to the verbs that go with them in the following paragraphs. Underline any two-word verbs.*

In most sports, such as baseball, football, and basketball, play <u>is stopped</u> when substitutions <u>are made</u>. But ice hockey allows unlimited substitution while the game is in progress, one of the features that make hockey such a fast-paced game.

It is the goalie's job to be a dispatcher, announcing to his teammates when traffic patterns <u>are changing</u> on the ice. For example, a minor penalty involves the offender serving two minutes in the penalty box. Some goalies bang the ice to signal to teammates that they are now at even strength. (David Feldman, *How Does Aspirin Find a Headache?*)

Chapter 20   Pronoun-Antecedent Agreement *(page 269)*

*Indicate **pronoun-antecedent agreement** by drawing an arrow from each pronoun to the previous noun or pronoun it refers to. You should have some long arrows.*

I was 54 years old before venturing beyond the shores of my native Japan. It was 1953, and Georges Ohsawa and I were leaving on our first world tour. I remember feeling as naive, excited, and hesitant as a young schoolgirl about to embark on her first voyage into a wide and unknown world. I knew that Georges, having previously spent some years abroad, could speak both English and French, and that I, limited to my native language, would have to rely on him to steer our course. So I firmly re-solved to accept in silence whatever fate had in store for us. We traveled by ship to Calcutta, arriving in November, and were engulfed by a surging crowd of beggars the moment we stepped ashore. Shocked and bewildered, I wondered to what kind of world my husband was so intent upon introducing me. (Lima Ohsawa, *The Art of Just Cooking*)

Chapter 21   Commas *(page 283)*

*Decide why the **commas** are used in each of the following sentences and write in the reason using this list: date, direct address, series of adjectives, introductory word, introductory phrase, introductory clause, title after a name, appositive, compound sentence with coordinating conjunction.*

1. Alina, I am writing this letter to congratulate you on your graduation.
   direct address

2. You have succeeded, and you have made us proud. *compound sentence with coordinating conjunction*

3. This date, May 20, 2001, should be your proudest. *date*

4. Now the words "Alina Martin, M.D.," will always have a special meaning for me. *title after name*

5. You are diligent, hard working, motivated, and compassionate. ___*series of*___

    ___*adjectives*___

6. As you continue in life, you will always remember this special day when you

    started. ___*introductory clause*___

7. After studying so much, you should find medical practice relatively easy. _____

    ___*introductory phrase*___

8. However, I hope you will not forget the loving family that now counts on you.

    ___*introductory word*___

9. In addition, remember the sacrifices that they made for you. _____

    ___*introductory phrase*___

10. My niece, the doctor, will always make me proud. _____

    ___*appositive*___

Chapter 22   Semicolons and Colons (page 296)

Circle the **semicolons** *and* **colons** *in the following paragraphs and note in the margin why they are used.*

CD
sentence   Wisdom is better than possessions and an advantage to all who see the sun. Better have wisdom behind you than money; wisdom profits men by giving life to those

CD
sentence   who know her.

avoid
confusion
further
detail   Consider God's handiwork; who can straighten what He has made crooked? When things go well, be glad; but when things go ill, consider this: God has set the one alongside the other in such a way that no one can find out what is to happen next. (Ecclesiastes 7:11–19, *The New English Bible*)

Chapter 23   Quotation Marks and Italics (page 309)

Write above each quotation the reason the **quotation marks** *are used in the following paragraph.*

A twelve-inch gold-plated disk containing twenty-seven musical selections had been placed in the Voyager 2 spacecraft and by 1990 had already left the solar system. The contents of the record were selected for NASA by a committee chaired by Dr. Carl Sagan. Among the selections, which included a Pygmy girls' initiation song, "Melancholy Blues" performed by Louis Armstrong and his Hot Seven, and

song title [above "Melancholy Blues"]

the Sacrificial Dance from Stravinsky's *Rite of Spring*, the committee had chosen the cavatina from Beethoven's "String Quartet no. 13 in B flat, Opus 130." . . . As Sagan

music title [above "String Quartet"]

noted, "The spacecraft will be encountered and the record played only if there are ad-

someone's exact words [above "The spacecraft will"]

vanced spacefaring civilizations in interstellar space.". . . . And how will they react to the middle section marked *Beklemmt*, which we of the human race find so mov-

ing? *Beklemmt* translates loosely into "oppressed" or "anguished." Will the aliens

translated words [above "oppressed"]

find it so? (Arnold Steinhardt, *Indivisible by Four*)

Chapter 24   Apostrophes *(page 321)*

In the following paragraph, circle the words with apostrophes and explain why each **apostrophe** *was used.*

Innovative architectural response to domestic change was especially strong in and around Los Angeles, where it had been led, since the 1930s, by the Austrian emigrés Rudolph Schindler and Richard Neutra. California's climate was perfect for

possessive noun [above "California's"]

the modernist ideal of thin-skinned houses, with a steel or wood frame and plentiful glass. But Schindler, Neutra, and others warmed up the International Style with brick hearths, wooden beams and built-ins, appealing to American ideals of tradi-tion. They revolutionized American housing while responding to its context and history. These architects' most widely imitated visual change was the flat roof. By

possessive noun [above "architects"]

the late '40s, the flat-roofed, single-story house had become an affordable, deus ex

contraction [above "40s"]

machina, not only for down-sized households, but also for thousands of G.I.s re-turning to a severe housing shortage. (Lisa Zeiger, "Natural Selection," *New York Times Magazine*)

Chapter 25   Dashes, Parentheses, Brackets, Slashes, Hyphens, *, . . . , &, %, #, @ *(page 335)*

Note after each sentence why the **punctuation** *(aside from commas and periods) is being used in the following sentences.*

1. Our modern world—the twenty-first century—has become reliant on symbols for identification instead of words. __*for emphasis, to call attention*__

2. Our world includes pictures (logos, icons) that we recognize instantly. _____
   added information, details

3. This symbol-laden world is not new, however. _____
   two-part adjective

4. Before literacy was widespread, all communication (stores, products, rulers, routes) was based on recognition of symbols. _____
   added information, details

5. A seller and/or buyer knew the pawnshop by the three hanging balls over the door. _____
   shortcut replacing other words

6. A would-be political leader would choose a sun or cow or hat to identify him- or herself. _____
   two-part adjective   partial word

7. So that people could swear their allegiance—an absolute necessity for any leader—they could just follow the symbol. _____
   emphasis

8. The alphabet (in itself a series of symbols) made written communications easier, but we continued to use other symbols. _____
   detail

9. One boss recently wrote this note to an employee: "Buy 6 of #2s @$8.00 & get a 10% discount.* _____
   symbols for number (#), each or at (@), and (&), percent (%), see note below (*)

10. *Buy 12 @$7.00 w/o discount." _____
    symbols for note below (*), each or at (@), shortcut meaning "without" (w/o).

Chapter 26   Sentence Fragments (page 349)

*Each of the following advertisements has one or more **sentence fragments**. Underline the fragments you find.*

Want to lose weight? Have friends? Get a good job? Find that special someone? Join the TopNotch Health and Sports Club and make all your dreams come true. It's a proven fact that thinner people have more fun and go further in life. Sign up today!

Join now and get the first month free. <u>Also a tee shirt with our logo.</u> <u>And two free</u>
<u>passes for anyone you know.</u> A great bargain!

      <u>The perfect jacket for all occasions.</u> <u>Dressy with a tie.</u> <u>Casual with a polo shirt.</u>
<u>Stain resistant.</u> <u>Waterproof.</u> <u>Inside and outside pockets.</u> <u>Secret pocket for important</u>
<u>documents.</u> <u>Roomy.</u> <u>Hand-turned lapels.</u> <u>Five-button cuffs.</u> <u>Comes in charcoal or</u>
<u>black.</u> Order now while supplies last. <u>One per customer, please!</u>

      Here is the famous Palm Light you've been hearing about. It fits into the palm
of your hand and lights with a touch of a finger. <u>Invaluable in hotel rooms.</u> <u>Perfect</u>
<u>for the theater.</u> <u>Makes dark staircases safer.</u> Read maps in the dark. Order one for
everyone in your family. <u>Each $3.95.</u> <u>Special for a limited time only: Five for only</u>
<u>$17.95.</u> <u>Big savings.</u> <u>Free shipping and handling.</u> Don't wait until you're stuck in the
dark.

      Subscribe to *Computer Casuals.* <u>The only magazine that tells you what to wear</u>
<u>while you work at your computer.</u> You'll feel better knowing you look right for
Games. <u>Chats.</u> <u>Surfing.</u>

Chapter 27   *Run-Together Sentences* (page 359)

*Underline the five **run-together sentences** in this paragraph and correct them using
punctuation.*

      Brazilians say that God created the world in six days<u>;</u> on the seventh day he *or period*
made Rio. <u>Rio de Janeiro is one of the most beautiful cities in the world<u>;</u> it has a *or period*
wonderful setting.</u> The city consists of a long beachfront, rocky islands jutting out of
the water, forested mountains rising inland, and a tropical rainforest within the city
limits. The world-famous beaches include Copacabana, Ipanema, and Leblon. <u>One
rocky peak is Sugar Loaf<u>;</u> the other is Corcovado.</u> Both rise spectacularly over the *or period*
city. The Tijuca National Park has hilly areas with lush tropical vegetation. <u>The
climate is generally very healthful<u>;</u> trade winds keep the air relatively cool.</u> The *or period*
coolest time is June, July, and August<u>;</u> the hottest times are in the winter when tem- *or period*
<u>peratures go over 100 degrees.</u> Being south of the equator, the seasons are reversed.

Chapter 28   *Words Often Confused* (page 369)

*In the following sentences, circle the correct choice among **words often confused.***

  1. There are many ways to (raise, rays, raze, rise) children.

2. The parents should decide (*weather*, *whether*) they want a large or small family.
3. The (*amount of*, *number of*) children in a family makes a big difference.
4. Parents must decide (*who's*, *whose*) in charge.
5. (*Some*, *Sum*) parents believe in strict discipline.
6. (*There*, *Their*, *They're*) are parents who believe that children should be left alone.
7. Others think parents should (*all ways*, *always*) be there.
8. They believe in (*fewer*, *less*) rules.
9. If (*your*, *you're*) thinking of starting a family, think hard about (*your*, *you're*) child-rearing philosophy.
10. But mostly you need to give (*a lot*, *allot*) of love.

Chapter 29   Misplaced and Dangling Modifiers *(page 379)*

*Underline the one **misplaced** or **dangling modifier** in each of the following sentences.*

1. Some people from the western part of France settled in Acadia, now called Nova Scotia <u>in the seventeenth century.</u>
2. When taken over by the British in 1755, the Acadians fled to Louisiana and eastern Texas <u>mostly</u> to settle in French-owned territory.
3. They became known <u>only</u> as "Cajuns," from "Acadians," after this move.
4. <u>Mostly fishing, trapping, and farming,</u> life was full of problems and difficulties in this isolated land.
5. <u>Already on the land,</u> the Cajuns were not welcomed by the local Creoles, who considered them invaders.
6. <u>Being Cajun country,</u> the culture's uniqueness can be seen and felt in the land, people, food, and shelter.
7. They have their own language that <u>almost</u> sounds like French, but some major differences in vocabulary, pronunciation, and grammar exist.
8. Bridges and highways forced them to assimilate with the rest of the United States <u>built in the early twentieth century.</u>
9. The state of Louisiana mandated that French could not be spoken in the public schools <u>even.</u>
10. <u>Almost eradicated in recent decades,</u> there has been a revival of Cajun language, music, dance, and cuisine.

Chapter 30   Pseudoerrors *(page 388)*

*In the following sentences, note **pseudoerrors** (constructions that are sometimes considered errors but are not) in the space following each sentence.*

1. Because she seemed to lead a glamorous life, many people envied Frida Kahlo, the Mexican painter.   starting sentence with "because"

2. But she really had a life filled with pain and suffering.   starting sentence with "but"

3. Kahlo contracted polio as a small child and then was seriously injured in a bus accident that caused her to spend months in the hospital recovering from the effects of a metal shaft that went through her body.   writing a long sentence

4. Yet she married Diego Rivera, the famous muralist, and participated in an active social and artistic life.   starting sentence with "yet"

5. Her many self-portraits depict the ills she suffered from.   ending with a preposition

6. Knowing about her life helps to really understand her portraits.   splitting infinitive

7. For they show her surrounded by such things as monkeys, gargoyles, and parrots, each symbolizing an aspect of her life.   starting sentence with "for"

8. Or she has a stone pillar instead of a spine, showing that she had a spinal fusion operation.   starting sentence with "or"

9. To completely recover from her many ills was impossible.   splitting infinitive

10. She died at the young age of forty-seven because of illnesses that she could not recover from.   ending with a preposition

Index